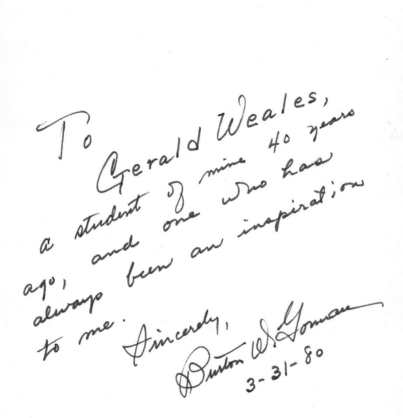

To Gerald Weales,
a student of mine 40 years
ago, and one who has
always been an inspiration
to me.
Sincerely,
Burton W. Gorman
3-31-80

Secondary Education

Secondary
Education

THE HIGH SCHOOL
AMERICA NEEDS

BURTON W. GORMAN
Kent State University

RANDOM HOUSE
NEW YORK

All rights reserved under International and Pan-American Copyright Conventions. Published in the United States by Random House, Inc., New York, and simultaneously in Canada by Random House of Canada Limited, Toronto.

ISBN: 0-394-31007-1
Library of Congress Catalog Card Number: 77-130186
Manufactured in the United States of America. Composed by Cherry Hill Composition, Pennsauken, New Jersey. Printed and bound by Halliday Lithograph Corporation, West Hanover, Massachusetts.

Designed by Marion Needham

First Edition

9 8 7 6 5 4 3 2 1

Dedicated to
Becky,
Ben,
Joe,
and John
and to
A great future for the American high school

Acknowledgments

For whatever character and quality this book may have I am much indebted to the inspiration and stimulation received from my colleagues. The senior partners in this organization include Robert White, Clayton Schindler, George Cooke, Harris Dante, George Lucht, Gerald Read, Roger Shaw, and Robert Wilson. Likewise, I am indebted to former colleagues Henry Perkinson, Paul Komisar, and Herbert Heller, and to my professors, especially to Harold Benjamin, W. C. Jones, Willard Goslin, Louis Armstrong, and Carl G. F. Franzén.

For the most thorough and critical reading of the manuscript I credit my scientist friend G. Leonard Bush. Dean Norton L. Beach, of the University of North Carolina, read and criticized substantial portions of the initial draft. Other helpful criticisms and suggestions were provided by my colleagues Paul Howells, Charles Chandler, Jack Durance, Ray Wilken, George Harrison, and John Ohles. John Baker, of the University of Vermont, deserves credit of which he is scarcely conscious.

Valuable help and counsel came from my sociologist son, Benjamin, and from my lawyer son, Joseph. The initial draft was typed by my wife, Rebecca. Other important clerical and typing help was generously given by Linda Mathia, Betty Sterner, Kathleen Lambes, Jonell Harvey, and Annette Ault. Robert Yoder, of Kent State's Audio-Visual Bureau, gave valued help in developing illustrations.

Kent State's sabbatical leave program made it possible for me to get the book along to the point where it could be completed on a part-time basis.

Miss Jane Cullen and others at Random House have made suggestions which have improved the text in numerous ways. The efforts of many have combined to make this result possible.

B. W. G.

Contents

Introduction

Ours is an era of extremely rapid change, change so rapid that even the most careful analysts and observers are confused. This change bears in upon the high school from a number of directions. The institution itself has changed, especially with respect to size; and its clientele has changed. In 1910 the average public secondary school in America enrolled ninety students. Today the vast majority of enrollees attend schools of 500 to 5000 students. Further, economic efficiency and citizenship sufficiency in the technological society of today demand the education of all.

The degree to which young people have changed is nowhere fully appreciated. They are today more mature than the youth of earlier generations in every imaginable respect, save in their experience of responsibility for themselves, for others, and for their community.

The problems of society have undergone overwhelming change. Awkward efforts to cope with the new internationalism of a shrunken sphere bewilder all. Environmental problems, both physical and human, seem to have moved in upon us with the pace of a hurricane. All this has come at a time when racial and youthful segments of the population have been making determined drives for their share of involvement and influence in society's affairs. These latter movements bear testimony to educational successes.

It is in this broad perspective that this book has been conceived and written. Can the high school continue to deploy its time and its human resources in a framework designed for less than a hundred students and successfully meet the challenge of this age? Change cannot deeply penetrate other segments of life and leave a social institution such as the high school untouched.

The need for high school reform has been widely acknowledged for twenty years. Innovation is a celebrated word wherever secondary school leaders gather. Change, however, has seldom been guided by carefully conceived and consolidated purpose. Even more seldom has reform effort been designed to serve all students or been directed at the school's basic or total structure. Rarely, too, has change been leveled at recently revealed needs of society.

This book deals with the change that must take place in the high school to bring it abreast of current challenges. Secondary schooling must help young people to gain maturity in the areas where they are now least mature. It must give greater attention to the development of social conscience. It must provide experience in the development of responsibility for self and for others. People who are to live so close together and who are to unite themselves to deal with so many common problems must develop an uncommon respect for one another. The school must provide them varied experiences in working together to solve problems of general concern.

Significant elements of the high school's education must be not only individualized but personalized for all students. They must become more fully involved, more committed in their own behalf. The potential initiative and resourcefulness present in all young people must be cultivated.

Preparation for responsible participation in a democratic society is a long-recognized aim of the high school. The school has failed to recognize, though, that one is not prepared for responsible participation in any society merely by talking about it, however analytical, logical, and philosophical that talk may be. Success crowns the effort of the high school that itself becomes a social laboratory for experience in such living.

The prejudice of this book is a better high school, one that believes itself capable of developing citizens equal to the problems of our times. It argues the case, and it dares to be prescriptive. It describes a high school in which teacher and student energy is directed toward these ends.

B. W. G.

Secondary
Education

1

The Long View
and the Large View

> People generally have more feeling for canals and
> roads than education. However, I hope we can
> advance them with equal pace.
>
> *Thomas Jefferson*

The smugness that we Americans felt just a few years ago about
our institutions, our values, and our future is no longer with us.
Over the last dozen years especially, that smugness has undergone one shaking after another. Such tremors, both foreign and
domestic, have jarred our society to its very roots. That the people
generally have become concerned is evidenced in a Harris Survey
that reports 55 percent feeling that "something is deeply wrong
with our society."[1] This survey might be considered a less than
valid measure in that it was made only a few weeks after the second Kennedy assassination; but actually, this jarring event served
to emphasize an already existing concern for the nation's well-
being, a concern over conflagrations large and small. Some of
these have been serious, and they have appeared in ever more
rapid succession over a number of years. There is a spreading and
growing ground swell that acknowledges the need for activity
beyond merely sitting in the driver's seat and steering straight
ahead.

[1] Louis Harris Survey, reported in *Cleveland Plain Dealer*, July 5, 1968,
p. 20.

While serving as Secretary of Health, Education, and Welfare, John W. Gardner in a 1967 speech at the University of North Carolina, captured the essence of both the great afflictions and the great challenges of our time when he said:

> We don't want an impersonal society in which everyone is anonymous, in which individuality is smothered by organization, in which rootlessness is the universal condition and irresponsibility the universal affliction.
>
> .   .   .
>
> The non-participant individual, without roots, without a sense of identity or belonging, is a hazard to everyone. He is always liable to lash out in desperate efforts to find meaning and purpose. And if he cannot find socially worthy meanings and purposes, he will seize upon whatever comes to hand—extremist philosophies, nihilist politics, bizarre religions, far-out protest movements.[2]

The implications of such an analysis for all institutionalized education ought at once to be clear. They are of special moment to that institution which at graduation or earlier is still terminal for most young Americans—the high school. The great power of the quotation turns upon its reference to the nonparticipant individual, to the dangers that attend the presence of those who are rootless, who are not fully and firmly identified with the organization of which they are presumed to be a part. Gardner is reminding us that such individuals do exist, as observing school people know, and they do exist in great numbers. He is trying to give us a measure of the threat he sees in the increasingly impersonal nature of our society and our institutions.

THE NATURE OF THE HIGH SCHOOL

The high school is as American as the Constitution, baseball, or the milkshake. It stands as one of the chief reminders of the American belief that there are no unimportant people, that every last individual—including the most humble and the apparently

---

[2] John W. Gardner, "But What of the Dream?" A speech at the University of North Carolina, October 12, 1967.

least endowed—counts. The high school has great traditions in its favor.

Conceived as "the people's college," the high school has been a great equalizer of opportunity, a great social and economic escalator for many. In 1950 Henry Steele Commager wrote a classic defense of America's educational goals. Its title sums up his message: "Our Schools Have Kept Us Free." This eminent historian credits the schools with providing American democracy with "an enlightened citizenry," "the creation of national unity," and "that which we call Americanization." Fourth, he declares that "In the classroom, the nation's children have lived and learned equality."[3] In the United States the high school has made the great difference, for elsewhere a number of nations have long subscribed to the idea of universal primary or elementary education. For example, the 1848 Constitution of Switzerland provided for free and compulsory elementary education for all.

QUESTIONS THE HIGH SCHOOL MUST FACE

The first question that must be raised in any serious study of today's high school is: To what extent has it stood by one of its staunchest and most American traditions, that of the extension of equal educational opportunity for all? Although the nation's 1967 public and nonpublic high school graduates numbered almost 2.7 million,[4] approximately one-fourth of America's youth do not yet acquire the high school diploma.[5] What is the high school to do for these people in the last third of the twentieth century? Likewise, what is it to do for the additional psychological dropouts estimated at 15 to 25 percent or more? They are forced by social and economic pressure to hang on and secure the symbol of persistent attendance, although they never really enter into the mainstream of the school's opportunities. Is the

---

[3] Henry Steele Commager, "Our Schools Have Kept Us Free," *Life*, October 27, 1950, pp. 46–47.

[4] *Digest of Educational Statistics, 1968*, U.S. National Center for Educational Statistics (Washington, D.C.: Government Printing Office, 1968).

[5] *Statistical Abstract of the United States Bureau of Commerce* (Washington, D.C.: Government Printing Office, 1967), p. 118. Of each 1,000 fifth-graders of 1959, 721 reached high school graduation in 1967.

school obligated to manage its program in such a way that these people can be motivated to participate more fully in both the activity and the academic life of the institution? Can the high school become in fact the people's college?

The problem encompasses a constellation of other problems that face today's high school. Among these are the following:

1.   Is it possible for a mass institution to organize its program so that it serves the student in terms of his own unique interests, goals, and individuality?

2.   Are the purposes of education in a democratic society best served when the school's student body is heterogeneous or homogeneous?

3.   Is it possible to reorganize the school and its learning tasks so that better results for both the most favorably inclined and the least favorably inclined students are obtained?

4.   Are there effective ways of more fully challenging both the top student and the ordinarily indifferent student other than by simply piling more work upon them?

5.   Is ability grouping or any other plan of differing content for differing sections in the basic studies a satisfactory and appropriate means of individualizing instruction?

6.   Is it possible in an age of such rapid change for the high school to keep its aims and its programs abreast of society's most desperate needs?

HIGH SCHOOL AIMS AND SOCIETY'S PROBLEMS

Education tends to reflect the faults of the society that supports it. Consequently, it tends to direct its efforts at the problems of yesterday rather than at the problems of today and tomorrow. Most high schools have made attempts at reform over the past two decades. It seems fair to state that such stirrings have tended to crest upon the heels of the most feverish concerns of the combined space and national defense interests. These efforts have been sustained by two influences: first, by the James B. Conant recommendations and counsel, which have centered upon academic rigor with slight demand for alteration in organization or method;[6] and second, by the pressures of parents whose sons and daughters must compete for places in prestige colleges. Some aspects of these amalgamated interests reached their ultimate in the early 1960s. Some have not yet reached it.

We are now more than a decade beyond the challenge of Sputnik. These years have brought an escalation of domestic problems. At the same time, the nation's chief faraway bout with communism has led mainly to frustration abroad and division at home. Thoughtful people both within and outside the school are no longer so sure of the motives upon which school reform is to be based. One notes in the morning paper that the Civil War, which he was led to believe ended in 1865, was renewed on the streets of another large city yesterday. This leads him to turn his attention to matters nearer home. As he realizes that his air is ever less fit to breathe, his water ever less fit to drink, his streets ever less safe by both night and day, he begins to think of his immediate environment. Brave school leaders and teachers have modified curricula somewhat, procedures less, to meet this challenge. The domestic crises, however, have provoked nowhere near the stir that international crises did earlier.

Even the partially enlightened citizen of today reflects upon the fact that American affluence has reached only two-thirds of her citizens. He notes the havoc and ruin that dissatisfied but organized minorities can bring about in city streets, on college campuses, in industry, and in economic life generally. Then he asks: How can we meet these problems and at the same time preserve the American respect for individual liberty and freedom? If he is exceedingly thoughtful, he may ask: How can we construct an educational program that will above all else teach men respect for themselves and respect for each other? It is again being generally realized that social solidarity, the common purpose needed by the community at all levels, cannot be expected to come about automatically. The possibility that we may have overstressed individual and corporate efficiency to the neglect of social man is occurring to many. Such persons find themselves

[6] James B. Conant, *The American High School Today* (New York: McGraw-Hill, 1959).

receptive to Ben Franklin's two-hundred-year-old counsel to hang together lest we all hang separately.

Today's high school needs to become stronger not only in quality. It needs also to become more universal in usefulness, more personal and individualized in its procedures, and more relevant to the individual's and to society's needs.

THE PHILOSOPHICAL PLATFORM

This work is based upon certain premises, not all of which the reader may be able to accept fully at this point. Among these are the following:

1. It is possible to have secondary schools that serve the masses of students and at the same time provide high-quality education.

2. The most highly motivated and the most indifferent students can be led to respond favorably to similar educational procedures when these are wisely chosen and well managed.

3. The American ideal of universal education requires that it now be made universally effective. Maintenance and expansion of our kind of civilization demand it. Such a conviction is a significant part of the motive for the federal government's intensified and expanded interest in public education in recent years.

4. It is both possible and desirable to individualize and to personalize to a considerable degree the instruction for all students. A willingness to make some modifications in organization and in the direction of learning procedures is assumed. Careful calculation supports the belief that these changes can be accomplished in present buildings that are adequate, and without prohibitive increases in cost.

5. There is a significant difference between the stated or generally avowed aims of American secondary education and their realization. Strenuous efforts must be made to close this gap at least partially.

6. The humanizing aims of education have tended of late

to be neglected, and there must be a reorientation toward these.

7.   The task of education is not only to develop intelligence. It is also to teach the application of intelligence to the problems of both the individual and society. The quality of an education manifests itself most clearly and most effectively in the behavior of a school's alumni.

There is here no pretense at treating either all issues or all sides of issues. Greatest attention is given to the issues and the sides that are seen as most often neglected, those most in need of attention. Emphasis is placed upon providing a guiding philosophy, a unifying philosophy that is relevant to today's learners and today's problems. An attempt is made to wrestle carefully with the elements that must be drawn together to implement this philosophy. An effort is made to show that the kind of high school advocated here is consistent with the traditional aims and hopes for that American institution. The program proposed is conceived as a response to the demands and needs of a changed youth and a changed society. The whole is characterized by a recurring emphasis upon the total institution and upon the individual student's relationship to it. The rootlessness of which John Gardner speaks must be overcome. The mechanics of the school must be organized to help the student identify warmly with it. A personalization of service and spirit must prevail.

HISTORICAL NEEDS

Since the potentials of the future are tied to the problems of the past by the anxieties of the present, it is appropriate that we look first at the institution's history. What ideas and what ideals called the high school into being? What hopes have been held for it? To what demands and pressures has it been responsive? What economic and social forces have impinged upon it from its inception in Boston in 1821 to its estimated 14 million students and over 800,000 teachers today?

The pages ahead weigh the assets and liabilities that the high school has accumulated in the nearly 150 years since its introduction to our society. Such an assessment represents the first step in any effort at refurbishment and revitalization of the institution.

Size of Enrollment

The most important fact about the American high school is its size, that is, the scope of the whole enterprise, the number of youth it takes in, the number of young people it graduates. Nowhere else in the world does some 7 percent of the population march off to one type of educational institution at the secondary level each schoolday morning. The open doors of the high school are in singular contrast to its American predecessors, the Latin school and the academy. The Latin school was a British transplant and the academy sought to remain more or less selective and European in outlook. The high school was different. Democratization of educational opportunity was from the outset an important part of its foundation.

Rapid Expansion

The second and third important facts about the American high school are its youth and growth. The institution is a newcomer on the educational horizon. As late as 1860, according to Cubberley, there were in the United States only 321 high schools,[7] as opposed to today's 25,000. The figures do less than justice to the dramatic increase, since so few of the earlier high schools enrolled more than 100 students. It is doubtful that the rise and expansion of the high school has parallel in the entire world's educational history. That is, no other educational institution, perhaps no social institution of any kind, has attempted in the long history of mankind to fit itself to serve such a large portion of the population in so short a time. Understanding this is quite important to the student of secondary education. It goes far to explain the mounting shortage of high-level leadership and of qualified and com-

---

[7] Ellwood P. Cubberley, *Public Education in the United States* (Boston: Houghton Mifflin, 1919), p. 198. Based on a 1904 report of the U.S. Commissioner of Education.

mitted teacher supply, the general lack of adequate and appropriate libraries and learning materials. It helps to explain the lack of suitable textbooks, books written by authors who have both depth in subject matter and an understanding of learning problems at the secondary school level.

The high school has had its chief development in the twentieth century, for its real period of expansion did not really commence until about 1890. Few except the closest students of secondary education realize that the academy remained the dominant form of secondary educational institution until at least 1880.[8] Both were in competition, of course, with an institution that called itself a normal school and that did not limit its attention wholly to future teachers but often took in all eligible comers who were able to pay the fees. There were at this time, too, numerous institutions that were called seminaries, institutes, finishing schools, schools of expression, business colleges, and military schools. Each offered secondary work that was more or less academically respectable than the offerings of the high school or the academy, depending upon which individual institution was being compared with which other. Stereotypes do not apply to educational institutions any more than they apply to groups of people. Leadership and staffing varied greatly both within and among types of schools. There have always been more average and inferior schools than good ones, whatever the labels under which they operated.

In the four decades following 1890, the growth of the high school, both in number of institutions and in students enrolled, was frantic, even at times reckless. The establishment of a high school became one of the chief community bandwagons of the day. Once a building was constructed to house the organization, it was soon outgrown, replaced by a larger one, and turned over to an elementary school or to the rising institution of the junior high school, a completely twentieth-century phenomenon.

One somewhat typical Indiana industrial community built a new building for high school purposes in 1893, a second one three times as large in 1903, and a third one in 1924 four times as large as the second. Careful reflection upon the pressures born of this

[8] *Ibid.,* p. 192.

kind of growth reveals one of the main reasons why school
boards turned more and more to the employment of "managers"
rather than educators to serve as superintendents and principals
of these burgeoning schools, a long-continued trend that is well
documented in Professor Callahan's *Education and the Cult of
Efficiency.*[9]

Persuasive personality replaced scholastic insight and interest
as the chief criterion for selecting a leadership that must constantly fight to keep its economic nose above water. The tasks of
providing housing, desks, books, some meager equipment, supplies, and teachers who had some sort of qualifications crowded
attention to the school's educational aims and design into the
position of a poor second. Unfortunately, such conditions still
prevail over wide expanses of the educational front. They compound the problem of tailoring curricula to individual student
needs and interests.

Recent Establishment

In 1890 the American high school enrolled a grand total of
202,963 pupils, approximately 1 for every 65 students enrolled
in our high schools today. For any institution to multiply its
accommodations by 65 in the span of a single lifetime creates
a strain almost beyond comprehension. The fact cannot be overstressed. Distortion of purpose, vast areas of weakness, inappropriate and inadequately prepared staffing and leadership—these
are the inevitable results of such rapid expansion in any social
institution, educational or otherwise. This is not to say that such
growth should not have taken place or that the high school should
or could have regulated its growth or limited the number of additional students admitted each year. To have done so would have
denied the very purpose that the high school was created to
serve. It does mean that the historical fact should be recognized
for what it says about the status, stature, and problems of the
institution today. It does mean that the high school need not

[9] Raymond E. Callahan, *Education and the Cult of Efficiency* (Chicago:
University of Chicago Press, 1962).

always live with the shortcomings accrued as a by-product of its rapid growth, however necessary the toleration of these deficiencies may once have been.

Even as late as 1900, the 519,251 pupils being taught in the 6,005 public secondary schools of the United States[10] represented only a little over two-thirds the number of teachers now employed by public high schools. Clearly the people's college had not yet arrived in 1900. It is useful to note that these figures reveal an average school size of 86 students. As an even more revealing contrast, the 94,883 seventeen-year-olds who were graduated from high school in 1900 were only 6.4 percent of their age group, whereas in 1965, 71.9 percent—2,640,000—of all seventeen-year-olds became graduates.[11]

Stage of Maturity

It might be useful to think of an institution as rising, growing, reaching maturity, serving many years, and eventually giving way to another, just as an individual does. No scientific validity is claimed for the comparison, but it helps to clarify certain ideas. Students asked to think in such terms estimate that the high school's maturity as an institution has not yet reached beyond adolescence. Adolescence is often characterized as the awkward age, early adolescence as the period of rapid growth. Applying this yardstick, the high school has just passed through early adolescence, is still very venturesome, often lacks judgment, and is earnestly struggling to attain some maturity, along with a clearer perspective upon its purpose. Keeping this perhaps crude and not wholly accurate figure in mind may help the reader establish a perspective useful in all reflections upon the high school.

Diversity of Student Body and Program

Europe is characterized by secondary schools that have been established to serve limited purposes and limited segments of the

---

[10] *Statistical Abstract of the United States,* Bureau of Commerce (Washington, D.C.: Government Printing Office, 1963), p. 113.
[11] *Ibid.* (1967), p. 131.

population. There are typically the academic secondary school, aimed at preparation for the university; the vocational school; and a kind of extended elementary school. Not so in America, where the secondary school serves a socially and economically diverse population. It also offers a *diverse, varied,* or *comprehensive* curriculum. Such a social and curricular mix was first supported by the American conception of equality of opportunity and later also by compulsory attendance laws, the first of which came in 1852.[12] It is doubtful that any other society supports a secondary school that under one roof attempts to do so many different things, both curricular and extracurricular, for so many different kinds of people. The roots and forms of such social and educational diversity will be examined in some detail in the paragraphs that follow.

Origins and Motivation of Students

What has caused the diversity of the high school's student body? This question cannot be thoroughly understood without reference to aspects of the national mind and character at the time the high school was beginning, let us say during the last quarter of the nineteenth century. The doctrine of Manifest Destiny had been at work for some years. Industrial expansion had given the nation confidence. The United States was recognized in many places as a rising world power. The citizens, surprised as they reviewed their accomplishments, came increasingly to feel that in America nothing was impossible. In a very real sense the high school was born of and flourished upon this spirit. In the land of opportunity and promise, every man's son and daughter must have his educational opportunity, a chance to develop his personal promise.

New European immigrants made up a growing and influential part of the nation of the 1880s, 1890s, and early 1900s. These people with rare exception were laborers, but they had grander dreams for their children. Consequently, they often and early

---

[12] Massachusetts passed an attendance law in 1852. Cubberley, *op. cit.,* p. 253. By 1885 fourteen states and six territories had done so. Cubberley, *A Brief History of Education* (Boston: Houghton Mifflin, 1922), p. 449.

developed a sharp appreciation for the open door of the American public school. These citizens, although often no more than barely literate themselves, quickly noted that the foremen, supervisors, or proprietors for whom they worked were better schooled and more confident than themselves. Such a better lot they coveted for their children. To that end they frequently became zealous and effective promoters of better educational opportunities. Like most citizens of today, these new Americans were unclear about what education was to do for their children, but their intuition told them it would help. They used the same arguments, reflecting the same limited vision, that many parents still use: It will get you a white-collar job; it will enable you to escape hard work; it will fill your pockets with cash. Many such persons denied themselves necessities that they might send to the high school their sons and daughters, who were urged on toward graduation.

Into the new high school often came the student of the greatest potential in the community. Typically he represented the community's most cultivated home; he was the product of travel and cultural advantage, highly sensitized and highly motivated. Through the same door came the son of the perceptive and sensitive but largely unlettered laborer. When the son could not match his father's intelligence or ambition, his father might insist, nevertheless, that the boy go to the school and that he persist in his attendance. Then as now, when the teachers got tired of seeing such a student around, he graduated.

Quality of Student Body

One of the commonly held myths, even among professional educators, is that the early American high school was a highly selective, college-preparatory institution, that it served a monolithic element of our culture. This is not true, as clearly revealed in Krug's thorough historical research, despite the number of professional books that imply if not actually state it as truth.[13] The high school student body was diverse. From the beginning it represented all strata of our society and culture. Who attended

[13] Edward A. Krug, *The Shaping of the American High School* (New York: Harper & Row, 1964), pp. 11–14.

was based upon the same factors that usually determine attendance at other institutions: accessibility, costs, and desire. Only a minority of its students were college-bound through most of the early days—fewer than 15 percent, for example, in 1900.[14]

Actually, today's high school is to a greater degree a college-preparatory institution than it has ever been in the past; only since the middle 1950s have more than 50 percent of the high school graduates been entering college. In fact, conscientious principals of the 1880s and 1890s worried about survival rates. In some whole states in 1890 the graduates represented as few as 6 percent of the high school enrollment. Nationally, the average was less than 11 percent.[15]

This is not to say that today's student body is the ablest and most highly motivated that the high school has ever had. There is probably no valid way to make comparisons between the average quality of American high school students in 1900 and more recent times, although some few comparisons have been made. The difference, when one has been discovered, is not in favor of the earlier students.

A study made in an industrial city in the Midwest in 1942 gave one kind of comparison with the student body in the same high school in 1923. The Miller Intelligence Test, Form A, had been given to the 651 pupils enrolled in the high school in April 1923, and the records were available. An imaginative and inquiring leader resurrected long-buried copies of the test and administered it to the enrollment of April 1942, now grown to 1,321. To the surprise of almost everyone concerned, the larger, later student body made an average score 4.5 raw points higher than the earlier group. All differences considered, the 1942 pupils showed an average of 9 months greater mental maturity, with relatively fewer of low ability. If there was an advantage to either group in the matter of vocabulary, it was with the earlier group. Someone will counter that the 1942 scholars were more test-wise than those of 1923. An examination of the records revealed, however, that in this particular school, as in many others, the students of

---

[14] Elmer E. Brown, *The Making of Our Middle Schools* (Longmans, Green, 1905), p. 472.

[15] Krug, *op. cit.*, pp. 13–14.

1923 were being subjected to psychological tests more frequently than were the students of 1942.[16] Psychological testing was one of the great educational fads and preoccupations of the early twenties, the Army Alpha of World War I having been the first important mass-administered paper-and-pencil intelligence test in history.

Evidence is lacking that the high school students of 1890, 1910, 1920, or any other earlier date that one might arbitrarily wish to select were on the average superior in ability or intelligence to the high school students of a generation later or of today.

FACTORS IN STUDENT INCENTIVE TODAY

It is possible that recent high school populations have included more of the indifferent or less highly motivated students than was true of earlier student bodies. Such differences appear to root in matters other than native intelligence or ability. These differences must be thoroughly understood by the teacher or administrator who would serve well his students and his society. Today's youth, like their parents, may be more preoccupied with a multiplicity of other things, more absorbed with the products of a highly materialistic civilization. Educational analysts differ, however, as to whether the impact of the mass media has been negative or positive. Many such students are convinced that the greater amount of serious reading is in favor of today's youth.

The cause of the greater indifference in today's student may be in part psychological in nature. Today's student is not impressed with the idea that his having a high school to attend represents a rare privilege. The institution is so much taken for granted that the thought does not cross his mind. In fact, he is often inclined to regard it as a sentence to be served rather than as a privilege to be enjoyed. Even the college-bound student may think of it as an obstacle between him and the college he hopes to attend.

[16] F. H. Finch, "Are High School Pupils of the Present Day Inferior to Those of an Earlier Period?" *The School Review*, 52:2 (February 1944), pp. 84–91.

The Teacher's Competition Today

The high school teacher's competition outside the school is today more formidable than that of the teacher of one or two generations ago. For example, a number of well-done television performances present literary, scientific, and historical themes in a logical and polished style. Even the teacher's pronunciation and grammar are compared with that of the nation's best and most sophisticated news analysts. He finds his students skeptical of the loose logic and looser generalities or half-truths that were uncritically accepted by pupils of an earlier generation. The teacher's out-of-school competition is undoubtedly a factor in the lower student incentive of the present.

Relative Teacher Stature Today

The level of the typical high school teacher's education has moved upward less rapidly than has that of the general population over the past fifty years. Similarly, it has advanced at a slower pace than the education of either the elementary or the college teacher. Teacher qualification has suffered especially since the close of World War II, as substantiated in detail in Chapter 7. It is a change that has been accented in the high schools of the large cities. The writer has taken the trouble to look at 1947 and 1967 state reports in two typical high schools in one large midwestern city. Here he found that in this twenty-year period the percentage of teachers holding the master's degree had declined in the first instance from 50 to 22.4 percent; in the second, from 56.25 to 19.78 percent.

As a result of the rise in schooling among the general population, it is infinitely more difficult for the high school teacher of today to be as far ahead of his average pupil's parent as he once was. Again his competition is less favorable to him than it was not too many years ago. It is for such reasons as these that teacher and leadership personnel are given the rather considerable attention they receive in this volume. Incentive for learning is so important that it must be considered from every possible angle.

Student Economic Motivation Today

The economic drive for education is not nearly so great as it once was. This may be the most important of all causes of indifference in today's student. The power of labor unions and the pressures they have been able to exert have stolen a most effective partner away from the teacher. This has been especially true in the years of unbroken prosperity and jobs for all since the close of World War II. Better wages are paid for numerous jobs of little or no required skill than are paid for many white-collar positions that demand relatively high levels of literary or mathematical ability.

One high school English teacher, trying to initiate one of her less inspired charges into the mysteries of grammatical construction, was reminded firmly by the young man, "My father drives a truck. He gits paid more than you, and he don't know nothin' about this stuff." Despite all this, the United States Chamber of Commerce and many school men still try to sell education with the dollar sign. This demonstrates how easy it is to become fond of a rationale and to lean upon it long after its usefulness has passed.

Today's high school pupil probably is more often indifferent or harder to reach than the pupil of one or two generations ago. This is one of the prices of full or almost full employment. However, there is no evidence that today's pupil is less intelligent. The American high school has always served a quite diverse pupil population: socially diverse, economically diverse, diverse in ambitions, and intellectually diverse.

Education is not helped by begging the interpretations of its history. Forthrightness and honesty must prevail even though educators find themselves thereby robbed of long-standing excuses for their gravest failures.

HISTORY OF PROGRAM DIVERSITY

Again contrary to popular and considerable professional opinion, diversity has long been characteristic of the American high school program. Pressures for the practical and the vocational have persisted in mounting volume for more than two hundred years. In 1749 Benjamin Franklin called for an education "both useful and ornamental." According to his belief in the practical, he put into the curriculum of the Philadelphia Academy geometry and astronomy as well as their then most commonly applied counterparts: surveying and navigation. His was the first secondary school curriculum in America to give major emphasis to instruction in the language of the vernacular, English.

Vocation and Adjustment in Franklin's Curriculum

Franklin's curriculum also included science, agriculture, perspective and scale drawing, accounting, and penmanship. Thus we see the early foundation of programs that became common at the secondary level more than a century and a half later. In fact, Benjamin Franklin was a devout believer in life-adjustment education, which became the great bugaboo of American education's most vocal attackers in the 1950s. Reflection upon Franklin's famous autobiography reveals that he not only urges the life-adjustment of the student but advocates a personal regimen and adjustment that will make the cultured, happy, and productive life possible.

Life-adjustment education, unfortunately, is one of those terms that mean whatever the user wishes them to mean. To some self-appointed educational authorities, it is to be shunned as snake venom. Its spirit has been present in educational circles since Plato, although its letter is a twentieth-century phenomenon. It is a matter that cannot for long be denied due attention, for where people lack consideration and respect for each other, where they lack capacity to adjust, the essential social solidarity crumbles. Today's needs in this area are obvious. They are given major attention in at least three later chapters.

Range of Studies in the Nineteenth-Century Academy

The American academy, a semipublic school and the high school's immediate ancestor, not only taught many subjects but taught numerous practical and life-adjustment subjects. For example, the Phillips Exeter Academy curriculum of 1799 included such subjects as surveying, navigation, and moral and political philosophy. Paul Monroe lists the following academy subjects reported to the New York Regents in 1837:

> Arithmetic, algebra, *architecture,* astronomy, botany, *bookkeeping, Biblical antiquities, biography, chemistry,* composition, conic sections, *Constitution of New York,* Constitution of the United States, elements of criticism, declamation, *drawing, dialing,* English grammar, *evidences of Christianity, embroidery, civil engineering, extemporaneous speaking,* French, geography, physical geography, geology, plane geometry, analytic geometry, Greek, Grecian antiquities, German, general history, history of the United States, *history of New York,* Hebrew, Italian, Latin, *law,* logic, *leveling,* logarithms, *vocal music, instrumental music, mapping, mensuration, mineralogy,* mythology, natural history, *navigation, nautical astronomy, natural theology,* orthography, natural philosophy, *moral philosophy,* intellectual philosophy, *penmanship,* political economy, *painting, perspective,* physiology, *English pronunciation,* reading, rhetoric, Roman antiquities, *stenography, statistics, surveying,* Spanish, trigonometry, *topography, technology,* and *principles of teaching.*[17]

Of the seventy-three studies listed, those italicized, thirty-three in number, are primarily either vocational or life-adjustment in nature, or both. The reader is not asked to accept this judgment as to which are vocational-adjustment and which primarily intellectual but is invited to make his own list of any sort. That both of these aims of education are generously represented in the list, however, is a conclusion that seems inescapable. In the final analysis, of course, education is not readily dichotomized, for as Whitehead says, "You may not divide the seamless coat of learning," and again, "there is not one course of study which merely gives general culture, and another which gives special knowledge."[18]

In the area of the extracurricular, the academies frequently

---

[17] Paul Monroe, *Founding of the American School System* (New York: Macmillan, 1940), p. 407.

[18] Alfred N. Whitehead, *The Aims of Education* (New York: Mentor Books, 1949), p. 23.

introduced programs similar to the lyceums and to the literary and debating societies of the times. The records also make reference to student government, school periodicals, and dramatics, among other activities.

Certain it is that diversity of the secondary school program, both curricular and extracurricular, became a well-established and general phenomenon long before the popularizing of the high school as an institution. Considerable evidence would argue, in fact, that diversity was easier to establish then than now, for the academy owed little or no allegiance to regulatory state departments, the pressures of accrediting associations were yet to be established, and the rigidity imposed by the Carnegie unit did not come until the close of the first decade of the twentieth century. Minus the pressure of state requirements for graduation, most of the academies and many of the earlier high schools probably taught whatever subjects their teachers knew or thought they knew and wanted to teach. Diversification of subject offerings is a long-established tradition of American secondary education. This tradition must be cherished and expanded. The ideal demands unique elements for each student, hence as many curricula as students.

CURRICULAR PRESSURES

The high school, being close to the people and directed by more or less democratically selected representatives of the people, has always been responsive to the people. This has not been a benefit in every case. Generally it has been helpful, both to the institution and to the student. The institution has gained in confidence and support. The student has gained by finding a frequent appeal to his interests. Thus he has been ready to join and willing to stay for graduation.

Influence of Diversity in College Programs

At the federal level, the Morrill Act of 1862, by which most states eventually established state colleges to teach agriculture and the mechanic arts, was exerting pressure on the high school curriculum more than a generation before the average community had built a high school. This pressure was born of an ever-wider vision of the potential industrial greatness of the nation, the subduing of the West to a European type of civilization, and the need for a nationwide network of roads, bridges, and railroads. Faith in technical education grew rapidly. To prepare young men for entry or advanced placement in the new technical colleges became an obsession in some communities. Consequently, the pressures for more and better mathematics, as well as for the natural and life sciences, quickly became irresistible.

As was true in the rest of the Western world, education in America long had been influenced, indeed is still influenced, by the Renaissance. The long-continued stress upon Greek and Latin reached into the twentieth century. By 1930, or approximately 100 years after the beginning of the industrial revolution in the United States, Greek had all but disappeared from the secondary school curriculum, and the portion of students studying Latin had been greatly reduced. The Morrill Act was one of the major influences in bringing about this change. New subjects always draw their support from the life-blood of the old. The "classical" diploma is almost a relic of the past. Americans have been required to *adjust* to the demands of a technological society.

Influence of Social Progressivism

It is a common error to attribute to John Dewey and his disciples, or to progressive education in general, the prepossession of American education with vocationalism. Such trends were clearly and firmly established before Dewey wrote his first professional word. For at least the last quarter of the nineteenth century, the more broadly progressive influences in American society had been at work on education. A people interested in subduing a wilderness and in building industrial greatness could scarcely escape a pragmatically oriented education. In addition, the kinds of influences that made themselves felt in the Populist movement exerted influences toward a more practical education. The farm magazines published in Iowa and Wisconsin, for example, espoused a rural education that would fit young people to become better and more profitable farmers, that would fit them for rural life. They favored a life-adjustment education, and they editorialized regularly in its behalf.[19]

How and when did what we now call industrial arts get into the secondary schools? This is something else that John Dewey and his followers had no chance to bring into being, although the error of crediting them has become very common, perhaps because they did espouse the project method in learning. The fact is that we are indebted to a Russian exhibit at the Independence Centennial Exposition of Philadelphia in 1876 for the inspiration that set us moving on this trail. John D. Runkle, the first president of the then-new Massachusetts Institute of Technology, was impressed by an Exposition display—working drawings, illustrated processes, and finished products—from the Technical School of Moscow. He began to write and speak about the importance of this kind of education to the future of America. In 1876 John Dewey was seventeen years old.

Pressure by Industrial Interests

Runkle, not Dewey, widely aided and abetted by industrial leaders and men of technical interests everywhere, was successful. Calvin Woodward, in St. Louis, established the Manual Training School of Washington University only three years later. Woodward's secondary school combined the manual with the academic. From the beginning, its aim was liberal, not vocational, a goal still held by many of the nation's most noted leaders in industrial arts education. The situation in Indianapolis, Indiana, was not atypical. There the Industrial Training School was established in 1895, although the name was changed to Emmerich Manual Training High School in 1903, Charles E. Emmerich, a German-educated man, having served as its first principal. Its establishment was due primarily to the persistent efforts of Otto Stecchan, a mechanic and manufacturer. Mr. Stecchan went to Europe at his own expense in 1888 to study technical and vocational schools that had been established there.

---

[19] For a full and scholarly treatment of this theme, see Lawrence Cremin, *The Transformation of the School* (New York: Knopf, 1961), Chapters 2–3.

INDUSTRIAL TRAINING SCHOOL,

INDIANAPOLIS, INDIANA.

C. E. EMMERICH, Principal.

F. L. EMORY, Director Technical Department.

PROGRAMME OF RECITATIONS.   FROM FEBRUARY TO JUNE, 1895.

TEACHERS.	Rm.	8:45 to 9:30.	Room	9:30 to 10:15.	Room	10:15 to 11:00.	Room	11:00 to 11:45.	Room	Noon Recess.	1:15 to 2:00.	Room	2:00 to 2:45.	Room	2:45 to 3:30.	Room	3:30 to 4:15.	Room
C. E. Emmerich		Office															Library.	
V. A. Denree	F	12 A English	F	12 B English	F	In charge of Room	2	11 A Virgil			In charge of Room	F	11 B History	F	11 B Virgil	1	11 A History	F
Wm. H. Bass	Shop	Wood-working II		Library		Wood-working I		Sen. Composition			Wood-working I	Shop	Wood-working I	Shop	Wood-working I	Shop	Wood-working I	
B. S. Foy	G	11 A English				11 B English	G	10 B Arithmetic	G		10 A English	G	In charge of Room	G	10 A English	G		
Theo. W. Smith						Chemistry I	7					5	Physics II	5			Physics II	
*Kate A. Thompson	C	In charge of Room	C	Civil Government	C	Civil Government	C	Civil Government	C		Civil Government	C	Civil Government		Library			
Paul H. Grummann	E	9 A Latin	2	10 B Latin	E	9 A Latin	E	9 B Latin	I		In charge of Room	E			10 A Latin	2	10 A Latin	
Wm. L. McMillen	B	10 B English	B	In charge of Room	B	10 B English	B	10 B English	B		In charge of Room	B	9 A English		Library	B	9 A English	
Elmer B. Bryan	I	Plane Geometry	I	Solid Geometry	I	9 A Algebra	I	Library	I		Plane Geometry	I	In charge of Room	I	9 A Algebra	I	9 A Algebra	
A. J. Bean	19	Mechanical Drawing	19	Drawing	19	Mechanical Drawing		Drawing										
A. J. Griffith	D	9 B English	D	9 B English	D	9 B English	D	9 B English	Libr'y	D	9 B English	D	In charge of Room	D	9 B English	D	9 B English	
W. J. Thissolle	H	9 A English	H	Book-keeping and Penmanship	H	9 A English	H	Book-keeping and Penmanship	E		Book-keeping and Penmanship	E	Book-keeping and Penmanship	E	Book-keeping and Penmanship	E	Book-keeping and Penmanship	E
F. L. Jones	16	Freeh'd Draw'g I	16	9 A English	H	In charge of Room		In charge of Room	H		Library		9 B English		9 B English			
F. H. Noyes	16	Freeh'd Draw'g I	16	Freeh'd Draw'g I	16	Freeh'd Draw'g I			16		Freeh'd Draw'g I	16	Freeh'd Draw'g I	16	Freeh'd Draw'g III	16	Freeh'd Draw'g I	16
R. A. Trees	5	Physics I	5	Physics I	5	Physics I					Geology	1					Botany	C
H. Ingersoll	2	9 B Algebra	D	9 B Algebra.				9 B Algebra	3		9 B Algebra	H	9 B Algebra	B	9 B Algebra	C		
James Yule											Iron and Steel	Shop	Forging	Shop	Iron and Steel		Forging	
H. G. Sturm	1	10 A German	1	11 B German	1	10 B German	1				9 B German	1	9 B German	1	9 A German	4	9 A German	
Mary C. Comstock	14	Sewing I	14	9 A Algebra	14			Sewing I	13		Cooking I	13	9 B German	4				
Kate Wentz	G	Library	G	9 A Algebra				9 A Algebra	9		10 B Arithmetic	8	9 A Algebra	8	10 B Arithmetic	9		
Anna Taylor	4	Stenography	4	Stenography	4	Stenography		Stenography	3		Stenography	3	Stenography	3	Stenography	3		

Absent by reason of illness: Mr. Wm. F. Harding will instruct Miss Thompson's classes until her return.

25

In his efforts to get the Indianapolis school established, he was eventually aided by an architect named Bohlen and by other manufacturers, especially by those engaged in the manufacture of furniture.[20]

It was no doubt several years before leading progressive educators even heard about the Indianapolis school. Many of them never did. The school, in its first semester, 1895, offered courses in woodworking, iron and steel forging, stenography, bookkeeping, penmanship, cooking, sewing, and freehand drawing. (See the copy of the spring semester program on page 25). In 1897 Mr. Emmerich, the principal, organized and directed personally one of the first high school orchestras in America. He brought with him from his native Germany a triple emphasis: the education of the head, the hand, and the heart. Thus another life-adjustment influence was imported from Europe.

Influence of Business and Feminism

Only a few schools progressed as far as the Indianapolis school during the eighties and nineties. By the 1920s, however, education for secretarial practice and office procedures had grown rapidly, stimulated by the further expansion of commerce and industry and by the women's rights movement, which began to result in increased employment opportunities for women. The typewriter, of course, had been a post–Civil War invention (1873) and by the 1890s was becoming widely used. The high schools in the larger centers were the first to compete with private business colleges in meeting the need for trained office workers. By 1920, however, schools in the smaller communities were establishing commercial departments, and the private business colleges were beginning to pass into history.

At the same time that these events were transpiring, electric washers and sweepers and an increase in the distribution of preprocessed foods were freeing women from much of their home drudgery. Consequently, an increasing number of young women

---

[20] The writer has drawn data from a number of Indianapolis newspapers and from archives in the school itself, which he served as principal from 1949 to 1951.

were wishing to take training in school that might lead to a pay check after graduation and enable them to continue their employment after marriage. Many parents, too, encouraged this kind of substitution of job training for what had formerly been conceived of as education. Business houses, profiting from the availability of more highly skilled office help, encouraged the trend.

One can readily imagine that in many communities an influential father of daughters, one who was designing and hardfisted, exerted pressure upon the local high school and school board to establish a commercial department, thus relieving him of the financial responsibility of possibly boarding his daughters away from home while they learned shorthand and typewriting at Madame Fitzencough's Business College.

The Response of Education to Society

There is no evidence whatever that high school commercial departments were spawned by educational philosophies. They represented the school's response to changes in technology, in business management, in the role of the female in society, and in patterns of life generally. Before condemning such a response to society's demands, let us concede that many young people may learn much about living while learning about the world of business. Many educators agree that the discipline through which young people view life is usually less important than who helps them view it and the conditions under which the viewing proceeds.

EXTRACURRICULAR PRESSURES

Not only have the curricular offerings of the school been subject to seemingly irresistible pressures, but the extracurricular as well. People everywhere crave entertainment and excitement. In the days before radio and television, even before the movies, they often looked to the local high school to provide it; in many respects they still do. In small towns, especially, the entire populace awaited the senior class play with anticipation. Some schools, to meet the demand, added a junior class play and a sophomore class play and eventually established dramatics clubs that were active all year. Even so, the developmental experience offered by participation in a full-length play is available to only a minor fraction of today's high school students. Community need has diminished. Student need has not.

The game of basketball, invented in 1893, just in the early morning of the high school's era of expansion, proved to be a game that any school which had five able-bodied boys could play. So great a community pressure was built up around the game that many high schools were kept open long after their educational and economic soundness could justify their existence. The basketball team was a community rallying point that could not be sacrificed to school reorganization. Only a few years ago, visiting professionals of a statewide school survey team in one Midwestern state found basketball practice in progress in the middle of the day and in some cases for a considerable portion of the day. It was state tournament time, and other educational matters must stand aside in the interest of the team's advancement toward championship. The extracurricular has sometimes been subject to the same excesses and distortion that have characterized statewide scholastic examinations.

In football the emphasis is often greater still, especially in the larger communities and in the larger schools. Community pressures are infrequently felt in connection with quality instruction in English, history, or mathematics. But such pressures are regular and persistent concerning the distribution of football tickets and the effectiveness of the personnel employed to coach the team. If the coach also happens to be able to teach something, that is well and good; but he must establish a winning record, and a bonus salary of as much as 25 percent above the teacher scale awaits the man who can deliver.

Success of Extracurricular Methods

No small number of instrumental music teachers have told the author that they are unable during the first third of the school year to work with their students on the great music of the world's eminent composers. They must instead work with their charges upon the fine points of precision drill, executed to the accompaniment of martial or jazz tunes. Meanwhile, the girls' physical education department is readying its most attractive charges for their part of the half-time show. In some schools the mathematics or drawing department is called upon to diagram band or dancing maneuvers, the home economics and dramatics departments to costume them, and so on. Under imaginative and enthusiastic leadership the enterprise can become an almost total effort.

Use of Extracurricular Methods in Academic Programs

The emphasis here is not one of condemnation for the high school's program of cocurricular activities. Progress is never made by fighting a source of enthusiasm. A far more useful approach can be found in seeking answers to such questions as: Why the enthusiasm? What are its identifiable elements? Can they be enlisted and capitalized upon in other aspects of the school's endeavor? If some areas are overemphasized, it is quite probable that there are in young lives certain voids to be filled. The school, therefore, might best turn its attention toward the development of more varied means of filling such voids. Can the academic and citizenship efforts of the school employ more fully and more wisely such factors as recognition, team effort, and a more highly personalized and informal encouragement to the student?

With considerable justification it could be argued that it is in the area of the extracurricular that the high school has made the greatest gains during the past fifty years. Ask alumni what made the greatest difference in them, and they often point to the extracurricular.

Thinking first of using the findings only as a teaching device in his secondary school supervision course, the writer recently asked enrollees in his courses, both graduate and undergraduate, to respond to the following question: "What single experience during your entire and total high school career do you now feel meant the most to you? That is, what helped most to give you a measure of your powers or potential, to raise your aspirations for yourself, to give you hope, confidence, and reassurance?" It may be of some significance that approximately two-thirds of the 147

people to respond to this question credited experiences connected with the extracurricular as being most valuable. A further
analysis of responses, whatever the area, revealed that these
people had been most helped or inspired when the teacher contact had taken the nature of a personal aside, when it had been
somewhat informal.

Certainly this modest study does not mean that the curricular
should be abandoned, that the extracurricular should be given
the full sweep of the program. It might mean, however, along
with other evidence that tends to point in the same direction, that
the method of the extracurricular might with profit more often
penetrate the curricular. It might argue for a school less formally
organized, for one that more generously fosters informal, individual, and personal contact between student and teacher,
between student and student. Such a view is implicit in the
assumptions stated in the next chapter and in the school
organization discussed in Chapters 5 and 6.

THE GUIDANCE MOVEMENT

Among those who early in the twentieth century foresaw the
danger of the individual student's getting lost in the mass activity
of the school was Frank Parsons of Boston. He saw the need for
personalizing the school's service to the student and for meaningfully relating the school and its pupils to the workaday world
outside the school. Thus the guidance movement was born in
1908, although it caught on in few places until after World War I,
in many places not until after World War II. Like other specialties that are developed to serve school clientele, its activities
have too rarely become thoroughly integrated with the school's
existing curricular areas and program.

The guidance movement is, nevertheless, one of the principal
additions brought into most high schools between 1920 and 1960.
It is perhaps more notable for the spirit it engenders and the
attitude toward students that it fosters than for its record of solid
and penetrating organization. The area has been characterized by
much patient struggle, often against visible odds, by experimen-

tation, and by a considerable professional alertness. Despite limitations, guidance people frequently have been quite useful to college-bound students, perhaps less often to those going directly from high school to jobs, least often to those whose personal problems are deep-rooted or psychopathic.

Shortcomings of the guidance organization, wherever they exist, are as often chargeable to the awkwardness of the school's overall organization and to the collective attitudes of other staff members as to any defect within the guidance staff itself. Guidance staff members, like social case workers, too often have to spend time cleaning up messes created by defective organization and inept staff persons, a condition that can be eliminated by insightful and alert leadership.

A question pertinent to this discussion and to the character and content of this book generally might be stated as follows: Can the high school be so organized and staffed that the spirit of a good guidance staff pervades the whole organization? Can the kind of organization that leads students to accept greater responsibility for themselves free guidance workers, administrators, and teachers from much of the emergency repair service all are now called upon to render, thus making possible the planning and execution of more constructive efforts? Isn't it possible that too much staff energy is today directed into elements of control, with the result that problems are as often made as solved?

THE VOCATIONAL AGRICULTURE AND 4-H METHOD

Federal aid to public education is no longer widely regarded as the threat that it was just a few years ago. The indirect influence of the Morrill Act upon the high school curriculum was mentioned earlier. In February 1917, just a few months before America began singing: "How you gonna keep 'em down on the farm, after they've seen Paree?" the U.S. Congress passed the Smith-Hughes Act. It provided support for the teaching of vocational agriculture, trade and industrial education, and home economics in the high schools. The immediate provocation of this act

was the U.S. commitment to feed the Allied forces of World
War I, who were in a sense seen as fighting for American interests
as well as their own. In reality, however, Congress was responding to a long-standing desire on the part of many for job training
and for education that would, hopefully, help to keep young
people down on the farm, making that farm life more livable,
more comfortable, and more rewarding.[21]

In many a school, especially in rural regions, it was the
teachers in agriculture and home economics who taught other
teachers the usefulness of the field trip, the experimental approach, the functionality of life-connected education. The 4-H
projects demonstrated the vitality of individualized instruction
and the advantages of developing pupil responsibility and initiative, how much can be accomplished on one's own, granted
appropriate encouragement. One of the incidental benefits of the
vocational programs frequently was better salaries for teachers
generally and for local administrators. Conscientious citizens
could not always tolerate the realization that the vocational
teacher was the only one who was able to live respectably.

The later extension of federal support to other vocational
areas, such as those in distributive education and diversified
occupations, have met with similar, although perhaps less startling, success. They, too, have set useful examples of learning to
do by doing and have tended to link the school more substantially to the community it attempts to serve.

The shortcoming of all such programs as these, collectively,
is that their services have reached only a quite limited portion of
the nation's high school enrollment. The school, therefore, can
probably profit most by taking what is good and applicable from
these programs (and much of it is applicable) and utilizing those
features in the remainder of the curriculum.

RECENT PRESSURES AND CHANGES

It is always less easy and more dangerous to assess the recent
than the earlier, but some assessment must be made. One must

---

[21] Krug, *op. cit.*, pp. 414–415. See also Cremin, *op. cit.*, Chapter 2, for full
background of this issue.

know where he is and which way he faces before he can move with assurance into further fields of progress.

World War II had not quite ended when a major and continuing barrage of criticism was laid upon education generally and upon the high school particularly. The high school received the brunt of this criticism for several reasons. It represented the highest and the most recent schooling of most of the soldiers. It taught the kind of mathematics, science, and capacities to communicate upon which the necessary technical training for managing and maneuvering war forces might be built. It represented the middle of the school system, and when one aims at a target he does not understand very well, he aims at the middle as a matter of general principle. Finally, the high school is closer to most people than either the elementary school or the college. They remember it better than their elementary school, they read daily about its activities, and it is more visible and more accessible to them than the college.

Hot and Cold War Pressures

Hence the high school mathematics program was blamed when a young aeronautical navigator miscalculated his target by 73 miles. That Einstein might have missed it also was never considered. Why didn't the high school teach foreign language the way the Army did? This question was asked repeatedly, although the vast difference in teaching resources (including the Army's ability to commission at whatever level necessary the high school's best foreign language teacher) was seldom noted. Criticism continued, with historians, admirals, and other notables joining in. Then came 1957 and Russia's Sputnik, creating an impact that spread and intensified the dissatisfaction many times over. The schools that had waited to see which changes might last and which would not now had to move, ready or not. And they must move on the front in question at the moment regardless of the fitness of their forces to conquer that front. One can honestly feel only sympathy and understanding for the high school principal or the superintendent of schools in those turbulent days.

Pressure to Innovate

Innovation became the order of the day, the sacred word, in the very institution that had for almost half a century generally refused to let it in, even by the side door. Principals went to national and state meetings and found it difficult to get within earshot of meetings that discussed the new math or the new science. One might not know the tune of the new songs, but he bandied the words about. Thus a good deal of hypocrisy and pretense was encouraged, if not actually forced, a kind of stance toward which educators always and everywhere have been inclined simply because of the fact that those more ignorant expect them to know so much, and one must try to live up to what is expected of him.

The position on change is now being reevaluated, and the innovations themselves are being reevaluated. The heyday of innovation for its own sake is now in the past. The tendency of several years' duration, that of celebrating the machinery rather than the purpose of innovation, is also subsiding. Teachers and principals are more wisely raising such questions as: What do we expect this plan to do that is not now being done? Is the expected result worthy of the pupil and teacher time and energy it requires?

Some Innovations Questioned

That such a shift of attitude toward innovation is taking place is evidenced by the address of Principal Allan A. Glatthorn at the 1968 national conference of the Secondary School Principals Association. Glatthorn flatly charges the new curricula of the past ten years, which he characterizes as produced by scholars and "packaged by large corporations" with three failures: (1) fragmentation, (2) standardization, and (3) worst of all, irrelevancy and blandness.[22] Addressing another session of the same conference, Henry S. Dyer, vice-president of the Educational Testing Service, cast doubt upon the value of recent curricular revisions

---

[22] Allan A. Glatthorn, "How to Sabotage 'Teacher-Proof' Curricula," *National Association of Secondary School Principals Bulletin* 328 (May 1968), pp. 159–174.

and pleaded convincingly for a "teacher-centered curriculum."[23]

John Goodlad has called attention to the disposition of the new curriculum makers (1) to ignore consideration of the great aims of schooling; (2) to chart their courses as if no one had before mapped the area; (3) to assume that proper programming can render materials "teacher-proof," and as a consequence to fail to make sure that teachers understand the intent of the new curriculum; and (4) to fail to provide for self-renewal of the program through appropriate preservice and in-service education of teachers, for college as well as high school teachers. He suggests that the kind of person the school seeks to produce be given priority attention in future efforts to upgrade curricula.[24]

Such evidence that the high school's problems have not all been solved and that its thoughtful students and leaders are not entirely happy with everything that has happened to it during the last ten or twenty years could be extended indefinitely. The examples used, however, appear to serve present purposes adequately.

While the nature and value of a number of recent changes have been questioned frequently, it is still widely recognized by students of the high school and by its agencies of leadership that the time for reexamination of goals and reconstruction of effort has arrived. The journals and professional organizations that serve the institution regularly reflect this in the titles of articles printed, the tone and language employed, the topics chosen for discussion, the questions asked. The problem is how to get the needed change, to overcome intervening obstacles, to relate it to long-range and worthy purposes, and to enlist both human and other resources in its behalf.

SUMMARY

In this chapter some of the justifications for this kind of study of the high school have been suggested. Some aspects of the history

---

[23] Henry S. Dyer, "The Art of Unwrapping Curriculum Packages," National Association of Secondary School Principals Bulletin 328 (May 1968), pp. 141–158.

[24] John I. Goodlad, R. Von Stoephasius, and M. F. Klein, *The Changing School Curriculum: A Report from the Fund for the Advancement of Education* (New York: Ford Foundation, 1966), pp. 91–144.

of the high school have been examined. Particular stress has been laid upon the collective effects of the high school's effort to rise to the service of so many students in so many different ways in so short a time. It has been suggested that such an effort could only find the high school today with unmet demands upon its resources, both material and human, with many unsolved problems, with many unfilled voids.

It has been suggested, too, that the high school, so preoccupied with problems of expansion, has limped along for too many decades with too little change in concept, too little change in basic organization, too little change in ambition. It has been noted that change is due or overdue. This is evidenced by numerous efforts at change during the past twenty years. At the same time, the nature and soundness of recently effected changes have been questioned, their overall philosophy has been found incomplete or challenged, their unification largely undeveloped, and their relation to purpose often unclear.

The chapter has shown that the history of the American high school reveals many assets as well as liabilities, although the assets have not been fully exploited for the benefit of the total institution.

If the high school is to meet the challenge that is now full upon it, weaknesses and strengths must be carefully assessed, the former minimized and the latter augmented in the light of clearly defined purposes.

It is not the purpose of this work to add another panacea to the current pile. No one makes a loaf of bread from a single stalk of grain, no matter how richly headed it may be. Further, one stalk does not stand well or do well by itself. It is the total bundle, the combination of needed changes, their common properties of principle and philosophy, their capacities to support and supply vigor to one another, that is of concern here. The interest is in a pattern of secondary education with which America can proudly close the twentieth century and march confidently into the twenty-first.

2

Which Way Forward?

... those who loved their institutions tended to
smother them in an embrace of death, loving
their rigidities more than their promise, shielding
them from life-giving criticism.

John W. Gardner

One of the main reasons, no doubt, for the confusion that has
existed about the secondary school has been too common a tendency for decisions to be made on the basis of expediency. The
employment of referents—whether they are called principles, policies, assumptions, or purposes—has been much too rare. The high
school frequently has been too willing, like Stephen Leacock's
character, to mount its horse and ride "madly off in all directions."

This work rests upon certain assumptions, eight of which are
listed here so that the reader may see where he is going. Some
are built upon or convert to challenges or premises listed in
Chapter 1.

1. Teachers and principals can and must influence educational direction, emphases, goals, and curricula.
2. The first task of the secondary school is to extend the
general education of all students.
3. Unteachable young people are few in number.
4. Secondary education, not unlike all other education, has
been more effective in improving man's skills, his scientific

and technical know-how, than in improving his social behavior or his citizenship.

5. The educational product is first-class only when it is tailored to the individual learner, so that it becomes personally relevant and significant to him.

6. The development of responsible maturity is a most important but neglected aim of modern secondary education.

7. The high school today is in the early stages of change that can become momentous and far-reaching.

8. The school must recognize that previously slighted people, including the young, are today engaged in a new reach for freedom, for greater participation in the control of their destiny, for a part in reshaping society's values, and for a place in the mainstream of society's business.

These assumptions are discussed in detail in this chapter.

Assumption 1: Teachers and principals can and must influence educational direction, emphases, goals, and curricula. It has been too frequently assumed that they cannot and should not do so. Not only are such persons in positions that enable them to influence what the school does, but they also have a professional and a moral obligation to do so. In the last analysis the teacher is the chief curriculum maker. The prescribed state course of study, the curriculum guide, the textbook: all these have been used far too often as excuses for the lack of educational invention or progress, for the school or the teacher not to do what is needed. These excuses can never serve as reasons.

Courses of study, curriculum guides, and textbooks all lie in the area of suggested outlines. All are designed as means of assuring the attainment of minimum aims. The misuse and misinterpretation of such guides is one of many ways in which the school has tended to level down rather than up. Such miscarriage of intent has a tendency to cause minimums to become accepted as optimums. Any guide worth attention urges the teacher to teach individuals, to administer to individual obstacles, problems, and potentials. The prescribed textbooks or prescribed supplementary book may have confused the pupil yesterday; hence the teacher must set him straight today. Tomorrow the problem will be different. If academic freedom means anything, it means that the teacher is free to modify and to make curriculum that is meaningful and developmental for the individual pupil *now*. What the teacher can do personally within the sphere of his own classes the principal or the supervisor can do in a larger sphere through all the teachers he is in a position to lead and to influence. Not only is this his opportunity; it is his duty. Every secondary school enrollee is entitled to a curricular exposure that undergoes the maximum alteration or tailoring *for him*. Such tailoring is possible only to one who knows and understands him well. The person best qualified to do it is the teacher, who often needs help and support from the principal.

Assumption 2: The first task of the secondary school is to extend the general education of all students. This view is applied to both the junior and the senior high school. Today's secondary school graduates go out into a speaking, reading, writing, listening, calculating, and thinking world. All of them will be eligible to vote, to participate in the means by which a self-governing people functions. Not only does each youth require a good general education to discharge his obligations to his society, but he requires such an education to satisfy himself. One who lives in a socially and intellectually sophisticated society is a thousand times disadvantaged and uncomfortable if his own sophistication is too far below that of the majority. In the last analysis the truck driver whose formal education ended with high school and whose job for hours on end often demands little mental energy has both more time and perhaps more inclination to reflect upon a Hemingway novel or Socrates' theory of immortal life than has the insurance executive who acquired a B.S. in business administration.

This assumption rests squarely upon a second one—that *a general education is the best education to insure the capacity to reeducate oneself*, a qualification that seems to take on added merit with each passing generation. It is axiomatic that nothing seems more boundless in today's world than change, change at an ever more rapid pace. A general education seems to be the best learning to prepare one for a world of change because it forms the foundation of all other learnings.

In addition, with the rapid passing of the need for unskilled labor in a technologically dominated world, the utter necessity for better general education for all becomes even more apparent. Today the hewers of wood and the drawers of water are ever more often symbols of the buried past.

United States Bureau of Labor statistics for 1966 show that laborers except farm and mine, and farm laborers and foremen combined constituted only 7.3 percent of employed Americans. In recent years these groups of workers have been declining in percentage of all American workers, faster than any other groups. Industrial workers, who probably constitute the next least skilled group, are experiencing the next fastest decline.

On the other hand, the ways in which more Americans each year make their livings are as professional and technical workers, as clerical workers, and as service workers (excluding workers in private households).[1]

All of this means that more and more often the citizen who is equipped to earn his own livelihood must read, write, calculate, and reason well enough to take and follow some kind of technical directions—that is, technical in the broadest sense, both involved and specialized. To the extent that the school fails to bring the citizen to this degree of self-realization, others will have to pay his way, although he will still be able to vote himself a more generous dole. This offers our society only the poorest of alternatives, certainly less than the foundation upon which to erect an increasingly stronger and more democratic world leadership.

Assumption 3: Unteachable young people are few in number. It is true that much broader range in the motivational and structural bases from which we start is required to reach many with whom the school is now failing or only very partially succeeding. The full acceptance of the second assumption implies acceptance of this one, too, for the second called for the extension of general education for *all* young Americans through the secondary school.

Perhaps man naturally tends to disregard any truth that he finds exceedingly difficult to implement and to live by until necessity drives him to its acceptance. A recent study conducted

[1] *Handbook of Labor Statistics,* Department of Labor, Bureau of Labor Statistics (Washington, D.C.: Government Printing Office, 1967), p. 29.

by the National Association of Secondary School Principals shows that about half of the senior high school principals do not accept this assumption or its necessity to our society. While 73 percent of them accept the broad principle of universal secondary education, only 41 percent of them, nationwide, believe that school attendance should be compulsory to the age of eighteen or until secondary school graduation.[2] The utter necessity of such acceptance, however, is at once one of the significant achievements, one of the chief challenges, one of the main perplexities of the twentieth century. So important is it that the nation's failure to recognize and deal successfully with the challenge could be disastrous to our most cherished social and political ideals. The full nature of this necessity will be examined a little later.

The belief that the unteachable child or youth is a rarity dates back at least to the Roman Quintilian, who lived in the first century. He was among the earliest to recognize the importance of method and of the careful nurturing of the pupil's favorable attitude toward his studies.

Quintilian expressed his faith in a widely disseminated capacity for thinking and for learning as follows:

> For there is absolutely no foundation for the complaint that but few men have the power to take in the knowledge that is imparted to them, and that the majority are so slow of understanding that education is a waste of time and labour. On the contrary you will find that most are quick to reason and ready to learn. Reasoning comes as naturally to man as flying to birds, speed to horses and ferocity to beasts of prey: our minds are endowed by nature with such activity and sagacity that the soul is believed to proceed from heaven. Those who are dull and unteachable are as abnormal as prodigious births and monstrosities, and are but few in number.[3]

The nature of the necessity for twentieth-century man reluctantly to accept this first-century idea was skirted in the discus-

---

[2] John K. Hemphill, James M. Richards, and Richard E. Peterson, *Report of the Senior High School Principalship* (Washington, D.C.: National Association of Secondary School Principals, 1965), pp. 53, 55.

[3] Quintilian, "Institutes of Oratory," trans. H. E. Butler, in Robert Ulich, *Three Thousand Years of Educational Wisdom* (Cambridge: Harvard University Press, 1950), pp. 103–104.

sion of the second assumption. The pressures to enable each man to make his own living in an advanced technological society are relevant also to the third assumption. Twentieth-century society's motives, however, are not so purely philanthropic or altruistic that the individual is helped to make his own living for his own sake. Twentieth-century society on every continent is possessed of another drive—an economic drive, that of raising the gross national product. Society wants the individual to be enabled to make his own living because he thereby becomes both a producer and a consumer, standing upon his own economic legs. He increases the GNP through the product that he helps to create or process; and he increases the GNP by stimulating demand.

The emphasis on consumers is a twentieth-century phenomenon. The trickle-down theory has been rejected by modern economists because it has been discovered that the power of man, multiplied enormously by machines, has produced shortages of consumers, not of products. The earlier economy of scarcity has been replaced by a modern economy of abundance. This economy of abundance is sustained by mass production, which in turn rests upon the technical understandings of many. Ours is an economy which must increase each man's power, to make him worthy of his hire and to make his hire equal to his becoming a respectable consumer. Only then can he buy enough to keep the goods he helps produce from rotting in the warehouses. In other words, our society can no longer afford the luxury of the ignorant man. It is another of those matters where there is no easy choice. We either educate everybody or drastically alter our civilization.

Thus twentieth-century society is finally being driven to accept a first-century idea, but with great reluctance and only after its repeated failure to discover that the respectable producer-consumer is the throttle force in a technological economy of abundance.

Assumption 4: Secondary education, not unlike all other education, has been more effective in improving man's skills, his scientific and technical know-how, than in improving his social behavior or his citizenship. This is certainly true of the past 100 or 150 years, a sufficient span of time to cover completely the era of the rise and spread of the American high school. This is not to say, however, that we have by any means achieved all that might have been done in reaching an apex of educational performance in the technical fields. It is simply to say that, whatever may have been our strengths and weaknesses there, we have been more effective in educating technical man than in educating social man.

This difference is perhaps quite natural, especially since the age of the high school has also been the age of the spawning of new scientific discoveries and new technical developments at an ever-accelerating pace. The brilliant English economist, Barbara Ward, summed up the resulting disparity in terms of today's most formidable problems when she said:

> Rational rules of behavior are what we lack. The drives and energies that have built our world society have been, on the whole, the energies of power and wealth and enmity. We seem to lack any comparable energy in building the institutions, the laws, the habits, the traditions which express our moral and social purposes—obligation, equality, dignity, respect, neighborliness in the fullest sense . . .[4]

Although this state of affairs is distressing, it is hardly surprising, for perhaps two reasons. First, it is surely more difficult to modify human behavior and values through education than to extend and refine human skills, including even powers of logic and analysis. Second, the development of values, attitudes, and character as an avowed or official aim of education is a relatively modern idea.

When John Ruskin spoke the following in an 1866 lecture, "War," he was stating a doctrine that was less than generally accepted. Indeed, it is not yet wholly accepted today.

> Education does not mean teaching people to know what they do not know. It means teaching them to behave as they do not behave. . . . It is not teaching the youth of England the shapes of letters and the tricks of numbers; and then leaving them to turn their arithmetic to roguery, and their literature to lust. It is, on the contrary, training them into the perfect exercise and

[4] Barbara Ward, *Spaceship Earth* (New York: Columbia University Press, 1966), pp. 15–16.

kingly continence of their bodies and souls. It is a painful, continual, and difficult work; to be done by kindness, by watching, by warning, by precept, and by praise,—but above all—by example.[5]

It may prove useful, in this connection, to compare the seven liberal arts of medieval education with the Seven Cardinal Principles given in 1918 in the classic statement of the aims of American secondary education. Although more recent statements and proliferations of these aims have been made, the classic seven generally are accepted as sufficiently inclusive. In this analysis the number seven has special magic and usefulness. Although the medievalists and the Commission on the Reorganization of Secondary Education did not use precisely comparable terms, the aim can be inferred, where necessary, from the indicated curriculum content.

TABLE 1
Implied Change in Educational Aims

Middle Ages: Seven Liberal Arts	Twentieth Century: Seven Cardinal Principles*
Trivium	
1. Grammar	1. Health and Safety
2. Rhetoric	2. Command of Fundamentals
3. Logic	3. Vocational Preparation and Guidance
Quadrivium	
1. Arithmetic	1. Citizenship
2. Geometry	2. Worthy Home Membership
3. Astronomy	3. Worthy Use of Leisure
4. Music	4. Ethical Character

Cardinal Principles of Secondary Education, Bulletin 35, Office of Education (Washington, D.C.: Government Printing Office, 1918).

From Table 1 it can be seen that the aims of medieval education were more limited than the avowed aims of American

[5] E. T. Cook and Alex Wedderburn, eds. *The Works of John Ruskin* (New York: Longmans, Green, 1905), XVIII, p. 502.

education in the twentieth century. There are those, of course, who take the position that the chief trouble with the American high school is that it has attempted to do so much for so many and that the school would do well to make little or no attempt in the areas of character and social development. Those of this school of thought are frequently inclined, too, to lay the responsibility for matters being otherwise on what they vaguely refer to as the disciples of the life-adjustment movement, or a little less vaguely, to the followers of John Dewey. Any who are inclined to give even limited and grudging credence to such a point of view are invited to look for a moment at the thinking of another great British thinker, a contemporary of Abraham Lincoln.

In the year that Lincoln was elected President in the United States, Herbert Spencer wrote in his great essay, "What Knowledge Is of Most Worth?" that "To prepare us for complete living is the function which education has to discharge; . . ." Acknowledging fully the difficulty of structuring and conducting an education based on such a premise, but stressing that the stakes warrant the undertaking of any difficulty, Spencer goes on:

> . . . in the order of their importance, the leading kinds of activity which constitute human life [are:]. . . . 1. Those activities which directly minister to self-preservation; 2. Those activities which, by securing the necessaries of life, indirectly minister to self-preservation; 3. Those activities which have for their end the rearing and discipline of offspring; 4. Those activities which are involved in the maintenance of proper social and political relations; 5. Those miscellaneous activities which make up the leisure part of life, devoted to the gratification of the tastes and feelings.[6]

The reader will recognize quite clearly in Mr. Spencer's analysis at least five of the Seven Cardinal Principles, stated, of course, in different words. The only ones of the seven not directly included are ethical character and the command of fundamental processes. If one reads, however, the whole of the Spencer essay, together with his others on education, he will see that full

---

[6] Herbert Spencer, *Education: Intellectual, Moral and Physical* (New York: D. Appleton and Co., 1860), pp. 12–14.

endorsement of these two aims is implied. Note the title of his essay includes moral education.

Among those, therefore, who would be unwilling to give up the broader aims for secondary education, besides the writer, are Benjamin Franklin (see Chapter 1, pp. 20 f.), John Ruskin, Herbert Spencer, and John Dewey. Among the practitioners in secondary education are a host of inventive and courageous people who are engaged, despite the difficulties, in carrying these aims to fruition. Some of them will receive attention in later chapters. Meanwhile, let the thesis of these last few paragraphs be reaffirmed: Today's high school is realizing far more fully its aims in the health-vocational-fundamentals trivium than in the citizenship-character-home-leisure quadrivium. Expressed another way, it is doing better with its tasks that relate to human skills than with its tasks that relate to social responsibility. It is doing better in the cognitive than in the affective domain. Expressed still another way, it is serving the interests of the individual, if the psychological is excluded, better than it is serving the interests of society. Is it not possible for a man to be at the same time an individual success but a social failure? This theme is the subject of an entire later chapter.

Assumption 5: Learning is first-class only when it is tailored to the individual learner, so that it becomes personally relevant and significant to him. Education at its best is not a service that is mass-rendered. It is a service to individual human beings. In the last analysis there is no such thing as teaching a class, for no class of any kind or level has a mental entity. Only the individual persons in that class possess a mental entity. Mental and emotional reaction to mental and emotional stimuli is a very personal thing. It cannot be expected to be characterized by precise sameness in any two individuals. This is surely what John Dewey meant when he declared that what the learner gets is novel, a synonym for "unique." How could it be otherwise, since new learnings can be interpreted only in terms of the learner's earlier learnings or experiences? The more significant the learning, the more lasting its effect, the broader its applications, the more personal and distinctive that learning is. The more limited its applications, the more narrow the skill, the less different or individual is the product of learning.

A simple algebraic equation may serve to clarify the point. If x represents what is taught on a given day and hour, and y represents the sum total of what pupil Y is on that same date and hour—that is, all of what his previous learnings and experiences have done to him—then the answer N represents novelty, a unique product. N can never be twice the same because there is no other Y in the class. The equation then, is as follows:

$$x \text{ (what is taught)} + y \text{ (all that learner } Y \text{ is)} = N \text{ (novelty)}$$

It is interesting and perhaps useful at this point to notice the patterns or prescriptions laid down by theorists in special education, whether their field is the so-called gifted, the slow learner, or whatever. Near the top of the list, with rare exception, will be such items as small classes, a great variety of materials and approaches, and the utilization of many field trips and resource persons. Clearly implied is a recognition of the need for individualized instruction, for capitalization upon the individual student's needs, questions, and interests. There is no intent here to quarrel with that viewpoint. This is good education. It is just as good, however, for the student considered average as for the superior or the inferior student, and it is just as essential that he get it. To an institution that has probably done as much as any in America to equalize opportunity for all its citizens, the responsibility is inescapable. The school must provide highly personalized and individualized instruction for *all* its students.

Such individually patterned education must not be geared simply to differences in ability or differences in pace. The student who can work the twenty-five problems in the textbook most quickly is the last student in the class who needs to work another twenty-five just like them from another text. Individual differences in student interest may be educationally more significant than individual differences in ability, although the latter have had much more attention through more than sixty years of exposition upon the subject. This means that the heart of the student's interest or interests may be exploited as the medium through which to teach him any subject. If music is a highly developed interest, then his English may, in the individualized part of his program, become a music-centered English, his physics music-centered, his history music-centered. Or an out-of-school hobby, planned travel, or a job may become the moving force.

None of this is to deny that group activity is also important, that students do learn from each other, that important aspects of learning are social by nature. These, too, are significant. However, they must be complemented not only by the utilization of individual idiosyncrasy but also by its planned and active promotion.

More than ever before in our history, bigness and mass threaten to engulf the individual. As the high school grows larger, it becomes more impersonal. The individual student is in danger of becoming a mere number, a line on the school's and the teacher's registers. Well-informed school architects are recognizing this danger, as does Donald B. Wines in the following:

> There is, perhaps, nothing more heartwarming than to observe the effervescent enthusiasm of a youngster beginning school. Unfortunately, too often this enthusiasm wears thin somewhere along the path of formal education. A number of unalterable factors may be accountable but one may be that the child is institutionalized in contradiction to his natural desires. The tendency of our computerized age is to place people, as well as things, in simple uncluttered packages. We are today labelled, titled, itemized and coded to the extent that our own singularities seem subservient to larger group classification. Our efforts in pursuit of education for all is an exemplary goal, but mass education must not be at the expense of individual identity and expression. Large numbers and sameness promote an institutional feeling which saps the individual personality.[7]

Whatever the organization, whatever the staffing, whatever the school population served by the school, individual personality must be served and must have the opportunity to express itself. This principle must be applied not only to elite groups, however selected or whatever named, but also throughout the student body. Some limitations, of course, upon both philosophy and organization are marked off by this dictum. The school must be

[7] Donald B. Wines, "A Challenge, Not a Choice," *The High School Journal,* 50 (November 1966), p. 76.

organized, for example, so that the teacher has time to service the individual student and so that the student has an opportunity to confer with the teacher individually. Emphasis must be placed upon teaching the pupil how to assume major responsibility for planning and directing his own learning effort. The school must stress its role as a motivating agent, pressing the individual student on to his best and most highly individualized effort.

Assumption 6: The development of responsibility is a most important but neglected aim of modern secondary education. One of the striking paradoxes of the twentieth century is found in the notably earlier physical and social maturity of youth, while the home and school environments have moved persistently in directions of prolonging childhood. The earlier maturity of today's young people is documented in Chapter 6.

The position here is that the capacity to carry responsibility is developed through the opportunity to exercise it. There is no other aspect of human development in which learning by doing is more essential. Certainly the elimination of child labor, largely completed during the first third of the twentieth century, represented a clear and needed social gain. An undesirable by-product of this gain appears to have been the development of too great a fear, on the part of parents and educators, of the exploitation of youth and children. The net result is the inhibiting of highly developmental educational activities of a variety of kinds.

The tendency to overprotect children and youth from the world of real work has come in the same two generations that have seen the domestic chores formerly assigned to them rapidly reduced nearly to zero. Farm youth throughout the nineteenth century had useful chores which they were usually required to perform. Today there are few farm youth because there are few farms and farm families. In the cities and towns most of the work that children formerly did has given way to electromechanical energy and to other forms of automation. In addition, chemical and other technological changes have eliminated the necessity for doing many domestic tasks. Wash-and-wear fabrics have eliminated the necessity of ironing clothes. Most of the work connected with the home preparation of meals now can be eliminated by purchasing processed foods that are ready or almost ready to eat.

These changes have been harder on our youth than is commonly supposed. Never before have so many of them had so much cause for feeling useless. Youth are not unlike more mature persons. They want to feel important to other people. They cherish opportunities to do something real, to render a significant service to their schools, their communities, their families, and their friends. Home and school life as now constituted generally denies them this opportunity or at best fails to encourage their real and active participation in projects of worth. Many of today's young people come to the high school graduation platform without ever having contributed any considerable amount of their own sweat to the common good. Is it surprising that as adult citizens they show relatively little concern with problems of pure water, pure air, urban renewal, and the development of human resources? They have rarely had real contact or personal involvement in any civic problem, large or small.

Not only is there minimal involvement of young people physically, either as participants or observers, even where their own interests and welfare are concerned. They are also far too often and too completely led by the hand in the pursuit of their intellectual school goals. Far too much of their learning activity is under the immediate and complete direction of a teacher. Independent study and independently designed study has been discussed a great deal in the past few years, but to date it reaches very few high school students in any really significant form. Pupils spend most of their school hours sitting before teachers who talk to them or who direct them to do thus and so for the next fifteen minutes or the next forty-five minutes.

Teacher assignments are typically short. They involve something that the pupil can do in ten minutes to two hours. Too seldom is a student encouraged to follow over an extended period of time a question or an interest that he has unearthed or conceived for himself, a proposition that perhaps the teacher may know little or nothing about. Pupils are given too little incentive or encouragement to design learning experiences for themselves, drawing upon teachers and all other resources of the school, as necessary, to reach desirable and rewarding goals.

All this is happening in an era in which young people are maturing earlier—physically, socially, and mentally—than in previous generations. It is happening in an era in which an ever-larger portion of the work force will be working at jobs that call upon them to assume some degree of personal and individual responsibility. In an era also of rapid and drastic change, people must know above everything else how to learn, how to tackle a new problem. The high school graduates who go on to college or other advanced training, now more than 60 percent, need desperately to know how to assume a much larger degree of responsibility for their own further progress. Those who go to jobs or to marriage need this capacity no less. Every town and city and every rural community in the nation needs citizens who will assume a more active interest in the pressing, unsolved problems of the community. The demands of the states and the nation upon their citizens are similar.

Clearly schools would do well to give more attention to the development in students of personal responsibility—responsibility for the common good and responsibility for their own self-development. In this all-important task, it would seem appropriate to remember that responsibility is best developed through practice in exercising it. Infancy and childhood must not be unduly prolonged if more responsible citizenry is the goal.

When emphasis is placed upon the development of responsibility through inner motivation, the school will find that it can release much teacher and administrator energy now diverted to policing. Rules and their troublesome paper work are no longer necessary. This viewpoint is strongly reinforced by widely divergent sources. Among these are certain highly respected religious groups throughout the world, including the Quakers; the noted scientist-anthropologist Ashley Montagu; the famous Johns Hopkins sociologist James S. Coleman; and some of the nation's highly respected researchers and theorists in management. One of these, Douglas McGregor, is cited in considerable detail in Chapter 12.

Implementation of this assumption is discussed in the chapters on organization, as well as in the last three chapters of this book.

Assumption 7: The high school today is in the early stages of change that can become momentous and far-reaching. High hopes cannot be cherished for change unless it is ordered, consistent with well-conceived aims, and supported by the alterations in personnel and financial policies necessary to sustain it and give it vitality.

It is perhaps not overstating the case to note that by the late 1950s, change in American secondary education was already overdue. In many respects it had changed little since the introduction of the Carnegie unit in 1909. The junior high school came upon the scene about the same time. Both of these innovations represented change in organization, in mechanics as well as in philosophy. It was early in the century, too, that the accrediting associations and the state departments of education began to establish and enforce standards and criteria for secondary schools.

Standards and criteria, very properly intended to ensure at least minimum educational standards and standard meanings, have at times tended to discourage experimentation and change. State department personnel and state association committees have not always been able to attract men of penetrating vision. Standards have been reduced to terms that are easily measured or quantified and as a result have often been restrictive and damaging. Furthermore, the structure of such standards is based upon a presumption of certainty about patterns of quality in secondary education that has little to support it except long and widespread practice. A very healthy aspect of the growing respect for change in recent years is seen in the increased employment of new approaches to subject matter, including different ways of organizing it, as in the humanities courses.

The effectiveness of change that stems from pressure, as recent high school changes for the most part have, is always subject to certain dangers or snares. The first of these is expediency. There is a disposition to turn to any port in a storm. This leads to others, such as fragmentation, superficiality, and an emphasis upon the mechanics or machinery of change. The latter has been encouraged by the new gadgetry, such as computer scheduling. When one is in a tremendous hurry, he tends to move without reference to or development of an overall philosophy, principle, or purpose. He overlooks, for example, what ought to appear obvious: that more efficient ways of scheduling pupils into classes is important only to the degree that it gives him additional time to work upon ideas that will make the programs into which they are scheduled more meaningful to them. A traditional program will be no less traditional by being set in motion with a minimum of frustration and inconvenience to those concerned.

Another tendency frequently found in change that is born of pressure is to do what is easy to do. It is often accompanied by a secondary weakness, having the form of change without the substance. Sometimes the change takes the form of a return to an earlier practice that failed to prove itself in earlier and sometimes widespread trials. A good example of all three of these aspects of change is found in the ability grouping reintroduced into many schools within the past fifteen years. For example, the writer recently visited a junior high school in which he found seven levels of ability grouping in American history. Yet all seven levels were using the same textbook, and there was no indication that significantly different procedures or materials were employed in any of the levels.

In his foreword to a recent book on secondary education, John Goodlad observed that "proposals to improve the secondary phase of education, whether on paper or in action, have been seriously fragmented, especially during the last two decades."[8] Lawrence Downey, the author of the same book, wrote in commenting upon change in the secondary school: "the innovations presently being tried out are not at all systematic; they are not guided by any comprehensive concept of the process of education; . . . their interrelations and implications for one another are not clear."[9] Downey further observed that the overall results of recent changes were nowhere nearly as effective as they might be and revealed a fear that the movement might die before significant long-range benefits were registered.

A unifying philosophy of change is intended as one of the most useful contributions of this book. If this philosophy can help a little, and if it inspires a number of others to make their contributions, large or small, in that direction, then the aspirations for it will have been met.

[8] Lawrence W. Downey, *The Secondary Phase of Education* (New York: Blaisdell, 1965), p. vii.

[9] *Ibid.*, p. x.

Assumption 8: The school must recognize that previously slighted people, including the young, are today engaged in a new reach for freedom, for greater participation in the control of their destiny, for a part in reshaping society's values, and for a place in the mainstream of society's business. From the earliest appearance of organized education, students have figured heavily in most revolutions of ideas. Collegiate authorities, taxpayers, commencement speakers, and viewers with alarm generally may label students rebels and may wail their hearts out. It will gain them nothing and avenge them nothing. Revolutions in ideas are not put down, especially when the ideas involve the extension of human freedom, of man's participation in the control of his own destiny. When those ideas seek the reshaping of society's values, as today's revolutionary ideas do, they are doubly potent and irresistible.

It cannot be assumed that student rebellion will be limited to the collegiate level. Sixteen-year-olds can think, too, and they will recognize when and where their high schools fail as social communities. They will understand the ways in which their schools engage in hypocrisy and pretense.

Students will insist on large measures of authority and determination, first in the custodial functions of the school—such as cafeteria, security of person and property, and the control of traffic—and in the activities that most intimately and personally concern them. In fact, many schools have already extended to students large measures of control in such areas. Not far away are the days when high school students will publish their own evaluations of courses and teachers, as is done in a number of colleges now. Likewise, their influence in shaping curricula, in defining the tasks upon which they are to work, will be felt increasingly in one way or another. The challenge to leadership is to harness this disposition to maximize its educational value and to increase the reality of the learning that takes place.

At the time of this writing, the Students for a Democratic Society had announced its resolve to propagandize widely and to seek to enlarge its membership at the high school level.[10] In a society so obsessed with organization, can it be expected that

---

[10] *Time*, June 21, 1968, p. 42; a report on the national conference of the Students for a Democratic Society at Michigan State University.

students will remain totally unorganized, oblivious to their interests and concerns as students? Specific organizations may change frequently at first, but organization is likely to persist.

Among the many thinkers of stature who have addressed themselves to elements of this assumption is Ramsey Clark, former United States Attorney General. He writes, in part, as follows: "All institutions ... must address themselves to change." Pleading for tolerance of dissent, he continues, "Dissent is the voice of powerless people. Historically, dissent has been the principal catalyst in the alchemy of truth. ... Can anyone really doubt that our attitude about the War in Vietnam has changed because of dissent?"[11] Clark seems unsure that human dignity is possible in a mass society, but he does seem to be sure that we had better give it every chance.

In the long history of the worldwide struggle of increasing numbers of people for freedom and for participation in their society's management, the growth of freedom has by no means followed a smooth and gently inclined plane. Rather, there have been times when freedom has done well to hold its own; times when it has lost ground; other times when the gains have been great. The school's principal and its faculty must recognize that human freedom is now in one of its sharper rises. The plea here is simply that the school's leadership and faculty be ready to capitalize, educationally, upon such phenomena, for they do exist and they will not be put aside. They will be reckoned with, increasingly, in one way or another.

SUMMARY

It is practically impossible for one to set down all possible assumptions about any enterprise. Some are so obvious as to require no special recognition. Others are so broad and significant that interpretation is required. In the chapters that follow, the writer does not limit himself by mechanics so rigid as to require direct reference to a given assumption. Frequently the discussion

[11] Ramsey Clark, "Man v. the State," *The Center Magazine*, 3:2 (March 1970), p. 72.

and the proposal will rest upon a combination or a blend of these. Any discussion of this kind is destined to be incomplete, to be subject to attack from many sides. Many whole books deal with the subject of this chapter. Even they leave entire areas untouched and others vulnerable.

The assumptions stated in this chapter call for no great revolution in the aims American secondary education has set for itself. They do call attention to an incomplete realization of some of these aims. They also call for a more spirited, deliberate, and organized effort to meet some of these expectations. Finally, they attempt to sharpen the focus on issues that are pertinent to the increased usefulness of the high school to today's society, today's problems, and today's students. It is hoped that the reader will find them helpful in the interpretation of the remainder of this work.

3

The Leaders
the High Schools Have

...the necessity of exercising judgment...is a
prime function of leadership.

Barbara W. Tuchman

Leadership is an important factor in carrying any institution from
where it is to where it ought to go. Obviously it is unfair to
suggest changes in leadership and leadership viewpoints without
first examining carefully the present leaders. What is the nature
of the typical high school principal's cultural and educational
background? What is his own educational background and
attainment?

How does the principal view the educational issues of the
day? What are his sophistications? To what extent do his opinions
about education tend to linger in the realm of folk wisdom? What
respect and what authority accompany his responsibility? How
does he view himself and his leadership role?

Examining the present situation enables one to see what
might be better. For making such an analysis, the best and most
recent source appears to be the *Report of the Senior High-School
Principalship,* a study completed and published by the National
Association of Secondary School Principals in 1965.[1] This report

[1] John K. Hemphill, James M. Richards, and Richard E. Peterson, *Report
of the Senior High-School Principalship* (Washington, D.C.: National
Association of Secondary School Principals, 1965).

involved what very probably was the most exhaustive study of the secondary school principalship ever made in America. The elaborate and rather complete questionnaire was broken into five forms, one of which was mailed to each of 23,555 secondary school principals of both public and independent secondary schools in November 1963. The study report was based upon 16,082 replies. Based upon returns received after the usable deadline date and other evidence, NASSP authorities believe that the bias in this study suggests that principals of small, rural, and poorly supported high schools are not quite fully represented in the sample. This probably means that the less well qualified principals are underrepresented in the study.

The writing of this chapter draws freely and frequently upon this NASSP study. It is quite likely that the investigation will get less attention and study than it deserves. No apology is made, therefore, for heavy reliance upon this significant study. All data of this chapter not otherwise credited are drawn from it. Permission to draw thus heavily upon the study was requested and was readily granted. The interpretations of the data are the writer's own and may or may not agree with those of the reporters of the study. Near the end of the chapter some important questions not mentioned or not covered adequately in the NASSP study are treated more or less speculatively.

THE PRINCIPALS AND THEIR BACKGROUNDS

Who are America's high school principals? They are predominantly male—just over 89 percent, in fact. The small number of female principals are found primarily in the cities, in independent schools, in specialized high schools, and in the Northeast.

How old are the principals? Only 4 percent are under thirty and only 8 percent are over sixty. Just over one-third of them fall in the thirty-five-to-forty-four age range; almost another third in the forty-five-to-fifty-four age bracket.

From what areas of the country do the secondary school leaders come? Twelve Midwestern states have contributed 37 percent of them. The second largest supplier is the Southeast, which has furnished 21 percent. Geographic areas supplying less than their share include the Far West and New England.

From these proportions one could surmise that rural environments furnish a disproportionately large share of the principals, and they do. Rural regions, plus towns with fewer than 5,000 people, have provided 59 percent of them. Only 12 percent grew up in cities of 250,000 or more. In other words, the high school principal is about three times out of five a country boy. Similar data no doubt would be characteristic of ministers, writers of books about education, and perhaps other kinds of leaders in American society. The rural or small-town boy has frequent opportunities to witness the performance of and develop respect for school and church leaders; but he has little contact with leaders and professionals in other fields.

Parents and Home Backgrounds

More revealing facts are found in the nature of the homes from which the principals came and in the educational levels attained by their parents. It is a striking coincidence that the percentage who came from the homes of farmers and laborers, skilled and unskilled, is the same as the rural percentage mentioned above, 59 percent. The 32 percent who represent the homes of laborers are, of course, only in part the same persons who came from the small towns.

Only 11 percent of the principals came from the homes of teachers, scientists, engineers, ministers, lawyers, physicians, and other professionals. This means that in almost 90 percent of the cases, the principals are first-generation professionals in their families.

How much formal education did the fathers and mothers of high school principals have? Only 3 percent of both the fathers and the mothers had finished four years of college. Only 8 percent of the fathers and 12 percent of the mothers had had some college or junior college work. This means that the principals overwhelmingly represent first-generation college education in their families.

High school graduation was reached by 11 percent of the principals' fathers and by 17 percent of their mothers. Grade school was not completed by 25 percent of the fathers and by 17 percent of the mothers. These figures, together with those cited in the paragraphs above, lead one to make some speculative but probably valid conclusions. Since a majority of secondary school principals came from rural and small-town homes, since only a minor fraction of their parents graduated from high school, and since their fathers were predominantly farmers and laborers, it is probable that the homes were proportionately limited in their encouragement of the scholastic life. For example, it is quite probable that the majority of these homes did not possess and use a good standard reference work. It is also probable that the periodical and other literature coming into these homes was rather limited in scope and nature. The mother or father in these homes who set an example of the wide reading of solid literature could be expected to be the exception rather than the rule. Thus, to the extent that today's secondary principals are scholars—and some of them are—they, with the help of their teachers and colleagues, have usually made themselves scholars. It was not often their home environment that pointed them in that direction, although they often may have received limited types of encouragement from their parents and others.

Environmental Advantages

Their rural and small-town environments offered these potential leaders certain advantages: the inspiration that comes from living close to nature, the constant invitation to study plants and animals, the opportunity to understand and to know a few people better and more intimately. Consequently, it might be expected that today's principals would be more effective in human relations than in curricular design or in educational purpose. Most careful observers of the secondary education scene would probably argue that this is in fact the case.

Tenure, Stability, and Commitment

At what age did secondary principals assume their first administrative or supervisory assignment? For 42 percent of them, more than two out of five, this came before age thirty; for 12 percent, before age twenty-five. This means that on-the-job training has played a large part in the development of principals now working at the job. It means that many took their first supervisory or administrative position with little or no specialized preparation for the job, because the job was acquired before there was time to prepare amply for it. It means that the principalship often has been its own apprenticeship, a job that many have learned by doing. This practice is surely destined to be less and less common in the future, because of the recent and continuing strengthening of certification requirements and the trend toward the requirement of an internship.

There is relative stability of tenure in the secondary school principalship, for 48 percent of the incumbents are still serving their initial principalship, while only 10 percent have held four positions or more, and none more than seven. The stability of the position is undoubtedly much greater than that of the superintendency. A further measure of stability in the position, though not necessarily in the same school, is seen in the fact that 43 percent have been serving as principals for ten years or longer, which is in recent years somewhat longer than the average teacher remains in teaching.

This study reveals that America's secondary principals are, with few exceptions, firmly committed to educational service. While 52 percent of them have never held any other full-time job (excluding military service), 32 percent more have held other jobs for periods of only one to four years. This is the more remarkable because public school teaching is a job of relatively short tenure, especially for men. (See Chapter 7.)

Education Through First Degree

Fully 83 percent of the principals are graduates of public high schools; the remainder are graduates of various types of nonpublic secondary schools.

The undergraduate work of 55 percent of the principals was taken at public universities and colleges, with 27 percent more earning their initial degrees at church-related colleges. As undergraduates, 29 percent majored in the humanities; 18 percent, in physical or biological sciences; 14 percent, in social sciences; 12 percent, in education; and 11 percent, in physical education.

Graduate and Professional Education

In graduate work, 90 percent hold at least a master's degree, 2 percent hold the doctorate in education, and 1 percent hold the doctor of philosophy degree. Of the 90 percent, another 6 percent have done all the course work for a doctorate but have not completed other requirements.

The major field of graduate work undertaken by 70 percent of the principals has been educational administration and supervision; another 12 percent have taken secondary education. Although 90 percent of the principals have had ten or more courses in education, graduate and undergraduate, only 25 percent have had as many as twenty-five courses in professional education. Most of the courses taken have been concerned with secondary school organization, curriculum development, tests and measurements, the psychology of learning, counseling and guidance, child and adolescent development, research methodology, and school finance.

It is interesting to note that, when asked to indicate the fields of professional study the principals consider most essential to their work, as a group they rate highest the supervision of instruction, personnel administration, and human relations. The philosophy of education ranks thirteenth among twenty-five listed categories; comparative education and the history of education are tied for twenty-second place; and political science and vocational education vie for last place.

Previous Experience in Education

Fully 56 percent of the principals have coached or served as athletic director at some time in their school careers, although only 14 percent came immediately from such positions into the principalship. In addition, 48 percent of them have served in guidance or counseling, 38 percent have been principals of elementary schools, 19 percent have been secondary school deans, and 13 percent have had at least one year as college teachers. There is, of course, obvious overlap among the categories of previous school experience; that is, often the same man has held two or more of these positions.

Among those who had secondary teaching experience prior to assuming their principalships, the largest number, 33 percent, had taught chiefly mathematics or natural science; the second greatest number, 26 percent, social sciences; and the third greatest number, 11 percent, English.

Other Qualifications

Principals tend to think that the vice-principalship is the most valuable prior experience, with the deanship, guidance or counseling, the elementary principalship, and the department chairmanship following in that order.

With regard to present certification requirements, almost three-fourths find teaching experience, administrative experience, and course work requirements satisfactory as they are. At the same time 72 percent of them say that they have found no set of theoretical or textbook principles of administration to be a useful guide for day-to-day operation of a school.

An important factor in evaluating the background of principals is the type of diploma granted by high schools. As shown by the NASSP study, the two most popular are for the college preparatory and the general programs of study. The third most popular, but lagging far behind, is the business diploma.

OPINIONS OF PRINCIPALS ON EDUCATIONAL ISSUES

What do principals think the most important tasks or goals of the schools are? What do they think the school should attempt to do for its students, or help them do for themselves? Here the NASSP committee listed nine goals and asked the principals to rank them in order of their importance. In Table 2 these goals are

TABLE 2
High School Goals as Ranked by Principals

Educational Goal	Rank								
	1	2	3	4	5	6	7	8	9
1. Acquisition of basic skills (e.g., reading, writing, computing)	52%	17%	11%	7%	4%	3%	3%	2%	1%
2. Acquisition of basic knowledge	11	36	16	12	9	6	5	3	2
3. Development of sound moral and spiritual values	18	12	14	13	11	10	10	6	5
4. Understanding of the values inherent in the American way of life	8	12	20	16	16	13	7	5	2
5. Development of skills and practice of critical intellectual inquiry	10	11	13	13	11	12	12	11	6
6. Development of positive self-concepts and a facility for good human relations	4	8	8	11	15	15	15	17	6
7. Adaptability to a changing world	4	5	8	13	13	14	16	15	11
8. Physical fitness	1	3	6	8	13	14	14	19	20
9. Training in the technical skills to run the country and/or development of appropriate talents (e.g., engineering, scientific)	1	3	3	5	5	7	12	19	43

Adapted, with permission, from John K. Hemphill, James M. Richards, and Richard E. Peterson, *Report of the Senior High-School Principalship* (Washington, D.C.: National Association of Secondary-School Principals, 1965), Table 51, p. 51. The items have been rearranged in the order principals ranked them, and the title has been supplied by this writer.

listed in the order of the relative importance which the principals, collectively, assigned to them.

In reflecting upon the accompanying table, it must be remembered that these data were gathered in the last months of 1963 and the early part of 1964. What differences might be reflected in a 1970 repetition of the study? In 1975? Might the "development of positive self-concepts and a facility for good human relations" move closer to the top? Might "adaptability to a changing world" similarly advance in rank? What effect do the problems society faces have upon the ordering of educational values?

Both from an overall viewpoint and from the fact that the principals place technical skills in last place, they appear to agree with the assumption, stated in Chapter 2, that general education is a priority function of secondary education. It is perhaps of some significance that the National Association's study commission, in setting up their values, made five of them represent the citizenship–character–whole person category. It is significant, too, that all of these rated above—and all but one well above—physical fitness and technical skills, even though the latter was obviously broad enough to include the technical aspects of prescientific and preengineering education.

Again it is useful to inquire what may be the effect upon this ranking of aims when the cold and hot wars of the present have been settled, and when the space race has been won, lost, or forgotten.

Opinions on Current Debates

How do principals think on the current and continuing educational controversies that plague American school boards, legislative bodies, courts, teachers, parents, and pupils?

Almost two-thirds of the principals (67 percent) are in favor of federal aid to public secondary schools, but only one out of five (21 percent) favors such aid to private and religious secondary schools. Only 34 percent agree with the Supreme Court about compulsory prayer and Bible reading in the public schools. This fact indicates a less sophisticated understanding of one of the American values the principals want taught (freedom from religious establishment) than one might hope. Precisely the same portion of the principals believe that there should be some limitations upon classroom discussions of political "isms" and "anti-isms," terms employed by the study.

Nearly three-fourths (73 percent) endorse Supreme Court decisions concerning segregation in the public schools, but only 17 percent agree with the critics who say that today's schools require too little academic work of students.

Opinions on School Programs and Universal Secondary Education

Only 26 percent of the principals feel it necessary to justify as practical every subject that is taught. Just over four out of five (81 percent) are in favor of ability grouping in such subjects as mathematics, English, and foreign languages. Here one wonders what the leaders would say now, more than ten years after the era of Sputnik, and the influence of James Bryant Conant.

While the principals usually have favored the introduction of scholastic rigor into the school program, only one-fifth of them (21 percent) are in favor of further lengthening the school year.

It is a bit shocking to discover that fewer than three-fourths (73 percent) of America's secondary principals accept the principle of universal secondary school education. In no part of the country nor in any type of secondary institution, furthermore, did more than 50 percent of them advocate compulsory school attendance to age eighteen or to secondary school graduation. In fact, only 41 percent of all the principals supported such a requirement. The questionnaire did not require the 59 percent who did not believe in such a requirement to say what agency or institution they would ask to take charge of the youth whom they would reject. The two items from the NASSP study table covering these points are given in Table 3.

Perhaps it is human for those in any area of endeavor to feel that the really tough problems should be handled by somebody else. One might hope, however, that more than 50 percent of the secondary school principals would take a broader view of their responsibilities to help their society solve its tough problems. To bring into the mainstream of American citizenship and responsi-

TABLE 3

High School Principals' Views on Universal Secondary Education (Percentage Answering Yes)

Question	Location		Type of School		Program		Region				Total Sample
	Urban	Rural	Public	Inde-pendent	Compre-hensive	Other	NE	SE	West		
Do you accept the principle of universal secondary school education?	77	70	75	65	75	67	78	66	73		73
Do you believe that school attendance should be compulsory until at least 18 years (or secondary school graduation)?	37	44	39	50	39	49	31	50	41		41

Adapted, with permission, from John K. Hemphill, James M. Richards, and Richard E. Peterson, *Report of the Senior High-School Principalship* (Washington, D.C.: National Association of Secondary School Principals, 1965), Table 53, pp. 53 and 55.

bility the majority of the youth that many schools are prone to reject is surely one of the pressing problems that threaten American society. This ought today to be evident to well-informed Americans, school people or not.

A degree of inconsistency with these attitudes appears in certain other responses made by the principals, for 71 percent believe that the public schools have responsibility for educating the physically handicapped and 58 percent, for educating the mentally handicapped. Some principals evidently draw sharp lines of difference between these types of handicaps and social, economic, and psychological handicaps. In other words, they draw a difference between accident-of-birth handicaps and accident-of-environment handicaps.

In other respects, principals do have a democratic outlook, as indicated by the fact that only 19 percent believe that the secondary schools should expend greater effort in educating the academically able than in educating the average student. This indicates, too, that many more principals feel the call of the average student upon their energies than are equally serious about their responsibilities to the inferior or indifferent student.

Hopes for the Future

From 37 to 40 percent of the principals approved of Lloyd Trump's suggestions about "schools of the future" as set forth in *Focus on Change,*[2] although 27 percent more confess unfamiliarity with these proposals on reorganizing the instruction, the buildings, the schedules, and the utilization of teacher time. Approximately half (48 percent) believe that important curricular changes should be preceded by the securing of community support.

In 1963 almost one-third of the principals (30 percent) were very optimistic about the elimination of illiteracy in American society within twenty years, while exactly 50 percent thought it possible, but not very probable. This reflects a marked degree of

[2] J. Lloyd Trump and Dorsey Baynham, *Focus on Change: Guide to Better Schools* (Skokie, Ill.: Rand McNally & Co., 1961).

consistency with their views on the degree of the school's responsibility to the indifferent or hard-to-reach scholar.

Agreement on Controversies?

From the past was drawn a persistent topic of educational debate: Are good teachers "born," or are they "made"? Almost half of the principals, 45 percent, indicated the belief that they are "born." Thus nearly half of America's secondary school leaders scuttled what many students of the secondary school believe is the most important part of their jobs, supervision. What is a supervisor of instruction doing if he isn't trying to improve teachers and teaching?

The principals were more liberal with respect to the importance of freedom of inquiry in education. Only 28 percent of them believed academic freedom for the teacher to be in conflict with good education, although even this would appear to be too many.

Exactly half of the principals favored "some system of individual promotion (e.g., on the basis of examinations) ... rather than the customary use of grade placement and continuous promotion." In fact, 5 percent reported that they already had something of this nature in operation in their schools.

Two-thirds of the principals indicated their awareness of the lack of satisfactory evidence on many educational problems, for 67 percent thought that educational research "can often be highly useful." Fewer (44 percent) rated psychological research as high. Only 3 percent believed that educational research "is pretty much a waste of time and money."

Surprisingly, 59 percent of the principals thought that national testing programs—such as the ACT, CEEB, and the National Merit Scholarship examinations—had either a desirable or a very desirable effect upon the instructional program of schools. Only 17 percent considered such efforts undesirable or very undesirable. Nearly all of them have found standardized test scores of value in providing useful information about individual students.

Principals are sharply divided on the advisability of telling parents what a child's I.Q. score is, with only a little over one-third (37 percent) believing that it should be revealed in all or most cases. Another 36 percent believe that the score should be revealed in unusual cases, while 21 percent believe that it should be standard practice not to give the score to the parent. On the other hand, 90 percent of the principals are ready to be more communicative about achievement test scores and to reveal them to parents in all or most cases.

As to the factors most often behind the earning of good grades—ability or motivation—44 percent believe the weight of these two factors to be about equal, while the rest are almost evenly divided between the two factors, with slightly more choosing motivation. The great study *Pygmalion in the Classroom,* discussed in Chapter 12, had not been published at the time of the principals' answers. Increasingly, however, the weight of evidence falls on the side of motivation.

Finally, the often-quoted observation credited to Socrates was given in the study as follows: "Children now love luxury. They have bad manners, contempt for authority. They show disrespect for elders, and love chatter in place of exercise." The principals were asked: "Would you say that these remarks also apply to contemporary American youth?" The division of opinion was almost even: 54 percent said yes; 46 percent, no. From this it might be concluded that principals are only half optimistic about their raw material and only half optimistic about their chances of success with it.

Similarity of Attitudes to Lay Beliefs

The information about attitudes shows that secondary school principals are about as divided on many of the important issues in education as the people generally seem to be. To what extent principals agree or disagree with a given proposition for the same reasons that laymen give for their viewpoints the NASSP study does not tell us. The reason or the lack of reason often may be similar. If this surmise is true, then it reflects to some extent the degree to which secondary school leadership has not yet become a profession, the degree to which the bases of its practice tend to linger in the realm of folk wisdom.

Some pages back the writer pointed out that the professional preparation of many principals was quite limited, many having taken their first positions before they had had much time to secure specialized professional preparation. That is, the high school principalship is an assignment that many of its practitioners have learned by doing. Their first jobs as principals have been their apprenticeships.

Looking back over the reported responses of principals to questions relating to educational issues, one finds grounds for arguing that principals' viewpoints most often resemble those of the lay population on issues that are theoretical or philosophical in nature. For example, there is the example of the 34 percent endorsement of the Supreme Court decision on prayer and Bible reading in schools. There is the notable failure, on the part of many principals, to support the social importance of universal secondary education. The potential cultivation of sophisticated thinking upon such issues lies in those very fields of professional education where the principals themselves rate their own preparation least valuable. These areas, of course, are the theoretical foundations: philosophy of education, comparative education, sociology of education, and history of education.

This weakness may have one or more of three causes. First, many principals may have had little introduction to the theoretical foundations. Second, the teaching in these fields in colleges of education may be weak and may fail to open up new dimensions of thought. Third, although the principals may have had enlightening exposure in these areas, they may have reacted only as students, using what they have learned only for examination and credit purposes. Their interest has not been aroused to the degree that they have continued to feed it, to read, and to relate their learnings to their professional behavior.

The conclusion seems to be fully justified, in light of the reported findings and this analysis, that the secondary school principalship, as exemplified by at least one-third to one-half of the practitioners, has not entered the realm of professionalism. Too many of the decisions of administration and leadership are made on the basis of folk wisdom. This is undoubtedly changing and is destined to change somewhat more rapidly in the years ahead. Means by which the processes of desirable change in this area can be hurried are discussed in the next chapter.

OPPORTUNITIES, HANDICAPS, AND REWARDS OF THE JOB

What chance do high school principals have to get their jobs done? What are the roadblocks and frustrations? How do principals spend their time? How much and what kinds of help do they have in achieving their purposes? To what extent does the central administration help or impede? What are the financial limitations of the school? How do principals view themselves? their opportunities? These are the measures of the principalship that the third section of the NASSP report attempts to explore.

A traditional measure of professional or executive stature, in the public eye, has been the number of people one has to get past to come face to face with the top man. On this scale principals do not rate very high. In fact, 17 percent of them have no secretarial help, and another 20 percent have only part-time secretaries. Only 25 percent of them have one or more full-time assistant principals. The small and the rural high schools rate most poorly on both counts. Only 26 percent of the principals have seven or more nonteaching personnel on their staffs, while the median number is three. This situation is surely destined to change markedly within the next few years, in response especially to the increased size of the average high school and to the advent of teacher aides.

Use of Time

Almost half the principals (45 percent) indicate an average work week of fifty to fifty-nine hours during the school year, although 29 percent of them indicate that they work sixty hours or more a week. Among the claims upon this time, and somewhat in order of frequency of major claim (more than 7 percent of the principal's time), are the following:

1. Administrative planning alone and with subordinate administrators
2. Meetings with students on matters other than discipline
3. Work with individual teachers on their proficiency

4. Meetings with teachers for curriculum or instruction
5. Correspondence
6. Classroom teaching
7. Supervision of extracurricular activities
8. Meetings with students for discipline
9. Private thought and reflection

Only one principal in five reports that he spends more than 6 percent of his time in reading professional literature.

In addition, 35 percent of the principals do regular teaching, with 9 percent of them doing so more than half of their time. The remaining 65 percent do no more than occasional substituting.

Obstacles to Progress

What do principals think are the most frequent roadblocks to doing the job they would like to get done in their schools? The factors designated most frequently, by from 88 down to 71 percent of the principals, are listed here in descending order:

1. Variation in the ability and dedication of teachers
2. Time taken up by administrative detail (at the expense of more important matters)
3. Lack of time
4. Inability to provide time for teacher planning and other professional improvement activities for teachers
5. Insufficient space and physical facilities
6. Inability to obtain funds for experimental activities
7. Quantity and quality of teaching staff

It must be noted that five of these seven roadblocks are problems that relate to professional personnel policy: the first and seventh to teacher personnel; the second and third to the principal's time and his use of it; and the fourth to teacher time for planning and in-service education. It is hoped that the reader will hold this in mind as he reads Chapter 4 and the two chapters that deal with teacher personnel in the high school.

Extramural Pressures on Principals

To what external pressures do principals feel that they and the schools they head are frequently subjected? Only minor fractions of the principals reported strong or frequent pressure from extreme leftists or rightists or from those seeking to censor books. Table 4 shows, in descending order, the percentage of principals who feel either "strong or frequent pressure" or "occasional or moderate pressure" upon themselves and their schools for the reasons indicated.

TABLE 4
Frequently Reported Pressures Exerted Upon High School Principals and Their Schools by Outside Interest Groups

Pressure Group	*Percent of Principals Reporting*
Citizen or parent groups other than PTA	56
Athletic minded persons, including alumni	51
State colleges and universities	46
Religious or church groups	35
Individuals, groups, concerning testing programs	33
Auto associations, insurance interests, concerning driver education	31
Local newspaper's editorial policy	31

Practically no principals reported more than one or two incidents over the two-year period prior to the study (1961–1963) in which individuals or groups became publicly angry over alleged anti-Americanism or lack of patriotism on the part of school staff members. In fact, 93 percent of the principals reported that they had had no such incidents. Incidents arising out of allegedly inappropriately assigned books were almost equally rare in their occurrence.

International crises and factors that may be related to the national defense probably constitute a source of more effective pressure upon schools. Nearly a quarter of the principals (24 percent) reported that in their schools there had been crash programs or revisions "more or less directly attributable to the

(real or alleged) Soviet scientific and technological advances."
The larger the school, the more frequently this had been the case.

Job Satisfactions and Rewards

Would the men holding high school principalships in 1963 go into
school administration again, had they their lives to live over?
Almost two out of five said no or were uncertain. Three-fifths said
yes. Did they expect to move out of the principalship eventually
"to another position in the school community"? On this question
28 percent said no; another 25 percent were uncertain; 12 percent
frankly aspired to a better principalship; 14 percent wanted a
superintendency; and 4 percent hoped eventually to reside in the
relaxed security of a college or university professorship.

How much is the public willing to pay for this job, subject
as it is and was to the frustrations and pressures indicated in this
chapter? In the school year 1963–1964 the most frequent salary
bracket (18 percent) was the lowest: $6,000 or less. Other fre-
quent brackets were $7,000 to $7,999, received by 16 percent, and
$10,000 to $12,499, received by 17 percent. Only 1 percent earned
more than $17,500. For the school year 1970–1971 these figures
might be updated by rolling them upward $1,800 at the bottom
and $3,600 at the top. Granted a continuing inflationary ten-
dency, salaries can be expected to continue to move upward at
least $300 a year at the bottom and $600 a year at the top. In only
36 percent of the communities from which replies came was the
principal's salary tied by ratio to the master's degree teacher
scale, which indicates that the principal's salary is in most places
negotiable.

Opinions of Status and Opportunities

Only 5 percent of the principals put themselves in the upper
class, while 49 percent rated themselves in the middle class and
38 percent in the upper middle. Only 6 percent rated themselves
in the lower middle or in the working classes.

Is the principal "accorded the professional status and prestige to which he is properly entitled by virtue of education, train-ing, and the work done?" One-third of them thought not, while 53 percent believed that NASSP should take steps to help its members attain appropriate status and prestige.

Almost half (49 percent) of the principals felt that they enjoyed considerable or very much job security. A somewhat larger portion, 71 percent, felt that their jobs offered them con-siderable or very much opportunity to be helpful to other people. In the matter of community prestige, they rated themselves less highly, 51 percent believing that they basked in a moderate amount of prestige or less.

How did the principals in 1963 feel about the opportunity their jobs gave them for independent thought and action? Only 37 percent indicated considerable opportunity while notably fewer, 11 percent, indicated very much opportunity. This point, upon which the situation of the principal apparently has worsened, will receive further discussion in the last section of this chapter and still more in Chapter 4. It is most important in the attraction of the type of individual the high school principalship demands.

All in all, only a minority, 48 percent, of America's high school principals in 1963 felt that their jobs provided them with considerable or very much opportunity for self-fulfillment.

These reported responses were geared to what the principals felt their jobs did offer them. These questions were followed by another set of questions on the very same points, but with the "does" changed to "should": What should the job offer? While the "considerable" and "very much" categories were seen as the appropriate ones by about 50 percent of the principals on most of these status questions, there is a distressing note in what the principals think should be their status. For example, only 72 per-cent of the principals thought that their jobs should provide them with considerable or very much prestige in the communities where they served. Why is the figure not closer to 100 percent? Does this mean that more than a fourth of the principals did not rate the principal as being a very important individual to his community? Should any position of leadership be assigned to a man who does not really believe in its potential? Do more than a fourth of the principals see themselves primarily as custodians of property and people rather than as educational leaders?

CIVIC, SOCIAL, AND PROFESSIONAL ACTIVITIES

How extensively do secondary-school principals participate in the civic and social life of the community? What about their membership in civic and political organizations (for example, the Chamber of Commerce) in 1963? While 27 percent belonged to no such organizations, 7 percent were members of four or more. Fairly equal percentages of the remainder belonged to one, two, or three organizations.

How many belonged to social or avocational organizations (for example, a country club)? Exactly half belonged to no such organizations, while only 6 percent belonged to three or more such organizations. Thus principals appear to be less social and avocational than civic- and political-minded. This observation carries no implied belittlement, for two reasons: first, social eminence is not a *sine qua non* of the principalship; and second, country club and other social club fees are not comfortably carried on the salary of many principals.

How active professionally had secondary principals been in the two years prior to the study? More than three-fourths (76 percent) had attended a statewide or a nationwide meeting of secondary school principals. In addition, 58 percent had participated in the activities of professional associations (local, state, or national). Two out of five had taken college or university courses in summer school or in extension, evening, or Saturday classes. Finally, 23 percent had been involved in conducting educational research; 59 percent had participated in workshops or educational conferences; and 73 percent had participated in community activities: service club, church, civic organizations, and the like. To some these latter activities might not be thought professional; but the report treated them under that classification, perhaps because they are seen by principals as enhancing their professional stature.

Opinions of the Profession

The marks of a professional person were listed by the questionnaire as follows: knowledge, dedication to one's job, dedication to human betterment, ethicality, and concern for the well-being of the profession. The principals were asked if they thought it appropriate to apply these five qualities to secondary school principals; 77 percent said that they did. Most of the remainder believed that one or more of the qualities did not apply, with 3 percent having no opinion and 1 percent indicating that they did not consider secondary school principals professionals by any definition.

Responses to the second and third stages of this question are more striking and more useful to a critical study. Table 5 shows which professional qualities principals as a whole think most in evidence and which least in evidence.

TABLE 5
High School Principals Rate Their Colleagues on Professional Qualities

	Percentage of Secondary School Principals Reporting	
Professional Quality	*Most in Evidence*	*Least in Evidence*
Knowledge	7	21
Dedication to one's job	56	5
Dedication to human betterment	23	15
Ethicality	1	25
Concern for the profession	13	32

Principals rate themselves, as a group, highest on dedication to the job and upon dedication to human betterment. In this judgment they are probably correct. In their low appraisal of the group's concern for the profession they are again probably correct.

OMISSIONS AND ANALYSES

Any study or investigation becomes famous, in part, for what it leaves out, for what it fails to examine or cannot examine. Valuable as it is, the study this chapter has drawn so heavily upon is no exception to this generalization.

How did present high school principals get their jobs? How did they happen to be selected over others who might have been available? Is the high school principal always selected objectively, purely upon the basis of the studied evidence and belief that he can handle it in the best educational interests of the boys and girls who are to attend the school? How many principals were placed in their jobs as a reward for handling well some other not-too-related assignment? How many were assigned the position primarily as a reward for faithfully serving the school system for many years? What criteria were set up for the selection? Did teachers or a teacher committee have a part in setting up the criteria, interviewing candidates, and in making the nomination? Consultants are often sought by boards of education who face the selection of a new superintendent. Is the selection of the high school principal, who is more directly in charge of an educational program, undertaken with equal care?

Job Motivation

Further enlightenment concerning the kind and quality of leadership secondary schools have might come from a knowledge of what motivated principals to accept the positions they now hold. How many were interested primarily because of the challenge seen in the job and a belief in their own capacity to meet that challenge? How many saw it as an escape from the rigors and the constant demands of classroom teaching? How many were interested primarily in the greater salary the position offered? How many saw it as a path to an earlier and more remunerative retirement, since retirement annuities are often tied to average annual earnings over a given number of best-paid years?

These questions are not intended to imply that a man should ever fail to act, at least in part, in terms of his own enlightened self-interest and the interests of his family. It is when these become the sole motives that they become damaging.

Questions Asked Before Appointment

Did the principal as a candidate inquire carefully and fully into the extent and nature of the authority that was to be granted to him along with the responsibility he was about to be asked to assume? How much room for the exercise of "independent thought and action," to use the words of the NASSP study, was he to be granted? How much support from the superintendent and board, spelled out in terms of hypothetical cases, was he to receive in effecting a program of educational leadership in the high school? To what ends would the authorities go in supporting, both financially and otherwise, a carefully designed program of instructional improvements? In short, did the candidate receive assurance of conditions that would enable him to handle well the job he sought?

Prestige

The thesis underlying these questions is that the way men behave when under consideration for a given position has much to do with the respect and prestige that position enjoys. The hypothesis is that many high school principals, as candidates for the positions they now hold, have not behaved in such a way as to enhance the prestige of the position. Too many principals, past and present, have been willing to accept their jobs under any and all conditions, conditions that often have made progress impossible.

The man whose interest in a high school principalship has been invited and who has turned the position down upon the basis of unfavorable conditions, which he explains, has usually done both the school and the position a greater favor than the man who has accepted under similar conditions. Superintendents and school board members ought to be very suspicious of principal candidates who make no demands and seek no concessions. A man who is readily salable does not sell himself so cheap.

The high school principal must be a man who thinks well of himself and who knows the kind of support and help he needs to do an effective job. This, however, is the theme of the ensuing chapter.

SUMMARY

The subjects of this chapter have been the high school principals of America, what they think, and how they feel about their jobs. The text has drawn heavily upon a 1963–1965 study conducted by the National Association of Secondary School Principals. The most favorable findings of this study, both direct and indirect, show the principals to be hard-working, dedicated to their jobs, usually quite effective in human relations, and enjoying favorable security and tenure in their positions.

The most alarming findings about high school principals are their lack of faith in the capacity of the high school to be useful to all American youth; their relatively low estimates of the stature and potentials of their own jobs (only 72 percent thought their jobs should carry considerable prestige); and their rating of themselves as a group relatively low in ethicality, knowledge, and concern for the profession. It can be inferred from other data, such as the number without secretarial help, that many high school principals show too little respect for themselves at the time they accept their positions. Many apparently do not see themselves as educational leaders.

4

The Leaders
the High Schools Need

Where there is no vision the people perish.
Proverbs 29:18

Of all the qualities needed by the high school principal, none outranks vision. The very word "supervision," the literal meaning of which is overseeing, might functionally be interpreted to mean the employment of superior or extraordinary vision. The principal must in truth be an educational leader. If he cannot see farther over the educational horizon than those he attempts to lead, he is ill fitted for leadership. Without such vision he can be a custodian, a caretaker of children, teachers, books, school equipment, and buildings. Without vision he can become an organizer of classes, a scheduler of recitations, and study halls, and an organizer of extra-class activities. Without vision, however, he cannot become an educational leader.

What does it mean to have vision? What are the component parts of vision? How can one determine when another has it and when he does not? Why is vision so essential to the leader in any field of endeavor? The answer is that vision enables one to see where he wants to go, where he ought to go. He is able to discern, as was implied in Chapter 2, which way is forward. Penetrating educational vision enables one to chart a dependable route to educational betterment. The man of vision is a man of ideas. He sees weaknesses. He sees the bases upon which they rest. He sees means of eradicating these weaknesses. Most important of all, he envisions strengths to put in their stead, and he sees ways by which these ideas of strength may be installed and implemented.

An educator, especially an educational leader, is a social engineer. He is also a designing engineer, not just an engineer who handles routine problems of engineering. When the high school principal assumes his post, he accepts responsibility for a unique school, one that is located in a unique community, which serves a unique student clientele, and which is staffed with a unique faculty. No other school in the entire nation has the same potential for becoming the kind of school this school is capable of becoming. If the principal is to be truly effective, he must envision the better kind of school that his school may become. The process is social engineering; the major ingredient, vision.

Uniqueness is a heavier factor in the world of education than in many of the nation's institutions. This is so because teachers and school leaders teach so much by what they are. They are by no means limited, cannot be limited, to what they know. Just as teachers teach in terms of what they are, learners learn in terms of what they are, in terms of all their previous experiences. Since the human element bulks so large in school operation, since teachers and pupils make up the greatest part of the institution's moving forces, and since these forces have by their unique environments been made themselves unique, the school's potential is unique.

Schools have often been asked to take their management cues from industrial successes. However, the job of the school is not that of turning out thousands of assembly line products, each like all the others. Industrial management techniques are not readily and profitably transferable to educational institutions. There is a level or a point, however, at which comparison is useful. Let it be supposed that one of the automobile manufacturers is seeking a new designing engineer. What qualities or qualifications would the concern's management seek? It would surely seek a man who holds penetrating views of the shortcomings or inadequacies of the cars that firm is now manufacturing. It would further seek a man who appears to have some sound notions of how the inadequacies or shortcomings could be overcome. It would want the new designer to have ideas about the building of a better car. It would seek and be willing to pay a good price for vision. In that sense the problems of building a superior car are similar to the problems of developing a superior high school.

The superintendent, the school board to the extent that it is involved, and the teacher or faculty committee must seek as their new high school principal a man of vision. The kinds of questions upon which their probing examination of the candidate should dwell are clearly implied in the above statements.

If the principal is not a designing engineer, if he has no clear vision of a better school, he thereby abdicates his greatest responsibility and neglects his greatest opportunity. He leaves his school to the direction of whatever breezes blow, to the whims and pressures of students, faculty, and parents. He resigns himself to doing office boy chores for a school that drifts, that either goes nowhere or that moves in undesirable directions, because no qualified person has charted a course or drafted a design by which the school might attain its own optimum selfhood as an institution.

PERSPECTIVE

Not only must the principal have some ideas about secondary education in general and about his own school in particular; he must also have convictions about what is more important and what is less important. He must have a hierarchy of values because his job has too many possibilities for him to attempt to do everything equally well. The high school principalship is no place for a perfectionist, for no man can wear all its hats with equal grace. A perfectionist has been defined as one who takes great pains and gives them to other people. The principal who tries to perform all the small and unimportant aspects of administration as a perfectionist will succeed in giving pains to his assistants and teacher colleagues. Some jobs he should slight or delegate rather completely to others. This is necessary to make possible the handling of the really important tasks with distinction.

Another question is whether the principal is willing and able to gear his handling of the principalship to a sound value scale. One of the important findings, possibly the most important, of the Kellogg studies of school administration related to this question. In essence, what the Kellogg studies revealed was that the goal orientation of the administrator is basic. What does he believe it important for the schools to try to do for the young people who attend them? For society? What is most important? The studies showed that the administrator who firmly believes certain values to be paramount will somehow show some progress in the direction of those goals.

Truman M. Pierce, one of the field coordinators of the Kellogg studies on school administration, in 1964 wrote to this author as follows:

> You have quoted me correctly. . . . This statement was made because of my conviction that what the school administrator is interested in doing and what he does to a considerable extent in the final analysis is determined by the beliefs he holds about society, about education and its role, about children, and about teaching. These, then, are expressed in his leadership performance.[1]

Such values, held by any candidate for the high school principalship anywhere, ought to have careful examination at the hands of any committee screening candidates for the position.

The administrator's belief about goals, of course, gives no index to his manner of operation. He may leave numerous ruffled feelings or disconcerted persons along the way. No advocacy of arbitrary procedures, of summary actions, or of ruthlessness is made here. Forward movement, nevertheless, even with some friction, is greatly to be preferred to no motion whatever.

There is a distinction, of course, between holding views that represent a highly cultivated sense of perspective and the ability and imagination to put them to work in day-to-day operation. Investigators of the potential high school principal must look at other aspects of the man's qualifications to obtain reliable indices on this point. Some very good theorists are quite awkward when

[1] Truman M. Pierce, January 20, 1964 (personal letter to the writer). Pierce was then Dean of Education at Auburn University.

placed on the front line of action. If, however, the man demonstrated persistence in pursuing his goals as a teacher, counselor, or lesser administrator, if he showed imagination and ingenuity in brushing obstacles aside in these other roles, the chances are good that he will do as well in the principalship.

At no point in the vast scope of school organization is one under more constant and more pressing temptation to get himself buried in the minutia of operation than in the high school principalship. Means of meeting this problem, some of which are not widely employed today, are discussed in Chapter 5.

The emphasis of this section has been upon two ideas. First, the high school principal who is to exert genuine educational leadership must have a perspective on the job and a hierarchy of justifiable educational values. Second, he must have ideas about how to organize a school to ensure that the less important essentials are handled satisfactorily while the factors upon which the realization of the school's important objectives depend are given major and recurring emphasis and attention by himself and others.

COURAGE

One of the great dilemmas of the administrator is that of the frequent but necessary choice between the easy thing to do and the right thing to do. The choice is further complicated by the fact that the right decision is sometimes, although rarely, the easy thing to do. For example, an innocent party is sometimes wronged if the obviously right thing is done. Here the right thing may also be the easy thing. A case that has no doubt been real in many schools will serve to illustrate. The clerk of records or registrar discovers, when the second semester is more than half over, that one of the candidates for June graduation has not had a second semester of work in the required subject of American history. It is obviously right to enforce state graduation requirements. It is also obviously right to hold all students to the same graduation requirements. Even more to the point, the school's failure to discover such an omission in a student's record until its correction is no longer reasonably possible to him (and it can happen despite great care), is a gross injustice to the student. The principal is called upon to have the courage to say that such mistakes are not "discovered" after it is too late to correct them. A scholar must never become the victim of a breakdown in the school's machinery. Courage is the sustaining force of good administration.

A second complication that may accompany such decisions is that the easy decision may be easiest at the time but the most difficult to live with in the long run. Courage, fortified by judgment, and willingness to accept the responsibility for serving the greatest good, are the personal qualities needed in these situations.

Courage serves the leader in a wide variety of situations. It is not to be confused with obstinacy or stubbornness, which are celebrated for their own sake. One of the places courage serves well is in the confession of weakness. It takes a degree of courage for a principal to say to his faculty, "I didn't serve you very well in this instance. I made certain miscalculations. In similar situations in the future, I shall try to bear these errors in mind and to do better." Such a statement takes courage, but it will build respect and it will strengthen followership.

The courage to confess weakness or oversight can at times be disarming to the administrator's would-be critic. For example, a young superintendent of schools was taken to task by one of his board members, who asked in a board meeting, "Don't you think you could have a better system of purchasing your janitorial supplies?" "Oh, yes," replied the superintendent. "The fact is that I have no system at all in this matter." Then the superintendent politely explained that janitorial supplies represented only one-half of 1 percent of the school budget, while teachers' salaries represented 75 percent of the budget. He further explained that he had given his major attention to working with the system's teachers in the betterment of the educational program, thus reflecting both courage and perspective. He made no promise about systematizing the purchase of janitorial supplies, nor was he pressed further on the matter.

The principal's courage probably serves his school and his students best when it represents his willingness to bet on an idea for improvement, to venture beyond the safeties of the past. The principal of vision and perspective knows when to take a calculated risk. His courage sustains him in taking that risk.

Every principal and prospective principal should read with care, and perhaps keep it near his desk, the late John F. Kennedy's Pulitzer Prize book, *Profiles in Courage*.[2] It will help him when he is inclined to vacillate, to equivocate, to yield to wrong pressures, to elect the unrewarding but easy route, to fear calculated risk or educational adventure.

There are issues that are broad enough, deep enough, and significant enough that the principal should be willing to lay down his job rather than yield to movement in a wrong direction or to refuse to move when he knows that educational advancement requires movement.

INTEGRITY

Integrity is the mucilage that holds the many aspects of a successful administration together. It is the quality without which vision, perspective, and courage cannot long be made effective. Mark Twain once advised, "Tell the truth; then you don't have to remember anything." The thought underscores the importance of integrity to the administrator, who can easily become entangled in his own web. No matter how careful his planning and how circumspect his every move, ulterior or selfish motives will often be ascribed to the principal's action by some. The way to be sure that no evidence of such motives is found is to be sure that no such motives exist.

Even before the principal is appointed, or while he is still enjoying the status of a candidate, he will give evidence of his integrity or his lack of it. Such evidence will reveal itself through the questions he asks or fails to ask. The man of immature integrity, as well as immature professional stature, will limit himself chiefly to questions about the range of duties, the routines of operation, and the expectations of superiors. The man who is truly professional, who will have the self-respect to turn the

---

[2] John F. Kennedy, *Profiles in Courage* (New York: Harper and Brothers, 1955).

position down if the conditions do not add up to an opportunity for educational leadership, will ask questions about willingness to alter unfavorable conditions for improvement, about the degree of authority or autonomy he will have, about the chances he will have and the help he can rely upon in building a better school. In short, the man with integrity and ability will make it clear that he wants an opportunity to render a significant educational service. The man without these qualities will make it abundantly clear, by what he says and does not say, that he wants only a job.

Professional integrity forbids a man to accept a position in whose potential and stature he has little faith. The NASSP study on the high school principalship, discussed at length in Chapter 3, appears to indicate that over one-fourth of the secondary principals serving in 1963–1964 did not believe the position should be one of considerable prestige and potential. The interviewing committee should make sure that the high school principal candidate has genuine respect for the position and genuine respect for himself. Finding either factor lacking, the committee members must themselves have the integrity to refuse to recommend him.

Granted the authority that he needs to carry out his responsibilities, the principal of integrity and courage is willing to exercise his judgment. He does not seek to manage a school by rule of thumb. A school that is to be run by a rule book does not need an administrator. A secretary who reads the rule book, at most a sort of parliamentarian, will do.

The principal who is worthy of his post is no parliamentarian. His behavior and his procedure resemble those of the judge rather than those of the policeman. If he is merely a custodian, he will behave more as a policeman. If he is an educational leader, his behavior will be more like that of the judge. He will have the integrity and the courage to make very opposite decisions in two cases that may look quite the same to the layman.

A man of integrity does not try to get out from under the load just because it is a difficult load or because defense of his action may be difficult. He only asks, "Is the decision mine to make?" He does not attempt to hide behind a rule or a regulation. Neither does he evade the issue or pass the buck. His eternal questions are: What is right? What is fair? What is just? What is best for this pupil or this teacher? For all these pupils? For all these teachers? What decision best becomes us as a teaching example?

OTHER LEADERSHIP CAPITAL

An educational leader must be a man of ideas, a generally informed person. He must give evidence of having made extensive and continuing effort to make himself a man of cultivated mind, of broad and rich cultural interests. While this is not as important as the four qualities discussed earlier, it is a component of vision and insight. It will also help him in securing the broadest possible support from faculty and in gaining helpful respect from the more articulate, better informed, and more influential of the community's citizens.

How well informed is the man who is being considered for the principalship? What serious and recently read books does he talk about? How would he stand up, pitted in debate or discussion against the community's more enlightened lawyers, ministers, and journalists, for example, on any or all of the great social, economic, or political issues of the day? What lay journals does he read and quote? Over what subjects does his social conversation range? How much at home is he when the topic moves beyond automobiles, golf, sports figures, and aspects of the consumer guides?

How does one identify the man of ideas, the man of imagination, insight, and vision? He is an individual who has some notions of the school's more important tasks. He is aware and can give a thoughtful recital of its neglected opportunities to serve youth wisely and well. He has some conceptions, which he can support, of ways in which the high school should be different and better ten or fifteen years from now. The idea man can tell you how he would like faculty members to be different ten years from now, what qualities and qualifications he would seek, provided that money and the supply of such persons present no problems.

The man of depth and ideas, the man whose personal and

intellectual stature is capable of bringing added prestige to the high school principalship, is able to relate theory to practice. He can state and explain the assumptions upon which his views about school strengths and weaknesses rest. He is keenly aware of existing roadblocks, and he has some conceptions of the patience, human relations strategy, and the recasting of administrative machinery required to remove them.

In short, the principal that each high school in the land needs is one who thinks constructively about the institution: its past, its problems, its needs, its potential, its staff, and its future. The next step, then, is to trace the trails that may lead to the discovery of such a social engineer, a twentieth-century Socrates.

SOURCES OF QUALITY

From what sort of background, influences, family, and education, is the kind of person just described most likely to come? Are there signals that lead with fair reliability to such attributes, such character, such erudition? Unfortunately, there are no absolute, always dependable signposts that lead to the selection of the potentially best man. In addition to the criteria suggested in the discussion of the basic qualities of character and disposition, certain indicators appear to be far more effective than acting solely upon one's feeling about the person. No one of the elements listed in this section is to be regarded, standing alone, as a must. It is the bundle that is expected to have usefulness, applied always to the total man and with the awareness that those without some low spots in either their professional or personal profiles are indeed rare.

Early Incentives

In Chapter 3 it was shown that most of the principals studied by the NASSP in 1963 came from homes that by today's standards might be regarded as relatively uneducated. This will be less and less true of the young men now coming to the principalship. Fewer and fewer of these will be first-generation college people in their respective families, simply because the general educational level of the population is rising rapidly. Whether the family of the prospective principal is one of little education or much, however, one should look for signs of intellectual interests and for signs of continuing inspiration, allowing always for the overcoming of early handicaps. Certainly the earlier intellectual and social interests take root, the stronger they are likely to become.

Early inspiration and incentive to learn need not have come from a parent. Sometimes it is just as significant when it stems from an older brother or sister, an aunt or uncle, a grandparent, or a good and wise neighbor or citizen who took an interest in this man as a boy. This is one of the places where both autobiographic material and close questioning are useful. What other inspirational forces were at work on this embryonic school administrator, and how potent were they?

What about his own high school days does the principal remember, and how well? To no small degree the success of the principal bears direct relationship to his capacity to put himself in the student's place. Further, it is to his advantage to have had some exciting and highly gratifying experiences in his own high school days, both scholastic and extracurricular. Such experiences are probably more significant than his own scholastic average in high school or the courses he studied. It is desirable, however, to find him with exposure to both the life and physical sciences, a foreign language, either music or art, and either speech or journalism. High school graduation requirements in most states take adequate care of English and social studies.

The man who is to serve as an exceptional high school principal, as is true of any other social leader of stature, must give evidence of commitment, and the earlier the signs of commitment began to appear in him, the better.

Collegiate Education and Interests

What should the undergraduate college record of the principal represent? What he did there and the interests he developed there are far more important than the reputed quality of the institution. Effective leaders have come from a wide range of collegiate institutions, although there should be striking compensations if his undergraduate school was one of the very weakest.

The undergraduate degree should, preferably, include a strong major in one of the great academic fields. Whatever the major, his studies should represent a good general or liberal education. After all, the man is to preside over an institution whose chief function is general education for most, if not all, its students. This seems to argue against his own too early specialization, although there are exceptions. There is nothing wrong with his having majored in industrial arts, the commercial field, music, art, or psychology, provided he has added a substantial number of courses from such fields as history, literature, economics, sociology, and languages and provided he has taken evident pains to augment his own general education through reading and generally educative experiences.

Preferably the principal's high school and college exposure combined should include at least two of the three commonly taught sciences, a substantial introduction to mathematics, a broad sampling of the social sciences, depth in one foreign language, music, art or industrial arts, and both literature and philosophy on the college level. Participation in speech, dramatic, or journalistic activities is an added asset, as is athletics.

In the principal's undergraduate college career, it is important that some of his learning experiences or scholastic contacts stand out vividly, that they represent memorable impressions or discoveries. These may have come from more than casual contacts with a good and wise professor in any field, a professor who was capable of communicating by some means a deeper understanding of life or learning, which for the true educator are almost synonymous. Practically all college students have exposure to such persons. Within many, however, the capacity for response is lacking. They cannot catch such inspiration any more than they can catch the measles a second time. The student who is susceptible, however, will be able to give evidence of the depth of his sensitivity to such influences years afterward. He will be able to discuss ideas and philosophies of his favorite teachers.

It is helpful to be able to find in a principal evidence that he has been incurably infected with an understanding of the countless powers that spring from insight and vision. To be impressed with the capacity in others, to view the social scene and find therein dimensions of ideas that most men miss is to cultivate the capacity for such perception in oneself.

Another common source of such insight-bearing experience for the young collegian is found in the scholastic or extracurricular activities that have given rein to his own creative capacities. Among these might be journalistic or speech activities, successful participation in essay contests, contributions to student magazines, or creative participation in music or art programs. The depth of the participation is significant. How much creativity on his part was involved? It is one thing to have written the play. A walk-on part, or two insignificant lines, to take the other extreme, is hardly of relevance to leadership potential.

Creative activity is of consequence to the potential leader, if for no other reason than that it affords him a measure of his own power. It enhances his confidence and his willingness to take risks. It is even more important as an indicator of the potential principal's approach to his job. One who has no history of creativity does not give promise of becoming suddenly creative simply by the bestowal of the title of principal upon him.

Graduate Study and Specialties

How much graduate study should a high school principal present? A doctorate is desirable but not readily achievable for all principals. Since 3 percent of the 1963 principals had a doctorate, and another 6 percent had done all but the dissertation, perhaps it is not unreasonable to expect that by 1978 nearly a fourth of them will have doctorates. Another ten years beyond that should bring the doctor's degree holders into the 40 to 50 percent range. This is not at all unreasonable in view of the larger number of institutions that have recently launched doctoral programs in education and the much larger numbers of assistantships and fellowships now available to doctoral candidates than just a few years ago. Even a man who has a family but who is willing to practice some self-denial may manage, since the assistantship or fellowship usually offers the opportunity for sustenance along with study and professional growth. Full qualification is today readily possible to any young man of ability, foresight, and determination.

It is natural that many of the older men who do not hold a doctorate, both principals and superintendents, should argue against its necessity. They have arrived despite the lack of extensive training, not because of it. Some of them point to holders of the doctorate who are not effective leaders. That it is no guarantee of leadership is fully conceded. That its possession is a handicap is denied. It is one of several highly desirable qualifications. Successful doctoral study usually represents more assurance of stature, for the screening processes of reputable institutions are not without their rigors. It always stands as testimony to added depth of interest and persistence in the pursuit of one's goals. It usually affirms uncommon initiative, creativity, resourcefulness, or self-propulsion, for the dissertation is both the main stopper and an effective measure of one's power to move on his own. Thus the doctor's degree demonstrates needed capacities, generates self-assurance and self-respect, and adds materially to the prestige of the assignment.

Only in exceptional cases, cases perhaps of men with considerable administrative experience, should any man be taken into his first principalship with less than two years of graduate study, the second year giving emphasis to secondary school supervision, curriculum, philosophy, and problems. Some states now require a second year of graduate study for certification of the secondary school administrator. The American Association of School Administrators demonstrated its faith in graduate study as a requisite of professionalism by requiring two years of graduate study of all new members taken in after January 1, 1964. It is hoped that the National Association of Secondary School Principals will, before many years have passed, establish similar requirements for its new members.

The Internship

The internship, preferably in a form similar to that sponsored experimentally by the NASSP since 1963, should be required of all, especially of any who have not had an administrative experience that afforded a broad view of the problems of school improvement.

The NASSP internship, in part foundation-supported since its inception, is characterized by certain salient features:

1. All interns are placed on salary, usually at 90 to 100 percent of the intern's position on the employing school's teacher salary scale.
2. The intern is paid by the school system, and he remains for the entire school year.
3. He must be given an opportunity to work in the area of instructional improvement, preferably where innovation is under way, and is expected to make a significant contribution.
4. The joint sponsor is a university, working through an appropriate education professor, who visits and advises the intern.
5. Representatives of the NASSP have conducted regional summer orientation conferences, visited the interns at work, and required interns to attend special conferences at the Association's national winter convention.

Teacher Preparation

The principal should be able to present superior preparation as a teacher. Hopefully, in addition to being an undergraduate major in his teaching field, he will have had at least some graduate work in that same teaching field. Such preparation ensures several desirable elements of his fitness to lead. First, it testifies to his depth of interest. Second, it indicates that he truly believes in superior teacher preparation. Third, it tends to ensure his interest in securing for the school teachers that are fully and solidly qualified in the areas they attempt to teach. Finally, it means that the principal himself has gone far enough in a teaching field to realize how much there is yet to learn, hence underscoring his appreciation of the need for continuing and in-service education of teachers.

The day has arrived when the first year of graduate study for all teachers should be dominated by the following kinds of experiences: (a) further work in the teaching field, (b) courses that sharpen one's understanding and know-how about teaching and learning, (c) other courses that help him to understand learners better, (d) sampling in the area of theoretical foundations of education, (e) work in supporting academic areas, such as sociology and philosophy, and (f) work in a field that supports the teaching field, such as literature for the history teacher. Administrative and consultant specialties should be developed in the second year of graduate study.

Theoretical Foundations of Education

It is really not too strange that in the NASSP study the secondary school principals of 1963 downgraded their courses in the theoretical foundations of education, as discussed in Chapter 3. The chances are good that few of them had taken more than three courses in the area. How much appreciation of the field of physics or mathematics accrues to one who takes three courses and quits? The theoretical foundations of education is a quite specialized but very important area, for it is here that the student of education gets his tools for thinking. Unfortunately, many who attempt to teach in the area, particularly at the undergraduate level, are not themselves qualified to be of great use to their students. At the same time, a small sample gives the area little chance.

Any professional who downgrades theory thereby undermines his profession. No highly respected profession has ever been developed that did not rest upon a broad and deep base of theory. Teachers and school administrators are guilty of doubletalk when they observe: "Yes, that is a very fine theory, but it won't work in practice." The acid test of any theory is the result obtained when it is intelligently and fully translated into practice. Well-conceived theory is the most practical phenomenon that can offer itself to an individual or an institution, for it is broadest in its applications.

The plain fact is that all in education are theorists. Both teachers and administrators make dozens to hundreds of decisions every working day. Consciously or unconsciously each decision is based on a theory. The only question concerns the quality of the theory. Upon what is it based? Does it rest upon reason and intelligence, upon a careful examination of the best that has been thought, expressed, and discovered in this area through the ages? Or is it a theory that springs from the top of a head, that has been sharpened only in the milieux of folk belief? To what extent then is the decision quite likely to be the same decision that the banker, the industrial executive, or the insurance agent might make, faced with the same question? The measure of this sameness is the measure of the educator's lack of professional fitness for his responsibility.

It is with the belief that the high school principalship holds the potential of a profession, that both it and high schools stand to profit by its becoming a profession, that the need of the principal for prolonged immersion in the theoretical foundations of education is here advocated. He should have at the graduate level a careful introduction, at the hands of qualified experts, to both the history of Western and American education, to the philosophy of education (at least two courses), to comparative education, and to the sociology of education. Further, the principal should give evidence that he is constantly renewing his learnings in these areas by reading books, monographs, and articles that draw on these fields or some combination of them, and that he is thereby bringing a distilled intelligence and reason to bear upon the professional questions he regularly faces and decides.

PREVIOUS EXPERIENCE IN EDUCATION

How the principal managed himself in his previous educational position is much more significant than what that position was. Did he demonstrate imagination, resourcefulness, initiative, a spirit of experimentation? Did he exert an effort to try some well-conceived approaches that most teachers do not exert? Was he a creative teacher, department chairman, counselor, dean, or assistant principal? Has he left a trail of progress, of forward motion, behind him? Were his achievements built on solid foundations, so that they persisted? Has he recorded progress without directly or seriously hurting others?

The man who has demonstrated imagination, experimentation, and creativity in his own classroom is likely to do the same in the principalship. The social studies department chairman who has led the teachers of that department in one fruitful teaching venture after another will usually have the same kind of influence upon other departments as the school's principal. Superior preparation and study for one's classes is an indicator of the same for the opportunities of the principalship, provided the man is interested in the job.

If a man in the deanship has shown himself to be persuasive, diplomatic, and respected as he deals with both students and teachers, he will be accorded the same allegiance and respect as principal. If, on the other hand, he has devoted his major energies toward the improvement of his golf game, toward establishing a reputation as a "good Joe," toward prominence in social organizations, he will continue to stress these values when he wears the title of principal. If his reading interests have been narrow and limited, they are not at all likely to broaden when he is given more responsibility. In fact, his lack of background will be a handicap in his capitalizing upon the professional meetings and professional contacts that the principalship opens to him.

Some kinds of experiences may represent a handicap to the imaginative handling of the principalship. For example, one who has been for several years an assistant principal in charge of discipline and attendance exclusively has a handicap to overcome, one of the reasons that no such position should exist in a well-conceived administrative organization, as discussed in Chapter 5. The reason for the handicap is that such a position tends to breed in the holder an unhealthy negative-mindedness. It gives him so much unpleasant work that inspiration and hope for humanity often become difficult to maintain. His work represents a seriously skewed perspective on the school and its students, if not upon society generally. The job does not afford experiences that develop fitness for the principalship itself, especially if it is retained by the same person for a considerable period of time.

A minimum secondary school teaching experience of perhaps three years should be expected of the man who is to be principal. It must be confessed, however, that there are weaknesses in all arbitrary and absolute requirements. The overall educational experience must be considered. The amount and kind of education must be taken into account. The individual himself is a tremendous factor. It may be appropriate to think in terms of a minimum age, perhaps twenty-eight to thirty, which would usually ensure some kind of minimum experience. Again, any such rule should not be inviolate. Who is to say how much maturity a man may gain from two years in Vietnam as an officer in charge of men, many only a little older than high school seniors? Each human being, especially the leader, is entitled to be judged in terms of the total self.

SUMMARY

In this chapter it has been suggested that the principal the high school needs must be a man of vision, possessed of a perspective on educational values; that he must be sustained by courage and characterized by integrity; and that he must be broadly and deeply educated in order to establish respect both inside and outside the school. He must be a proven and well-educated teacher, he should have at least two years of appropriate graduate education, and in most cases he should have had an internship of one year in a secondary school of quality where his duties were directed mainly at the improvement of instruction and curricula. The principal's professional education should involve a strong emphasis upon the theoretical bases of education, so that his knowing the difference between forward and backward in educational progress may be assured.

Personally and culturally, the principal the high school needs will be of such stature that he compares favorably with the leading industrial, business, and professional leaders of the community on every count. Finally, his professional integrity must be in evidence when he is under consideration for the job. He will seek and demand from his employers the autonomy, the assistants, and the conditions that make it indelibly clear that he seeks an opportunity for educational leadership, not merely a job.

With such leadership the kind of high school advocated in this volume has a chance of success.

5

Organizing the Staff for Effective Teaching

> We cannot live simply by the conservation and perpetuation of the past; we must be critical and creative.
>
> *Sterling McMurrin*

A theory of organization must be preceded by a theory of purpose—more precisely, by a theory that concerns itself with the values and priorities to be sought. Schools are organized to serve people, to bring about the development of people. The schools must, of course, serve their people (students) in terms of certain functions, but the people come first, and the areas in which they are serviced come second. This priority is fundamental. It is ignored at the peril of the institution's integrity.

One eminent secondary school principal has remarked that guidance has been organized to cover up the school's failures. While it is readily conceded that this observation is debatable, it does serve to underscore the principle stated above. Guidance certainly does put the individual student at the heart of its consideration. Unfortunately, general school practice and school organization has not always done this. The importance of this consideration is underscored by the very rapid increase in the average size of the American secondary school. This means that it becomes ever more easy for the individual student to be lost in the mass. It means that he is in danger of becoming merely a number on the record. It means that his chances of informal, personal contacts with his teachers are sharply reduced. The chances of his being well known, understood, and appreciated by either teacher or administrator in the school are diminished.

PURPOSES OF ORGANIZATION

Not only are the psychological and social consequences of an impersonal school awful to contemplate, but the educational ineffectiveness of such a school is to be abhorred. Today's huge universities and growing colleges are exploring means of dealing with the problem, which has on a number of campuses already taken nasty turns. An education from which the personal touch has been wrung out is at any level less than a satisfactory education. If there is any legitimacy to university students' complaints that they do not experience sufficient face-to-face relationships with their professors—and there probably is—how much more important is such personal and individualized help to the less mature high school student?

The reader may recall that the theme of this work was to some extent announced in the first chapter by a quotation from John W. Gardner, former Secretary of Health, Education, and Welfare. Here again his help is sought, in the form of a speech to the NEA convention in the summer of 1966, entitled "Education and the Great Society":

> Everything that we do, all that we achieve, must finally be measured in terms of its effect on the individual. We set out to create a free and just society in which the individual could flourish.

> But our modern, highly organized, technological society carries its own threats to individuality. There is the danger that people will become numbers and statistics; that they will be pressed to conform before there is order in conformity; that their jobs and lives will be fragmented, in the factories as in the professions; that they will lose all sense of being whole.

> It needn't be so. We can't do without bigness in our organizations and institutions, but we can design them so that they serve

the individual rather than the system. We can't avoid complexity, but we can organize the work of society so that people can fulfill their need to be needed. Our goal should be a society designed for people; and if we want it badly enough, we can have it.[1]

Most of the nation's high schools are now probably large enough to offer a reasonably varied curriculum. There are those who still concentrate their concern upon the tiny school that typically is impoverished in staff, curriculum, equipment, library —in almost everything. The great secondary school problems, however, no longer center in the small school. While there is even yet a sizable number of them, the total portion of America's high school youth attending them is a small fraction of the whole, and it grows smaller daily. The battle against the small school is mostly behind us. The battle to make the large and the medium-sized school relevant, personal, and individual is now before us.

Educational institutions at both the college and secondary levels in America have grown so rapidly in the past few years that it is not at all surprising to find that rarely have effective and satisfactory patterns of organization evolved in these institutions. Few principals of large high schools, few presidents of large colleges or universities, would fail to agree readily that their plans of organization might be restudied and reworked with profit. But often when such study is undertaken, if anything at all is done about the findings, it is in the nature of patching the old organization. Too seldom is the basic structure reexamined. Too seldom are the assumptions upon which the organization rests questioned. Too seldom is the question raised, Does our organization serve well our most significant purposes?

The purpose here is to raise such questions as these and to suggest possible answers. The following assumptions and principles are in further support, of course, of the assumptions laid down in Chapter 2. At this point they are stated as they apply to organization, and are examined and defended in terms of their demands upon organization. Partial defense for some of them has already been provided.

[1] National Education Association, *Addresses and Proceedings* (Washington, D.C.: 1966), p. 34.

The leadership of a secondary school that seeks to provide its students with a superior educational opportunity will test the soundness of its organization in the iron of the following principles:

1.   The structure is designed to serve individual students.
2.   The plan encourages frequent, informal contacts between teachers and students.
3.   The organization is flexible enough to promote varied and individualized learnings.
4.   The organization itself encourages teachers to initiate, invent, and experiment.
5.   The organization cultivates pupil participation in the structuring of his own learning.
6.   Educational purposes are never sacrificed or impaired by the machinery of organization.

The rationale for each of these principles is discussed in the paragraphs below.

The organization is structured in terms of individual students to be served. In other words, the organization is designed to serve students as individuals, rather than as students of this or that subject or curriculum. It places strong demands upon the organization to individualize and personalize as nearly all of its services to students as possible. It means that the routes of contact to the student are simplified and are as direct as it is possible to make them. The office where his crises are settled does not seem to the student to be far away, cold, and impersonal. He is given the feeling of being dealt with as a whole person, a unique person, and a special person. It means that he does not feel so segmented or subdivided into microscopic parts, with one part of him dealt with in this office, another in that. It means that the frustration that all human beings in our modern society feel, which comes from being buffeted from pillar to post, which comes from subservience to too many bureaus, too many offices, too many agencies, is minimized in the school organization that serves him. He is required to seek directly the services of few specialists, aside from his teachers. Failure to observe this principle causes many students to drop out of school and causes others to wish they could drop out. Such failure leads thousands of others to extract from their school experience less than the best possible education.

The organization must foster and encourage frequent and informal individual and small group contacts between students and teachers. Such organization seldom prevails in today's high school, where both students and teachers often find their school day stuffed quite full with classes and study halls. Furthermore, only a small minority of today's high school buildings provide the teacher with an office or other quarters where he can sit down and talk with a student in some degree of privacy. This is one of the conditions that depreciates teacher dignity, compounds teacher frustration, and materially adds to the problem of attracting and retaining the quality and quantity of teachers the schools need. An education that is anywhere nearly as good as today's understandings make possible is going to remain unrealizable until greater emphasis is placed upon the individualization and personalization of assignment and instruction. Such assignment and instruction is not encouraged by an organization that makes individual contact between teacher and student difficult.

The organization must be flexible enough to encourage and promote varied and individualized learnings. This is a corollary of the second assumption. If teachers are to be encouraged, even to find it possible, to do the things for individual students that they find advisable as a result of individual conferences with them, they are going to need to be released from a number of strictures that now make it difficult to promote the individual tailoring of pupil assignment and activity. For example, temporary alterations in the student's daily schedule frequently will be advisable. More library time, more laboratory time, more gathering of data outside the walls of the school building may be necessary to the effective pursuit of a student interest that is at white heat. Furthermore, the teacher must be able to effect the change with a minimum of ritual, for delay in such a case may be fatal to that interest. The teacher's judgment must be accepted as that of a professional person.

The organization must give rein to teacher initiative, invention, and experimentation. The teacher must feel not only free to seek better ways to promote learning, he must also be encouraged to do so. In a number of ways the secondary school teacher is expected to operate within more narrow limits than either the elementary or the college teacher. The college or university teacher, for example, would in no self-respecting institution ever submit his instruction to supervision at the hands of a general supervisor. He is most likely to be subject to no supervision at all. The college professor offers a given course, and it is his course. He follows his own outline, alters it as he chooses, and usually selects his own textbook. If the course has multiple sections and other teachers, he usually participates in drafting the syllabus and in choosing the text.

The high school teacher is much more pressured by college and university expectations than is the elementary teacher by any higher educational level. He is normally expected to have subject-matter expertise, as is the college teacher, but with less than the college teacher's freedom of judgment to interpret the subject in his own terms. He faces the rigidities of schedule that characterize the work of the college teacher, but with no basis for assuming the elasticity of library and laboratory hours that are characteristic for the college student. The self-contained elementary classroom teacher usually makes her own schedule, within broad guideline limits, and is at liberty to make alterations in it. The high school teacher needs elbowroom and freedom to use his own judgment. If changes in the school laws of the states are needed to reassure and to protect the teacher in the exercise of his judgment, then such changes must be sought. The teacher must be made to feel responsible for favorable results, but he must be given the professional autonomy that make such results achievable.

The organization must cultivate pupil interest and participation in the structuring of his own learning, so that he may become his own best teacher and strictest master. No educator will argue against the thesis that the best discipline is self-discipline. No one will disagree that the greatest of all masteries is self-mastery. No one who understands learning will deny that the individual in the last analysis teaches himself. No one will deny that the learner truly learns only what he wants to learn. No one who conceives of the rapidity of change in our era will fail to realize the practical value of knowing how to instruct oneself. All who have thoughtfully studied the matter realize that the capacity to carry responsibility successfully is developed by practice in exercising responsibility.

Despite all these realizations and understandings, secondary schools continue to organize so that most of their time is given to teaching students to follow directions. The student experiences little encouragement and little opportunity to exercise his own initiative. The approach is, rather, "You do these things, and we'll give you a unit of credit." Consequently, he graduates all too frequently with no significant consolidation of interests, at least partly because he has had little encouragement in exploring the by-ways that beckoned to him through his secondary school years.

The junior high school was established early in the century (1909) with a primary aim of helping young people find themselves. About the same time (1908), the guidance movement was conceived in Boston and set upon its way, although its rather general development had in some areas to wait until after World War II. Despite these two great movements, each of which holds tremendous potential for good, a very large number of young people each year reach the high school graduation platform with no idea whatever of how they want to invest their adult lives. Many are also lacking any scale of values by which they may be guided through those lives. Is it possible that this picture might be improved by an education which designedly and deliberately (rather than incidentally) placed a central emphasis upon the student's responsibility for pursuing his educational goals in ways that were meaningful to him?

Surely one of the most useful qualities, useful to himself and to others, that any college freshman or any young employee going out to assume his first full-time job could possess would be a highly developed capacity for self-direction. The young housewife and the young husband need it no less. Few will deny that responsibility is a broad and significant aim of all education. The plea here is that it be moved closer to the top of the hierarchy of all educational aims and that it be consciously and fully planned for in the design of the high school's organization.

Whenever and wherever the school's well-conceived educational purposes come into conflict with the machinery of organization, it is the machinery that must bend, not the purposes. This is no doubt just another way of saying that first things must remain in first place and must not be crowded into second, or third, or into any position of lower estate. It is really quite easy for the reverse to happen in any school, the temptation to confuse means and ends being forever present and frequently great.

Robert K. Merton discusses this problem, drawing an analogy between the natural inclination of the bureaucrat (administrator) to have just a little more organization, just a little tighter rule, than he needs and the bridge engineer who specifies greater strength in the supports than his calculations indicate necessary.[2] The difference is a kind of insurance. He wants to make sure. The school man often refers to this disposition as "running a tight ship," failing to recognize that the ports at which the ship calls rather than its tightness of operation are the real determinants of educational quality. Obviously, the ship must be tight enough to make sure that it remains afloat. It is possible, however, to place such extreme emphasis upon tightness and safety that the ship never raises its anchor. The educational horizon is then limited to the wharf and immediate environs. The result is dullness and eventual stultification for both crew (teachers) and passengers (students). There is no way to remove all risk from an education that is to be exciting and rewarding.

Much to the point of the argument here are the words of a great educational leader and thinker of a generation ago, William Satchel Learned, who in his Harvard Inglis Lecture of 1932, spoke as follows:

> The point escapes us that education can rarely be genuine and also tidy in the administrator's sense. He thinks of school and college as a sort of formal garden. The close-cut lawn, the precisely trimmed hedge, the standardized tulips set in patterns are an administrative delight. Educationally they are impossible, and would be hideous to contemplate even if we could achieve them.[3]

---

[2] Robert K. Merton, "Bureaucratic Structure and Personality," in Amitai Etzioni (ed.), *Complex Organizations: A Sociological Reader* (New York: Holt, Rinehart and Winston, 1961), pp. 52–53.

[3] William S. Learned, *Realism in Education* (Cambridge: Harvard University Press, 1932), p. 10.

THE STATUS OF PRESENT SCHOOLS

How well do most presently existing high school organizations meet the demands of these stated principles? Not very well. How much encouragement do they get from state departments of education and from accrediting associations in moving toward types of organization that might meet the above criteria? Not very much. Reflection upon the story of the high school's problems and the pressures to which it has been subjected over the past eighty years helps us to understand the limiting factors that bear upon this uniquely American institution. The rapid expansion of high school opportunity lies wholly within this eighty-year span. By far the most formative years, the most decisive of the institution's history, were those between 1890 and 1910. One who would understand the high school and its present problems must understand thoroughly its history through those years. By 1910 certain significant dies were cast. They were not always the wisest choices in terms of long-range developments, but they were probably the best that could be devised at the time. At least they were expedient. No institution, however, should be called upon to live forever with its mistakes of the past, especially when ensuing developments have magnified the proportions of those mistakes.

Since about 1910 the high school and the authorities and agencies that influence it most have suffered from a chronic ailment that might be called "hardening of the categories." Different interests have sought to elevate high school standards through standardized mechanics of organization. Chief among these have been the colleges, the accrediting associations, and state departments of education. Their criteria have too often been the clock and the calendar, not because these are the chief determinants of educational quality but because they are readily quantified. An office clerk without educational vision or insight can count and see whether standards are satisfied. Thus what is easy to measure often takes precedence over what is good to measure.

The leaders of the high schools themselves are not blameless in the patterns of rigidity that have been frozen upon them, although they are to a great extent forgivable. It must be remembered that high school principals were terribly pressed with problems of growth, especially between 1890 and 1930, and that staffing always runs somewhat behind the demands of growth. Under these conditions, and usually lacking the assistants and the secretarial help they needed, it was easier to accept the hardened categories, to pigeonhole the students who could be made to fit into existing slots, and to forget the rest of them. By 1930 the strictures that had been fought earnestly by numerous able principals in 1910 had come to be accepted. They were taken for granted, almost as if there were no other ways. So it remained for almost another thirty years. It is chiefly within the last decade, since the arousal of interest in such matters as independent study and flexible scheduling, that alert and able principals have begun to chafe under certain regulations. These regulations appear to many to be obstacles that stand in the way of well-conceived efforts to find paths that lead to more effective instruction.

To set the stage for the recommended high school organization described in the latter part of this chapter, it is appropriate to turn now to a rather detailed account of the problems and developments that overtook that institution in the first twenty years of its rapid growth period.

THE FORMATIVE YEARS, 1890–1910

It may be something of a surprise to many to note that in matters of organization the high school shifted from one pole to the other in a period of less than twenty years. The high school of 1892 was quite a freewheeling organization, one with very little closely followed pattern. A tenth-grade class in English might meet five days a week in one high school, three or even two days in another. The American colleges, themselves governed much by the clock and the calendar, found it difficult to compare one freshman candidate with another. Freshman candidates must be compared, of course, for such purposes as making decisions on admissions and scholarships, and in such a way, if possible, as to make the decisions more or less automatic and to shift the ultimate responsibility for them to others.

The collegiate-inspired pressure for more uniformity in high school courses and credits was one of the factors that led to the establishment of the now famous Committee of Ten on Secondary Studies[4] by the National Education Association in 1892. The committee was chaired and dominated by President Charles W. Eliot of Harvard University, who, ironically, had reduced scholastic rigidities at Harvard by promoting the elective system. The report of this committee led to the high school's first important strides toward uniform standards of curricula, organization, and program. It recommended, for example, that high schools abandon the practice, then very common, of giving many short courses on a wide variety of subjects. It is not here argued that such abandonment was all bad; or all good. Surely more than a persuasive teacher's current interest and fancy should lie behind the introduction of a new course into the school's standard curricula. Yet there is perhaps a legitimate place for such developments in a secondary school of quality.

The source of President Eliot's highly motivated interest in the secondary school was a strong feeling that young men could profitably start and finish their college careers earlier. He complained that Harvard's typical freshman was nineteen years old, that there was too much dallying in the twelve, in some places thirteen, years of public school education. The chaff, he said, should be winnowed out, and the young man should enter college a full year earlier. While he complained "Uniformity is the curse of American schools,"[5] it was his work, ideas, and influence, perhaps more than of any other single man, that led to the introduction of much greater uniformity in the machinery of operation in the nation's high schools.

The Committee of Ten Program

Thirty thousand free copies of the Eliot committee's report were distributed widely by William T. Harris, the first commissioner of the U.S. Bureau of Education and a member of the committee.

---

[4] Charles W. Eliot *et al.*, *Report of the NEA Committee of Ten* (New York: American Book, 1894).

[5] Charles W. Eliot, "Shortening and Enriching the Grammar School Course," in National Education Association, Department of Superintendents, *Proceedings* (Washington, D.C.: 1892), p. 623.

Its net effect was to encourage every high school to reduce its fringe curricula and to center the work of each student upon five or six academic areas in each of the four high school years. The committee recommended four curricula: classical, Latin-scientific, modern languages, and English. The classical curriculum called for three languages: Latin all four years; Greek, the last two; and German or French, three years, starting in grade ten. The Latin-scientific curriculum required four years of Latin and three years of German or French. The third curriculum, modern languages, called for two modern foreign languages, one for four years, the other for three. The English curriculum required one foreign language, ancient or modern, for all four years.

All four of the committee's curricula called for the study of English for two to four periods a week in all four years. Academic mathematics appeared in all four years of all curricula, history being an alternate in the senior year, with bookkeeping and commercial arithmetic indicated as an acceptable alternate to algebra in either the second or third year. History appeared in all four years of all curricula, but only as an alternate to mathematics in the senior year. With the exception of the second year of the classical curriculum, science was suggested for each student each year, in the following order: physical geography, physics, astronomy (a half year), meteorology (a half year), and chemistry.

Under the committee's prescription only Latin and Greek classes met five periods a week. The one exception to this was eleventh-grade English in the English curriculum, which also met daily. Most of the classes were to meet either three or four times a week, with English and history classes in a few instances limited to two meetings. Each student was to attend twenty prepared classes a week each year. Although no such thing as a unit of work had been spoken of at the time, the foundation for the present four units a year is seen in this pattern.

These recommendations of the Committee of Ten introduced the mechanics of the European academic secondary school of both then and now and added a curricular rigidity equal to that of the German gymnasium or the British grammar school.

Because of their great reliance upon the educative values of foreign languages, particularly the ancient, one must not be too ready to mark Committee of Ten members and their supporters as educational imbeciles. First, the attainment of mere literacy was a more dominant aim of schooling at that time than in recent years, and the study of any foreign language does contribute to literacy. Second, it must be recalled that in 1892 and for several years thereafter, the theory of formal or mental discipline was at the very top of educational thought. Edward L. Thorndike's revelations and those of other psychologists were still several years in the future. In the elementary school of the time, heavy emphasis was placed upon such matters as endless drill in spelling words the pupil did not know or understand. In geography he located places he was taught little or nothing about because such exercises were presumed to develop the mind. The same ends were served by the study of foreign languages, especially Latin, which as a secondary school study remained near the top until at least the time of World War I. For example, a state-wide study in Ohio in 1913 showed that Latin preempted more than one-sixth of high school pupil time there.[6]

The Report of the Committee of Ten became the center of an educational debate, journalistic and otherwise, that lasted for more than a decade. Those of the conservative right declared it gave a reckless latitude to the elective system. Those of the left saw it as a blueprint for the ruthless domination of the secondary school by the colleges and universities, whose purposes they felt it was designed to serve. It was criticized, even by one of its own members, for its neglect of the industrial and commercial subjects and for its evident encouragement of uniformity. Eliot persistently maintained that the pattern was not presented as *the* plan, but as a suggested approach to a secondary education of solid substance.

Attacks on the Report

One of the hardest fights was aimed from the right. This was a futile effort to place three years of Greek in the classical curricu-

[6] Ohio State School Survey Commission, *Report of Ohio State School Survey Commission: A Cooperative Field Study* (Columbus, Ohio: F. J. Heer, 1914), p. 13.

lum rather than two. It came in the 1894 meeting of the New England Association of Colleges and Preparatory Schools. A second fight was aimed at amendment in favor of five-day-a-week Latin in the third and fourth years of the Latin-scientific and classical curricula. Nothing came of the proposal, although Latin enrollments did rise in the years following the report. Perhaps it was the last great surge of American neoclassicism, for secondary school Greek faded rapidly in the first third of the twentieth century, and Latin followed the same route at a somewhat slower pace in the second third of the century.

The attack upon the report from the left was slower in gaining momentum but was more violent and more persistent. Its champion by 1900 had become G. Stanley Hall, the articulate and persuasive leader of the new pedagogy. Hall's criticisms were directed at what he saw as three fallacious assumptions of the report: first, that every subject should be taught in the same way and to the same extent to all pupils, regardless of their probable destinations; second, "that all subjects are of equal educational value if taught equally well"; and third, that the same education that fitted one for college success also fitted him for success in life. Hall bore down heavily on the evils of college domination, urged secondary teachers to establish and control their own organization, and accused the committee of ignoring the interests of hordes of young people who lacked the ability to profit from their curricula. In the light of recent experiments which have demonstrated that learning potential may be more related to acculturation and to incentive than to inherited capacities passed with the genes, history may eventually render the verdict that Eliot was closer to the truth than was Hall. Professor Hall appears to have been more prophetic when he observed that "subjects should be approached in as many different ways as there are ultimate goals."[7]

From the narrow curricular outlook with which the Committee of Ten sought to cloak the high school, it has been able to effect certain limited escapes. In truth, it was here and there

[7] G. Stanley Hall, *Adolescence, Its Psychology, and Its Relations to Physiology, Anthropology, Sociology, Sex, Crime, Religion and Education* (New York: D. Appleton & Co., 1916), Vol. II, pp. 510–512.

escaping such strictures even while these men were preparing their report. That escape has continued to take varied forms or routes ever since. From later more rigorous and more mechanical strictures, it is just now wriggling loose, getting a little elbow-room here, a little chance to vary the approach to learning there. We now turn to the strictest limitation upon freedom to experiment which the American high school, or perhaps any secondary school anywhere, has ever faced—to the rise and influence of the Carnegie unit.

LOSS OF FLEXIBILITY

In light of the recent concern for flexible scheduling, it is pertinent to examine how the high school lost the flexibility it once had. Under the Committee of Ten curricula, prescriptive as they were, the student studied five to eight different academic subjects each year. This was possible for two reasons. First, only Latin, Greek, and eleventh-grade English (this latter only in the English curriculum) met five days a week. Most classes met three or four times a week, and some only two. Second, more use was made of semester-length subjects than now. The least one can say about this program is that it provided the student with a broader range or variety of subjects, within its prescribed limits, than is the case today. It is worthy of note, too, that European academic secondary schools still retain this type of flexibility.

Under the Committee of Ten program, the student might present for graduation work in thirty or more different prepared classes, all carried for at least a semester, most carried for the entire year. Today's high school graduate, by comparison, typically offers prepared work in twelve to eighteen classes. Somewhere along the way almost everything taught has got itself accepted as a "solid," which has come to mean that it meets daily and that it presumes out-of-class preparation. This is a variation of the kind of uniformity spoken of in Dr. George H. Reavis' "Animal School." All the subjects are taught all the time; that is, they are given the same degree of emphasis. How did such uniformity get stamped upon the American high school? How did the clock gain such respect as a measurer of educational results? It was not true as late as 1908, but by 1920 the pattern was fixed and nearly universal. Today it would scarcely occur to a secondary teacher to propose that any prepared or academic course be offered fewer than five days a week.

Ellsworth Tompkins and Walter Gaumnitz, in their definitive study of the Carnegie unit, start their report by observing that "the Carnegie unit, unique to the American system of secondary education, is being reexamined."[8] That was in 1954. What is the Carnegie unit and where did it spring from?

The Carnegie Unit

During the last years of the nineteenth and the early years of the twentieth century, the colleges and universities were experiencing increasing troubles in matters of admission and scholarships. Due to the idiosyncrasies of the high schools, colleges found the comparison of students difficult, especially in the light of their own mounting efforts to improve standards and to upgrade the quality of their respective student bodies. The problem was further complicated by the fact that most American colleges were then fighting for students, not fighting them off as has so often been the case in recent years. In this scramble for students, the colleges often admitted young people who had not finished their high school work. The situation remained somewhat chaotic and was characterized by much guesswork until 1909, when an entirely different college problem had the effect of forcing a decision of expedience upon this one.

That different problem was what to do with the senile college professor. Professorial salaries did not at that time provide an affluence that permitted instructors to lay aside funds for their old age. As a consequence, many an instructor was retained on the teaching staff, out of sympathy, long after his days of effectiveness were past. In 1905 Andrew Carnegie gave the Carnegie Foundation for the Advancement of Teaching the sum of

---

[8] Ellsworth Tompkins and Walter Gaumnitz, *The Carnegie Unit: Its Origin, Status, and Trends,* Office of Education Bulletin 7 (Washington, D.C.: Government Printing Office, 1954), p. 1.

$10 million to endow a pension fund for college professors. The trustees of the fund found it necessary, in determining eligibility, to define a college professor, to define a college, and in that process, to define a high school, and they did. They decided that fourteen units of secondary school work should be a minimum preparation for college work, and they defined a unit as a five-period-a-week class that was pursued throughout the school year. The problem was complicated by the fact that many colleges then had their own preparatory or secondary school divisions and that many instructors taught at both the preparatory and collegiate levels. Furthermore, the line of demarcation between the two was at times not clear. The Carnegie unit decision was made in 1909. Thus the high school Carnegie unit became the by-product of a pension plan for college professors. Whatever its other uses or distinctions, the Carnegie unit did mark off for the first time a clear line of division between the high school and the college.

The Basic Assumption Underlying the Carnegie Unit

The introduction of the Carnegie unit undoubtedly raised both high school and college standards at the time. Particularly did it have the effect of raising college admission standards, but it has had the long-range effect of placing educational emphases upon quantity rather than quality. In their need to find a measure of educational progress, the trustees may have made an assumption that was not then valid, and one that is even less valid today.

The Carnegie unit appears to rest upon an assumption that may be stated something like this: The learning of a high school student in a given field is directly proportionate to the hours he spends in an organized class in that field. This assumption remains unsubstantiated to this day. On the other hand, much has been learned about negative learnings since 1909. It has been demonstrated, for example, that additional hours spent by some students in the classes of some subjects may result most notably in a mounting distaste for the subject, that is, in a determination not to study the subject any more, anywhere, under anyone.

What might be the result if we put the student in the class

not five but three days a week, and then put him in a richly equipped and related laboratory or library for the other two days? Do college students of the same age and reputed intelligence, who meet most classes only three days a week, learn less or more than high school students? In how many high schools has a modified approach under favorable conditions had a fair trial? Can all the benefits of such a plan be registered on an achievement test in the subject? What about the incidental interests or ideas the student has developed as he searched for subject-related ideas, through his sampling of this book with the fascinating title, his handling of that piece of laboratory equipment with its inexplicable appeal? What about his capacity for self-direction, for the exercise of initiative? In which situation do these benefit most?

It appears that the time has arrived for the Carnegie unit not only to be reexamined, but for it to undergo modification. Failure to meet the challenge of this need may jeopardize the high school's future as an institution. Other agencies or institutions, yet unimagined, and unfettered by tradition, could conceivably arise to meet today's needs for a flexibility that will enable secondary education to shift its emphases toward the development of responsibility and the enlistment of the student's own powers in the shaping of his own educational objectives. To do less is to give all talk about education for individual differences a hollow ring. To do less is to fail to meet the most pressing challenge of the age of rapid change, that of equipping young people with a heightened regard and capacity for self-instruction.

ORGANIZATION FOR RESPONSIBILITY

The key to effective organization in any enterprise is responsibility. The principal, the teachers, and the students of today's high school carry too little responsibility. The principal must be given more responsibility for his school, responsibility in terms of end results. The teacher must be given more responsibility for his teaching, again in terms of end results. Finally, the student must be given more responsibility for his learning, for this is the surest route to his adequacy for the problems of his day.

Autonomy, authority, and freedom to act are essential to responsibility. Today's high school principal, with rare exception, is not granted the autonomy he needs to become an effective educational leader. This is probably the chief reason why the job often attracts men who are fitted to be custodians of teachers and youth, but not leaders.

Today's high school teacher is often not granted the autonomy he needs to do his best possible teaching. This is surely among the reasons for the dropout of teachers the high school would do well to retain, and likewise, for the retention of too many teachers who do not like to think for themselves but prefer merely to follow orders, thus being able to blame their failures upon the system.

In the matter of student autonomy, there are here and there teachers who encourage the student to participate in the tailoring of his own assignment. The teacher who does encourage the student to follow his own bent, to try out his own ideas, however, often runs a risk that the administration would rather he would not take. Often, too, he is reminded of this. The pursuit of pupil idiosyncrasy is often so disturbing to the organization, is so much discouraged and so little encouraged, that the inventive teacher frequently gives up and the student stops trying to become thoroughly and absorbingly involved. It is so much easier for all to beat the same rhythm on the same drum.

ORGANIZATION OF THE PRINCIPAL AND HIS OFFICE

He who would organize others must first organize himself. Let us assume that the principal has assured himself that he has an honest interest in and a developed capacity for educational leadership. Let us assume that he has assured himself of the autonomy he needs to exercise leadership before he accepted the post. Let us assume that he has a written copy of the statement that spells out the extent of his authority and has the further assurance that his authority will not in any way or any time be reduced or curtailed without his written agreement. Let us further assume he has been given broad powers to set up his own administration, his own organization in his own way, and that the budget allocated to his school is adequate to finance a good school. What does he do now?

The Principal's Office

Among the principal's many roles is that of office manager. He must organize an office, one that should be businesslike if possible, but always functional in educational leadership. With this in mind, his office should be located, if possible, apart from other offices, preferably in a different part of the building. Though unorthodox in terms of present practice, this arrangement will have certain advantages. First, it will help to make the principal's office thought of as the office of educational leadership, not as a place where one stops by on the way, having deposited a purchase order with the activities bookkeeper. Second, it will tend to keep the endless traffic of housekeeping minutia out of the principal's way, thereby giving him a better chance to center his attention on aspects of educational leadership. Third, it will help the principal to develop strength and responsibility in his assistants, for they will find it less easy to turn to him to make or reinforce decisions for which they should accept full responsibility. This, too, will conserve his time and energy for the important tasks. Fourth, it will add to the dignity and prestige of the principal's office. Only problems that cannot be handled satisfactorily in the office of assistants will reach his station.

The Principal's Secretary

Attached to the principal's office should be his secretary, a person of some education and executive ability. Such a person can, under his direction, perform many of the principal's lesser tasks for him. She can, for example, read his correspondence, brief him on it, and determine which pieces require his personal and careful attention. She can answer much of the correspondence without specific instruction from the principal. Other letters, with a sentence or two of instruction, she can compose for him. Not more than half a dozen letters a week should require his personal dictation. It is said that Fiorello LaGuardia, some years ago the colorful and able mayor of New York City, spent but thirty minutes a day on his correspondence. His secretary took it from there. If such will serve well what is reputed to be the second heaviest executive position in the United States, it is quite likely that most high school principals spend too much time on their correspondence. Some, of course, like many college professors, ignore their mail.

An efficient secretary, who can and should be trained by her chief to assume more responsibility than merely doing what she is told, can in numerous ways extend the principal's efficiency. Under optimum conditions she serves as his official reminder and as the manager of his calendar. She places upon his desk, in priority rank, the items that she knows need attention on any given date, and with each folio she places any additional papers needed for him to make decisions. She jots notes about who can be of special help with each problem and further notes when each can be available.

Secretaries grow in their power to serve, just as do teachers and students, by being given responsibility. Unfortunately, many principals never learn to harness secretarial potential for building a more effective school. However, caution is pertinent here. The secretary must learn to carry her duties without appearing too officious, and the principal must make clear to his staff what authority his secretary has been granted and why.

The Principal's Conference Room

Adjacent to the principal's office should be a conference room that will comfortably seat at least fifteen persons. It should be much used at all times of day by faculty groups of varying size, and the principal should be present at many of these sessions, for this is one of the places that he can discover where there are real chances of educational gain. He can sense where his encouragement and aid will be fruitful. He can be alerted to promising potential. The conference room may serve, too, as the escape hatch through which he occasionally avoids seeing a caller whom he is not yet ready to face personally, at times a wholly legitimate maneuver.

ORGANIZATION OF THE PRINCIPAL'S ASSISTANTS

Most of today's high schools and colleges are awkwardly and inefficiently organized. A casual examination of the history of these institutions reveals the reasons. The first reason is found in the extremely rapid growth of the institutions, particularly in the average size of the individual school. This has taken place chiefly since 1920, since the era of the school bus, and since the beginning of the rapid flow of population from rural to urban and suburban centers. The second reason for inefficiency is found in the approach to the expansion of the school's services. This requires more careful explanation.

In meeting the needs for new services, the high school has been indiscriminate in applying the principle of specialization. Administrators have been inclined, mistakenly, to look upon themselves as specialists, when in fact the nature of their work calls upon them to be generalists, requiring them to develop and maintain the broad view. It is the principal who thinks of himself as a specialist who most frequently gets in his teachers' hair, who most frequently reminds them that they don't understand the problems of administration. Seeing the need for a new service, such principals have found the easiest way to meet the problem to be that of establishing a new office with a specialized function. In this they have failed to reckon the long-range cost in negative effects upon both teachers and students.

One of the probable reasons for widespread teacher discontent today is that the teacher is answerable to too many bosses. Likewise, one of the reasons for the discontent of students—some of whom drop out physically, others psychologically—is that the student is too much partitioned, is answerable to too many different persons, and must visit too many stations to get a problem solved. No one works best when his allegiance is divided among many persons.

This does not at all mean that the high school should have no specialists. All of the school's teachers must be specialists. The school also needs a number of other specialists, such as librarians and specialized teacher aides, to be discussed later. A fairly sound rule may be stated thus: Subordinate and auxiliary positions may represent specialization, while superordinate positions should rarely be specialist in nature.

Industry may be able to survive the introduction of numerous specialists at the management level, for in industry it is common to disregard the production worker's interest in the reasons for a given decision. Many industrial leaders realize the value of the development of a sense of community, but they generally tend to consider the problem insurmountable. Even here we are told that this attitude is changing, that concert of interest is a matter of growing industrial concern. The school's organization, however, must hold high reverence for the fact that the school is a social community before it is anything else. If the school's teachers and administrators are to be held even partially *in loco parentis,* the pupil must not have too many parents. One can notice the ill effects of such when young children find themselves subject to orders from uncles, aunts, and grandparents, as well as parents, all at the same time. Failure to respect this view leads to the sharp reduction in efficiency of all, from the principal to the most timid student. For the insecure student it is fatal. For teachers, students, and administrators alike, it leads to needless confusion.

The Cost of Specialization in Administration

Why is the assignment of administrative chores wholly in terms of specialties inefficient? The reason lies in the generally recognized fact that the wise decision on a student concern or problem is dependent upon knowing as nearly all about him as it is possible to know. As the majority of today's larger high schools are organized, the assembling of such data is a colossal and wasteful chore. In the process the student, usually required to do the leg work for his own case, often gives up in disgust. The school's machinery has convinced him that he does not have a problem, but he is seldom really convinced or happy about it. He is quite sure that he has been given a runaround.

An organization is ineffective when it exhausts administrators, teachers, and students in threading the gamut of organizational procedures. This is what happens when one person does the counseling, another makes the student's program, a third handles problems relating to discipline and attendance, and a fourth supervises the pupil's instructional program. Time is lost and misunderstandings arise in getting needed information from the person who has possession of it to the person who needs it at the moment. Because of the difficulty of getting the needed data, decisions are often made without it, and the student suffers. Furthermore, it is possible to imagine that the best cumulative pupil records will not overcome these disadvantages, for two reasons: First, it is impossible to commit to paper fully and accurately what is known about a student. Part of it is intuitive, and feelings are significant but often extremely difficult to describe in written words. Second, the person making the decision, for one reason or another, often fails to read the pupil data that is at hand.

The Functions of Assistant Principals

In the light of these observations, and in the further light of the need to organize the school so that students will be served as individuals, so that personalization of the school's effort may be uppermost, what is the best organization?

The pattern here recommended is not untried. It is, in fact, only a slight modification of an organizational plan that has been in effect at high schools like the one at Oak Park, Illinois, for forty years, more or less. There a four-year high school of about 3,600 students is served by 12 deans, who are assigned about 300 students each. No brief is held for the titles. Titles are unimportant, but function is all-important. The division dean takes his 300 freshman boys and goes through school with them. This gives him a chance to understand his students, a chance to serve to some degree *in loco parentis*. The freshman girls' dean this year becomes the sophomore girls' dean next year, and so on. An important feature of the Oak Park plan is that a meeting of all 12 principals or deans is held every Tuesday morning at nine o'clock. The meeting, presided over by the director-principal, serves to clear problems, to acquaint all with incipient developments, to effect reasonable consistency in administrative policy, and to give the school needed unity.

The plan recommended here is an extension of the Oak Park organization. It provides for further refinement of the unit, or house, as a social and educational community, for more attention to individualized and personalized learning.

It is here recommended that the student body of the large and medium-size school be divided into houses of 150 to not more than 300 students each. If the unit can be as few as 200 students, superior results should follow, but such a size must not be achieved at the expense of other needed services or personnel. Each house is to be presided over by an assistant principal-counselor, who will be responsible for his 200 students and the direction of their education. These persons might well be called principals, while the head of the total school might be referred to as the director or some other title. Again, terminology is unimportant. Each house principal will do or direct the scheduling of his students, will handle the discipline and other problems that arise in his unit, and will serve as counselor to his students, at least to the point where more highly specialized services, such as those of a trained psychologist, are deemed necessary.

Qualifications of Assistant Principal-Counselors

It is assumed that the house principal-counselor will have educational qualifications similar to that of the principal-director. He will be an individual of strong personal qualifications and judgment and will be a proven teacher, with strong teacher preparation. He will have extensive graduate work or continue to get more after appointed until he has at least two years of graduate study. His graduate program should reflect considerable work in guidance, the foundations of education, secondary curriculum and organization, and in human growth and development or adolescent psychology. Preferably, to strengthen his bond with teachers, he will continue to teach at least one regular class.

Other Staffing Considerations

Why a maximum of 300 students? While this number has no absolute sacredness, it represents a number that one person finds it possible to know rather well and to think about as individual persons. This number also meets guidance standards of accrediting associations, such as the North Central Association.[9] If the avenues of access to parents are open, it is possible for one person not only to know 300 students but to know at least one parent of each. This is an added advantage. Moving along with his students will give the unit or house principal a real opportunity to develop a degree of informal camaraderie with them. They may be able to laugh a little, each about the foibles or idiosyncrasies of the other, even when the subject of the conference is an awesome one.

So far as possible and practical, teacher assignments should be limited to their units, and some teachers should move with their units to the next grade level. Thus in the ninth grade of a four-year high school, it might be possible to hold the necessary different teacher contacts of the unit principal to as few as twenty to twenty-five teachers, while most of the classes taken by his unit's students might involve no more than twelve to fifteen teachers. This is assuming a ratio of about twenty pupils per teacher. The point is that every effort must be made to establish a community or family unit that promotes security, intimacy, personal interests and attention, and informal contact between teacher and student, between student and student, as well as continuity of experience. The arrangement makes for efficiency because what is learned about the pupil this year is useful in serving him better next year.

Insofar as practical, each unit should be housed in its own classrooms or section of the building, with all units using in common an auditorium, a general library, an audiovisual center, a graphic arts center, and other highly specialized laboratory and service facilities.

This means that the high school of 1,200 students is to be broken into not less than 4 student bodies, that of 2,000 students into at least 7. It means that each principal-counselor specializes in a given number of students, not that he specializes in attendance, discipline, counseling, or academic supervision. Units or houses might well be named after retired and highly respected

---

[9] North Central Association of Colleges and Secondary Schools, *Policies and Criteria for the Approval of Secondary Schools* (Chicago: 1960–1961), p. 17.

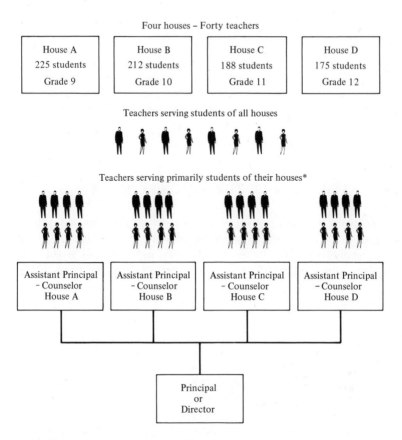

Four houses – Forty teachers

House A	House B	House C	House D
225 students	212 students	188 students	175 students
Grade 9	Grade 10	Grade 11	Grade 12

Teachers serving students of all houses

Teachers serving primarily students of their houses*

Assistant Principal – Counselor House A	Assistant Principal – Counselor House B	Assistant Principal – Counselor House C	Assistant Principal – Counselor House D

Principal
or
Director

*These teachers would tend to be, for the most part, those teaching the subjects taken by large numbers of students: English, social studies, mathematics, the basic sciences, foreign languages, and physical education.

Organization of a Four-Year Senior High School of 800 Students teachers, thus giving long and dedicated service to the school deserved recognition. The aim of the plan is to retain the advantages that larger schools can offer, while restoring the advantages that the much smaller schools of earlier days provided—to personalize and individualize the school program to a degree that many believe no longer possible. The chart on page 129 reveals the simplicity of the flow of responsibility in a school so organized.

ORGANIZATION OF THE TEACHING STAFF

Teachers, like other professional persons, if they are to approach maximum effectiveness, must spend some time with their clients as individuals. To make this possible and practical is the most important consideration in any reorganization of today's high school. Physically, this means two things. First, the teacher must not be so solidly booked with classes, study halls, and other assignments that he is inaccessible to students individually or in small groups. Secondly, the teacher must have a place where he can talk to the individual pupil, the individual parent, another teacher, or another citizen.

It is assumed that no teacher will be assigned study hall or monitorial duty of any kind. These, so far as they may be necessary, are functions to be served by teacher aides. The study hall will be supplanted, as explained in Chapter 6. That change will free teacher time for individualized and small group instruction. Then the teacher must either have his own office or one that he shares with no more than two other teachers, and he must have a desk there and easy access to a telephone. This little piece of the school he can call his own, as the dignity of his service demands.

Finally, the twenty-five classes a week that the academic teacher now meets must be reduced to no more than fifteen, with the possible exception of certain kinds of classes where the work is now of a laboratory nature and already by many teachers highly individualized. These might include such areas as physical education, art, typewriting, mechanical drawing, and certain industrial arts or shop classes.

In the reorganized school, of course, the student will be in formally organized classes fewer periods a week, giving the laboratory-library approach to learning a better chance to work. (A blueprint for this arrangement is provided in Chapter 6.) For example, a teacher of tenth-grade history may still teach five sections, but he meets each section as a total class only three times a week rather than the five that is now common practice. This will give the history teacher ten more hours a week, plus whatever further relief he gets from monitorial and study hall assignments, to confer with individual students, to talk with small groups in the history work-study laboratory, to work with other teachers in revamping the course or planning a field trip, to mine the library for motivating sources, for items that will make contact with this student's interest or that one's peculiarities. Four of the weekly teacher periods will be committed to whole house activity, an element of the proposed organization explained in the next chapter.

SUMMARY

The reorganized high school requires variations in traditional concepts of organization. This chapter recommends that the functions of counseling and administration be merged. Efficiency, intimacy, and cohesive social community are sought. To this end it is recommended that the high school be broken down into houses of 200 to 300 students. Each house is to have its own leader and to a considerable degree its own faculty.

Faculty time must be redeployed to encourage the personalization and the individualization of instruction. This is made possible by reducing the weekly meetings of classes from five to three, thus giving teachers and students time for individual conferences and a variety of small and large group activities.

A further development of the reorganized school is the subject of the chapter that follows. There special attention is given to the work-study laboratory and to the house organization and activity.

6

Organizing Students for Effective Learning

> The secondary school we need, then, is one where acceptance and love replace rejection; where there is enough consultation with youth so that they feel some ownership and involvement; where somebody cares about every single one of them; where there will be no second class citizens.
>
> *Earl C. Kelley*

School organization must be designed to serve all the students, and it must be designed to serve their effective learning. It is very wrong, as has been suggested by some, to organize any school merely upon the basis of what is best or presumed to be best for what is thought to be the ablest 25 percent. It is just as wrong to organize any school upon the basis of what is necessary or what is presumed to be necessary for the most indifferent 10 or 20 percent of the students. Curricular revisions have too often in the past twenty years been dictated by the first of these wrongs; and for more than fifty years, organization and the machinery of management have too often been determined by the second.

PRIORITY OF GOALS

If students are to be organized to achieve certain developmental goals that are of priority importance to our day and time, we must be most careful to keep those purposes near the top of the list. Failure to do so explains why the school deed is so often and so far separated from the school word. The belief here is that the school's first obligation is to help the student develop responsibility, to help him find himself, to appraise himself, to get himself pointed in the direction of his own promising and useful potential.

The belief here is that the school has an obligation to personalize and individualize the instruction, to work for excitingly unique results in the case of each individual student. If faculties are to do this, they cannot for one moment forget that what the student is and what he is becoming cannot be separated from what he is learning.

CONTRADICTIONS BETWEEN GOALS AND PROCEDURES

It is assumed that the reader can accept the development of the individual as central among the school's goals. If so, he will find little difficulty in accepting the ten hopes and aspirations that are listed below. It is probable that they now have general acceptance. It is equally probable that the sharp contrast between acknowledged goals and common practices is not generally recognized. Hence the contrasts as listed.

1. *We expect the student to become responsible*—but we provide little practice in the exercise of responsibility.
2. *We hope to develop initiative*—but we seldom give the student the opportunity to initiate significant phases of his own learning.
3. *We expect the student to demonstrate resourcefulness*—but we do not set him free with a rich variety of resources.
4. *We hope the student will cultivate a capacity for self-discipline*—but we keep him busy following our orders.
5. *We want a graduate capable of self-direction*—but we usually deny him the chance of discovering for himself false paths, of suffering the consequences of his own choices.
6. *We cherish for the student inner motivation*—but we continue to emphasize grades, the report card, and school requirements.

7. *We expect the student to discover and cultivate self, his own potential*—but we present an impersonal and stereotyped curriculum.

8. *We seek the student's respect and appreciation of others* —but our highly formalized and routinized organization gives him little chance really to know others, either students or teachers, let alone appreciate them, understand them, take from them and give to them.

9. *We claim to serve the individual student*—but we continue to aim our teaching at the mass, in the mass.

10. *We pay much lip-service to preparing the student for democratic citizenship*—but many practices of the school are among the most autocratic to be found in American society.

The high school organization of recent decades has been based too often upon the premise that all students are suspect. Never are we to be excused for treating all students as prisoners simply because 10 percent of them violate the law. Such a practice is very wrong. Any organization that lets a small minority of its constituents dictate the policy that governs all is wrong, no matter how indirectly that dictation may be effected. If special checks and guards are necessary to control the 10 percent, then let us place such strictures on that 10 percent, and let us be courageous enough to draw the line. Let us not deny, however, to the 90 percent the freedom they need to develop the self-discipline, inner drive, and depth of interest that are the hallmarks of the real and honest student at any level.

PRETENSE IN THE SCHOOL

It must be remembered that much pretense exists in the typical school situation, especially at the high school and college levels. The school game has rules, ordinarily unwritten, but rules nonetheless. The school record profile of the student who follows the rules meticulously tends to overrate him. That of the student who pays little heed to the rules is invariably underrated by his formal record. One has been a successful pretender; the other has not. This has been substantiated, among other places, in the great William S. Learned study of the 1930s, referred to in some detail later in this volume. In the study it was revealed that a high-achieving young man who was also cantankerous was about to flunk out, while a low-achieving young woman of cheerful disposition was about to graduate with honors. Any school that seeks to upgrade its service to students will reexamine itself on this issue. For a look at the extent to which students play the game of school, the strategies they employ to give the impression of learning, the reader is urged to turn to John Holt's *How Children Fail.*[1]

Faith in All Students

One of the shocking realizations that is forced upon the careful observer of the school scene is the large number of teachers and leaders who seem to have little faith in young people. Why should one who lacks faith in young people set himself up as a teacher of them? Of what use can such a person be as a teacher? He may be of use as a policeman, a custodian, but surely of no great use as a teacher. Young people sense our lack of faith in them, and they respond in kind. As a result, too much teacher energy and too much administrator energy is diverted from education to policing. Policing is like cancer; it feeds and grows upon itself. The more policing we do, the more we shall have to do.

It is surely of some significance that every year in America we find it necessary to place uniformed policemen in more of our senior and junior high schools. And every year we find that school vandalism by students increases. Could these be indications of need for modifications in organization and procedure?

The social and political climate in America has changed in the past thirty years. Have our schools caught up with the spirit of that change? There is a new emphasis upon human freedom, new interpretations of the nature of that freedom. Insistence upon the observance of some of its finer nuances has been trying and embarrassing at a number of colleges and universities in recent years, less noticeably so in scattered high schools. To reckon with the basic problems of such behavior at the high school level

[1] John Holt, *How Children Fail* (New York: Dell, 1964).

before it reaches the epidemic stage would be a great achievement for secondary school leadership. (See the eighth assumption in Chapter 2.)

Responsible Handling of Freedom

The chief argument here, despite the problem just discussed, is that the high school student must have more freedom for positive reasons, not for negative reasons. He must have the freedom required to learn how to educate himself, to develop some solid and substantial interests, to find himself, and to appraise his potential. At the same time he must be made to feel responsibility for using that freedom wisely. If we do less than this for him, we are letting both him and the supporting society down. In the process, we seek to develop in him not less but greater and more genuine application. We transfer much of the energy that we have been using to check up on him to helping him to get a conception of what it means to be responsible, to developing an appreciation of the satisfactions derived from behaving responsibly. We give our energy to assisting him personally and individually to find the route, the best sources for sharpening a spark of interest that he has expressed or that we have detected. We put him into contact with people outside the school who can help to anchor his interest and lengthen his reach. We help him to find and use both library and laboratory resources that induce the growth of his interest.

To this end we give him some degree of responsibility for making his own schedule. Beyond a minimum number, we let him decide how many periods a week he shall spend in the biology study laboratory, how many in the shop laboratory, and so on, but we make it abundantly clear that if his plan does not enable him to make demonstrable progress, then he will be responsible for altering it so that he does get results. We need desperately to make it clear that no one can learn for the student, that no one can stuff genuinely useful learning into him, that we can only give him the chance to learn for himself. And we err when we fail to recognize that most students want the chance.

READINESS OF ADOLESCENTS FOR RESPONSIBILITY

Many school people doubt the adolescents' capacities for responsibility, although the high school regularly teaches driver training, a program widely supported by both state departments of education and state legislatures, and one that turns the sixteen year old loose with a vehicle that vastly enlarges his scope of operation and his potential for destruction. The supposition is that he is prepared to use this privilege responsibly.

Is the modern adolescent capable of responsible behavior? What help has he had, what help does he need, in becoming so? If the modern youth is less equal to responsibility, the reason is only that he has had less experience in dealing with it. A hundred years or more ago, when formal schooling covered fewer years for most, it was not uncommon for a seventeen-year-old groom and a sixteen-year-old bride to take the responsibility of a farm, the wresting of a living from which required considerable self-discipline and ingenuity. The young man had a long apprenticeship in farming behind him, his responsibilities having been regularly increased since he was about eight. The same held for the girl. A technological society has left behind the tasks of such apprenticeships.

In the last hundred years, or five hundred, what has happened to the biological and social maturity of the individual? Does such data have a message for schooling?

Earlier Maturity

The data physically comparing America's World War I soldiers with their counterparts of World War II is well known: Those of the later date were both heavier and taller. A more telling comparison is found in the physiological data on maturation, which is sufficient to show that young people, at least in Europe, North America, Japan, and parts of China have been reaching puberty ever earlier over the past one hundred years.[2]

[2] J. M. Tanner, "Earlier Maturation in Man," *Scientific American*, January, 1968, p. 21.

Among other pertinent data brought out by J. M. Tanner in 1968 is the following:

> Puberty arrives two and a half to three and a half years earlier than it did a century ago.
>
> Menarche in girls has appeared earlier by three to four months per decade over the past one hundred years.
>
> Full height is now reached earlier, notable growth in the male after age nineteen being rare.
>
> Children of various ages show a greater increase in height and weight over earlier counterparts than do adults, a further indication of today's earlier maturity.
>
> Fifteen-year-old Swedish boys of 1938 were an average of five inches taller than their counterparts of 1883.

What evidence can be found to support the earlier social maturity of today's young people? Here perhaps the average age of the first marriage provides the most useful precise data. Although there are temporary exceptions, the general trend since 1920 has been as shown by Table 6. This prevails despite the deterrent factor of ever larger college enrollments.

TABLE 6
Median Age at First Marriage (United States)

Date	Male	Female
1920	24.6	21.2
1940	24.3	21.5
1960	22.8	20.3
1966	22.8	20.5

Source: *Statistical Abstract of the United States,* Department of Commerce, Bureau of the Census (Washington, D. C.: Government Printing Office, 1967), p. 64.

That there are other evidences, less tangible, of earlier maturity in today's young people, can scarcely be denied. Numerous writers point to the maturing effects of the mass media, to the exploitation of sex by the business world. No small number believe that the tendency to prolong childhood and to exclude youth from the decision-making processes are partially responsible for a variety of forms and expression of rebellion in today's youth. The position here is that adolescents are ready for more important responsibilities than are ordinarily entrusted to them and that both they and society stand to gain by change in that direction.

WORK-STUDY LABORATORIES

The work-study laboratory and the whole-house or unit program (to be described later in this chapter), are regarded as extensions of the classroom, especially as extensions of the subjects that make up the constants for most high school students. That the high school may be guilty of overteaching, of depending too much upon the formally organized class, is a growing feeling among thoughtful leaders in secondary education.

Dr. Paul B. Diederich, Senior Research Associate with the Educational Testing Service, for example, has long been convinced that high school students spend far too much time listening to other people talk. He says, ". . . nearly all students report that they learn more per year in college, where each class meets only two or three times a week." Dr. Diederich, in further reference to the endless sitting and listening to which high school students are subjected, makes this observation:

> All of this dreary, ineffectual round is based on the assumption that learning proceeds best when administered in doses of five periods a week plus homework for all academic subjects. This assumption is unsupported by a shred of evidence in all experimental literature, contrary to common sense, and contrary to the practice of almost all colleges in every country for hundreds of years.[3]

Teaching is an art of such delicacy and difficulty that Diederich predicts that the next century's experimentation will demonstrate

---

[3] Paul B. Diederich, "The Conant Report, July 6, 1959," in John A. Dahl *et al.* (eds.), *Student, School and Society, Crosscurrents in Secondary Education* (San Francisco: Chandler, 1964), pp. 63–64.

conclusively that an individual can do it effectively no more than two hours a day. He believes academic classes should meet only twice a week. Persons who have had more extensive contact with the high school on an experimental and evaluational basis than has Diederich would be hard to find.

In another paper Diederich tells of his experience with high school English teachers in Detroit, where he helped install a program in which classes were to meet in the traditional fashion only two days a week, two additional days being devoted to reading under the supervision of assistants, and the fifth to either large group instruction or programmed learning. When teachers began to wonder how they might cover five days' work in two, he asked them to suppose they were turning to college work, where such is the general practice, and to estimate how long it might take them to adjust. One was quick to state that he thought he could adjust in about thirty seconds. Diederich reported that once the plan was in operation, teachers "liked it better; their students liked it better; and no one missed the junk that had to be discarded."[4]

Diederich's paper also calls attention to the fact that Helen Parkhurst of the famous Dalton School in New York experimented in the 1930s, with favorable results, with two weekly class meetings in all fields except music and foreign language.

Nature and Purpose of Work-Study Laboratory

In the reorganized school the work-study laboratory becomes an important agency of learning. Each is set up on a subject-area basis; each should contain, if possible, at least 1,200 square feet of space; and each is equipped with maps, charts, books, apparatus, and realia related to the field. Each is staffed with a teacher aide who has had at least two years of college work, who has a keenly developed interest in the field, and who is often a prospective teacher, one who looks upon his assignment as a kind of apprenticeship. This teacher aide receives further attention in Chapter 8.

[4] Paul B. Diederich, "Adapting a College Type of Schedule to High Schools," (Princeton, N.J.: mimeographed release of Educational Testing Service, December 1966), p. 1.

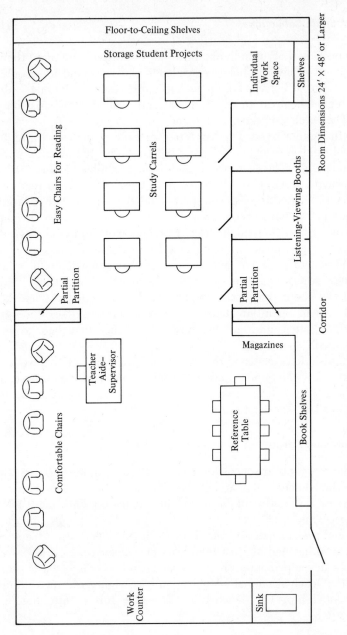

Diagram of a Work-Study Lab in English or Social Studies

It is in the work-study laboratory that the small discussion groups are expected to develop, but they should develop more naturally and spontaneously than is the case with many of the present highly structured approaches to team teaching. Each teacher in the department spends some time in the work-study laboratory each day, talking and visiting with groups and individuals, encouraging here, putting the student in touch with another source there, criticizing or helping to reconstruct a design somewhere else. The teacher also works through the aide in charge of the study lab, thus serving his students through another who can be more often available. A teacher would be expected to give aid and attention to any student in the laboratory, whether his or not. Thus another aspect of team teaching becomes incidental to the design. A diagram of one potential type of work-study lab is shown on page 142. Experimentation will develop a number of useful variations.

Replacement of the Study Hall

The recent warfare on study halls, justified on many counts, nevertheless overlooks some very important considerations. It is quite important that the high school youngster learn to study on his own. It is quite important that he have some time and a place to experiment, to play with an idea, or with an idea and a piece of equipment. It is quite important that there be at least some place in the school where he can be the initiator, since we wish to develop in him as much initiative as possible. It is quite important that he have a chance to come into contact with his teachers in informal ways. Thus the student can draw most fully upon the inspirations his teachers have to offer. All of these purposes the study laboratory, under insightful direction and leadership, is capable of serving.

The mass study hall of the past and present has been a makeshift affair, for it has tried to wring its life out of both facilities and personnel ostensibly provided for other purposes. It has been less than ideal in part because it has been a mass arrangement.[5]

---

[5] See Burton W. Gorman and William H. Johnson, "Pupil Activity in Study Halls: An Inventory and Implications for Progress," National Association of Secondary School Principals, Bulletin 293 (September 1964), pp. 1–13.

The reorganized school will avoid bringing more than a hundred pupils together at any time, for any purpose, except to see a play, an auditorium program, an athletic contest, or a film, or to participate in other appropriate whole-house activity. Lunchrooms that seat 400 or 500 persons or more are proving the point, for they are responsible for more than their share of today's problems.

INCREASED EMPHASIS ON LIBRARIES

The library's full educational potential remains unexplored in too many of today's high schools. Although a central library is appropriate and desirable and although the school's head librarian should be assigned overall responsibility for all its libraries, a school of 1,500 students might profit by having three libraries rather than one. Each library should have a maximum capacity of approximately 100 students. Assuming an eight-period school day, this would provide a maximum of twelve thousand pupil library periods a week. If the average student in the school spent three periods a week in one of these libraries, the demand would tax the facilities to an average of less than 40 percent of capacity. In this case two of the libraries might be specialized to a degree, or two of them might merely duplicate holdings most often in demand. Each should have good reference works and the country's best daily newspapers and periodicals.

Emphasis is placed upon the desirability of three library stations rather than one because the effect is to personalize the school's service to all students. The best school will have as high as 20 percent of its students doing library work at times, and a hundred pupils at a time is enough for any one station.

Certainly the emphasis of the recent past upon library holdings—that is, upon the different titles and volumes available—is important. Few libraries have anything like the holdings they ought to have. How far most high school libraries have to go can be seen in the fact that the Phillips of Andover Academy has over 80,000 volumes in its library for its 1,400 students.[6] That is an

---

[6] Letter from Andover Academy Librarian (October 1968).

estimated ten times the number found in similar size high schools generally. The time has arrived, however, to emphasize much more the accessibility and the usage of those materials by both students and teachers. The library offers the single greatest hope of liberation from the wearying kind of education that is chained to a textbook. This viewpoint provides one of the most cogent reasons for the type of daily school program that permits and encourages both teachers and students to get at the sources of inspiration and insight. A high school student who does not profitably spend some hours in the library each week is in truth less than a student.

Most schools also may find it profitable to scatter about the school, in a variety of patterns, individual study carrels (some even in certain corridor areas) in the ratio of perhaps one to each ten students. Some students work best in relative isolation.

INDIVIDUAL STUDENT ACTIVITY

The type of organization here envisioned is one in which almost every student in the school will on almost any school day in the year have one or more individual projects under way. One of the most promising innovations of recent years is the one that concerns itself with independent study, the possibilities of which have been scarcely scratched. The concept will receive attention in the second chapter on innovations, but a sketch of one kind of potentiality is needed here.

Student projects ideally spring from student interests. They need not and preferably should not be limited by subject-matter boundaries. In this way we get a team of teachers serving the student project. The phenomenon that fascinates the student may be more or less trivial. By the time his investigation is finished, however, he has gone far beyond trivialities on perhaps a number of fronts.

Let us suppose that a student becomes fascinated with Robert Manry's story of his Atlantic crossing in the miniature *Tinker Belle*. This could become a project that might profitably occupy him from a matter of weeks up to the greater part of a school year. How much of life might such a problem reveal to the student? What happens to a man's mind when he spends many successive days and nights totally alone? What mathematical and navigational phenomena are involved? how much oceanography? what meteorology and understanding of weather and winds? What is the chance to get greater insight into the sustenance and health of the human body? What are the human motivations that inspire a man to undergo such risks? What are the rewards, aside from money? Possibilities are almost without end. They could lead the student to draw upon the thinking and insights of three dozen or more different teachers, countless volumes in the library, and numerous additional persons in the community. Furthermore, a number of different students might start with the same stimulation or takeoff point, yet develop very different aspects of it in very different ways. One might emphasize the mechanical, another the psychological, and so on.

The student pursuing his individual project should have access to open courses that he could enter for as little as a few days or as much as several weeks. Suppose he finds that he is not satisfied with his illustrative ability. He should be able to go into an art class where he could get individual help from a skilled teacher as he proceeded to develop his illustrative material. His purposes served, he would then be free to leave. Or he wants to understand and use graphs better. He then goes into a helpful mathematics class, one that is designed to serve such purposes, where the learning is on an individualized basis, and where the teacher is there to serve him.

STUDENT SCHEDULES

A further word about student schedules is necessary. The proposed reorganization might well affect some school departments or subjects less than others. It is the standard academic areas that stand most in need of reform, for they are more tradition-bound and usually have made notably less use of the laboratory method than has art, shop, or music. In typewriting also, for example, and to a lesser extent in home economics, classes are often work or practice sessions. Such classes might go on much as in the past, or two of their five previous sessions might be placed in the study laboratory schedule, in which case the student might be placed in his work sessions with students at various stages of development in the field. Even in these areas a flexibility of 40 percent of previous class time should be introduced so that the other objectives of the program may be realized.

THE WHOLE-HOUSE PROGRAM

Each 200- to 300-pupil unit, or house, of the school should be scheduled with a given half day uncommitted each week, thus making room for field trips for any group without the problem of class conflicts. The school composed of five pupil units or fewer could schedule these unassigned half days by half units, making possible still smaller units, if this seemed desirable. Diligence in planning for the constructive use of each such half day for each group is a matter of first importance. Appropriate special assembly programs, group guidance plans, and educational films that support the subjects being studied might well utilize some of these days. No such half day could be permitted to arrive without definite plans and program. To allow this would be to promote disintegration of the entire schedule and plan. It would also tend to escalate pupil absence. Few schools find it easy to tuck away on short notice 10 percent of their students, the maximum number that might be so scheduled on any given half day in a large school. General faculty agreement on this point should precede the launching of any such program.

Most of the school's large group instruction would become a part of the weekly program of the unit. Some of this instruction would feature faculty members, some of it would feature students, and some of it would represent imports: community persons, both near and far, and other types of local learning resources.

Let it be supposed that the house is a tenth-grade one with practically all members enrolled in biology. One of the school's biology teachers has an excellent lecture on heredity. His lecture becomes a part of one of those half-day sessions. Perhaps he is assisted by some students, who themselves illustrate certain points, or who have helped him work up illustrative material—

overlays for the overhead projector or one of numerous other possibilities. The teacher's lecture is no less likely to be enjoyed and appreciated by one of the few students not enrolled in biology as by the others.

Many worthwhile field trips require the whole or the greater part of a half day. Arranging such in the normally scheduled school presents many problems. With the plan suggested here, it becomes easy. Occasionally a whole school day is a desirable unit of time for a field trip. In that case the problem is only half as great under this plan as it might otherwise be.

Greater Understanding of World of Work

Guidance people and high school principals have in recent years made some headway in their efforts to acquaint students with the world of work. Consequently, with considerable effort, they have arranged for the observance of "Careers Day." This has usually involved the use of a half day for seniors, sometimes for the entire student body. The weakness of this arrangement is dual. First, it is such a pitifully small effort, considering what is involved in understanding the world's work. Second, it is presented almost solely for employment opportunities, ignoring the potential for illustrating the curriculum and giving it relevance. Educationally, it might be far sounder to center upon the curriculum and let the guidance come as an almost certain by-product.

Few principals would deny that the high school graduate's understanding of the world of work is less extensive than one might hope. It is here suggested that as many as one-fourth of the thirty-six uncommitted half days of a nine-month school year might well be devoted to this objective. The program might include field trips, films, and talks by outside speakers.

The Social Importance of the House Plan

Let it be remembered that an important purpose of the house plan is that of building a base to which the student can firmly attach himself, a unit with which he can fully identify both socially and psychologically. With this basis, certain other potentials are advanced.

If the students in the unit are to know each other, they must play as well as work together. Each unit might well invest two of its half days, one in the fall and one in the spring, in field day exercises and games for both boys and girls. Committees representing both faculty and students should be involved in planning these as well as all other activities of the house.

Dramatics Opportunities

In most high schools today only a handful of the students get the opportunity to participate in dramatic activities. Each house might well produce as many as four different full-length plays each year, each play with a different cast, thus spreading the participation. Thus sixty to one hundred people from each unit might have the experience of satisfying their yearning for acting during the course of the year. All teachers who coach a play need not be experts in drama. The aim is social development, self-fulfillment, not vocational, for dramatics activities give many young people confidence. Most of the coaching might well be done, in many cases, by students who are somewhat expert. Participating students, even though not talented, would learn something of diction, much about how to work together, and perhaps many other skills of use in numerous ways. The remainder of the unit would constitute the audience. An evening performance for parents might be added.

The House's Town Meetings

Each school house should have its own self-governing body, with its elected student officials and appropriate committees. Occasional sessions of the whole house should be held. Teacher control should ordinarily limit itself to making sure that responsible students are fully organized and are ready to carry forward the meeting in a businesslike and responsible manner. These would constitute the unit's town meetings, at which the concerns would be those of the unit and of the total school.

Under reasonably imaginative leadership the possibilities of the school unit's class-free half day are almost limitless. Furthermore, its success or failure would be immediately self-revealing. If the unit's attendance rose on the program day, success could usually be taken for granted. If it fell, the program committee had best get to work.

Each unit's program committee would have important work to do. It might well be composed of three to five teachers and two to three times as many students, with some new members joining the committee each nine weeks, so that different students might get such experience during the course of the year. With rare exception all programs and activities should be planned several weeks in advance. Thus during the last few weeks of the spring, the committee would be working on the unit's programs for the early weeks of the fall semester, senior groups excepted. A substitute program, readily available, should always be held in reserve in case of a necessary last-minute change in plans.

HOUSING THE UNIT MEETINGS

Housing the unit meetings would in many schools not be at all difficult. If the school has an auditorium, the problem is solved. At the same time the housing of all other activities of the school is eased, for if on a given half day, one-tenth, one-fifth, or one-third of the school's students spend their time in the auditorium, or abroad, the load and traffic in all the rest of the school is thereby lightened. Thus the school gets higher efficiency from its auditorium.

If the school has no auditorium, other possibilities must be explored. Is the room that has previously served as the study hall large enough to house the unit meeting? Is it possible to utilize half or more of the cafeteria for this purpose, perhaps turning a number of regular classrooms into dining rooms at cafeteria periods? The cafeteria is often another low-utility room, one that does not pay its way educationally. The school that has in mind the richest service to the student cannot afford some of the space wastes that are often by-products of traditional patterns of organization.

INDIVIDUAL STUDENT FLEXIBILITY

Finally, individual student flexibility of program should be applied when educationally appropriate, and especially to those students who by past performance have indicated that they have earned the confidence of the teacher. For example, a student who has become absorbingly and honestly involved in the pursuit of a project or an idea might well be occasionally excused from attending his regular class for several successive days to take full advantage of a rising personal enthusiasm or an especially available source. The underlying thesis is that sitting in a formal class is not the only route to learning. For a given student on a given day and hour, it may not be the best one. The principal who grants a teacher the right of judgment in such matters is enhancing both his own and the teacher's professionalism, although he must be ready to deal with the teacher who exercises such judgment lightly or imprudently.

If the kind of scheduling proposed in this chapter cannot be handled by presently employed electronic devices, let such devices be discarded, for the personalization and individualization of student programs and the movement toward the laboratory method are first considerations. Scheduling presents no great problem for the assistant principal with 200 students, regardless of the method employed.

STUDENT PARTICIPATION IN MANAGEMENT

It is not really very strange that high school students seldom find themselves wrestling with potential solutions to school problems. The quickest way to solve any problem is to assemble the facts in the front office and to hand the decision down from the front office. Democracy is slower; and the high school throughout most of its existence, as explained in Chapter 1, has been in a hurry. If it is assumed that preparation for democratic participation is a part of the school's business, then involvement of students in democratic processes is essential, even if it is less efficient than autocratic management and even if it results in more answers that appear to be wrong, at least at the time. It is easy for the school administrator to take an unsophisticated view of his own responsibility. He sometimes fails to realize that he who develops responsibility in others is thereby best meeting his own responsibilities.

If students make some wrong decisions, this will not be the first time that wrong decisions have been made in American schools. One cannot refrain from observing, for example, as he visits high schools that have made rules limiting the frequency of student locker visits, that this whole situation represents a colossal adult management error. It was no doubt a mistake to permit the first steel locker to be brought into a school building, and the mistake was compounded and perpetuated when lockers were installed in school corridors, the better to police their use. Schools thereby created endless headaches for pupils, teachers, and administrators. The problem is the protection of student property and its convenient access, with a minimum of noise. Adult management has completely flunked the anti-noise requirement and made less than *A* on the other two.

Hand such a problem as this to any high school student body in America, and it will often come up with more practical answers than adult managers have devised. Practical-minded adolescents in many schools will find ways to assure security in lockers from which the noise-making doors have been removed. What is more important, students will have had experience in making a decision that serves the general welfare. Of further value to all concerned is the fact that, having participated in designing a solution, students feel a responsibility for making it work.

Opportunities Offered by the Cafeteria

The kind of problem best shared with students is the kind of problem that concerns them as a community, one whose effective solution serves their comfort, welfare, or convenience. This does not mean that students should wrestle with no other kind of problem. Rather, it means that they should have experience with at least this kind. The cafeteria, always a source of problems, is another matter to which student attention might be turned, with a view toward getting educational mileage out of both the problem and the solution. Perhaps the lunch hour could in more schools become the enjoyable part of the day that it ought to be rather than a necessary evil to be endured.

One warning is needed about student participation in the solving of school problems. Solutions must not be expected to hold forever. Students respond best to decisions they have helped to make. Like the school tax levy, renewals must be voted from time to time or amendments endorsed. What should be remembered above all else is that participation itself is a realistic education for active citizenship in a democratic society. Students will begin to see in it some relationship between what we preach and what we practice. It also extends the laboratory method.

CULTIVATED CREATIVITY, SHARED RESULTS

The kind of student programming described in this chapter will not only give rein to individualism, to the personalization of learning, but it will also encourage creativity of a variety of kinds. One of the most promising ideas recently thrust into the educational mainstream is the one calling attention to the fact that creativity has been seldom assessed and too seldom employed in the educative effort. The kind of organization suggested will promote and encourage more creativity in all learning activities by both students and teachers.

Numerous ways will be devised for the student who has done exceedingly well with his project to share his findings with his classmates. He may be more inclined, for example, to use a variety of audiovisual aids than is his teacher. The school whose students are engaged in a variety of individualized projects will have need for the production of a wide variety of student publications. Here is the best possible motivation for composition, as the school newspaper has often proved. A new kind of yearbook composed of excerpts, including pictures and illustrations from the projects of students, might provide a worthy substitute for the present memory-book type of effort. It would surely portray more of student individuality and show a phase of school work now completely neglected by yearbooks. Numerous digests of student work, preferably one or two at a time, might be circulated among the students. The various new duplicators and devices for illustration may be put to work in a variety of ways, higher standards being easier to exact when the aim is student creation and student consumption.

PERSONAL AND PERMANENT LEARNING

Let the reader reflect on his own high school days. What does he remember most vividly? What learning experiences meant the most to him? Were these experiences not, with rare exception, highly individualized in nature? More often than otherwise, perhaps, they were connected with an extracurricular activity rather than with the organized classwork, perhaps an oratorical contest, a project that left something tangible and visible with the school, a musical performance, a play, an assembly program, work on the school paper, an essay contest, personal achievement in a sport. Did they not usually represent individual encouragement and coaching by a teacher?

Knowing the power of such experiences to move young people and to change them, why should such involvement be left to chance? Why should such experiences be reserved for just the obviously more able and the more aggressive? All teachers of considerable experience can recall finding surprisingly bright lights under rather dull-looking bushels.

A school organization can be designed to foster bright and highly individualized experiences for practically all of its students. Such rewards will be reaped, however, only by schools whose leaders and teachers believe it important and are willing to work without stint toward that end. To teach and to learn in such a school is highly rewarding to both teachers and learners. The school can become a lively place where life and learning are relished rather than one where regimentation is tolerated or endured.

SUMMARY

In this and in the previous chapter the emphasis has been upon the need for taking a look at the typical present high school organization, upon analyzing weaknesses that prevail, and upon the attempt to present something of a blueprint for a new organization designed to overcome those weaknesses. The recasting of organization has aimed at placing a much greater emphasis upon the following:

1. More responsibility and more autonomy for the principal, the teacher, and the student
2. The intrinsic or inner motivation of the student effort
3. The spurring of student initiative and resourcefulness
4. A greatly enlarged emphasis upon personalized study
5. The active encouragement of spontaneous small group discussions
6. The individualization and the personalization of instruction
7. Individually tailored and self-structured student assignments
8. More opportunity for individual and informal contact between students and teachers
9. Heavier emphasis upon the laboratory method of learning in all fields
10. The preemption of less teacher time and less student time a week in whole-class activity
11. Expanded library usage by both teachers and students
12. The institution of work-study laboratories in all fields where the activity is not now laboratory in nature
13. Significant expansion of library facilities
14. The complete elimination of study halls as now known
15. Short, individually tailored courses to serve developed or sporadic student interests
16. The division of the larger school into units or houses of about 200 pupils each
17. The simplification of school machinery and the reduction of the official persons each student sees
18. A reduced emphasis upon policing but more upon the development of student responsibility
19. Heavier reliance upon teacher initiative, invention, and judgment
20. The gradual but certain discard of the Carnegie unit as the sole measure of progress toward graduation
21. A flexibility that puts student service and intrinsic

motivation ahead of any system, any rule, any bookkeeping, or any organization

22. A daily and weekly schedule that encourages wide usage of local resources and persons in the educative effort

23. Student participation in school community problems to provide practice in democratic processes

It is realized that the changes outlined in this and the previous chapter constitute major readjustments. It is also suggested that any principal or faculty seriously concerned with the problems facing today's high school and its students will realize that any attack upon those problems, in order to be genuinely rewarding, must be launched upon a broad front.

7

The Failure of Teacher Personnel Policies

> In the school, an accomplished teacher is the one thing needful.
>
> *Horace Mann*

Three reasons argue for the inclusion of careful attention to problems of teacher personnel in a work like this and at a time like the present:

1. The teacher is the single most important ingredient in any recipe that is to result in a quality school.
2. For twenty-five years the average high school has had little choice, often employing the unqualified teacher. Today's apparent surplus in some fields greatly increases responsibility for selection and retention of the creative teacher.
3. An expanding employment of both technology and paraprofessionals (aides), which will increase in the years just ahead, demands extensive reexamination and redeployment of the teacher's energy, services, and insights.

Contrary to widespread opinion, the teacher personnel problem is in many forms most acute at the secondary school level.

The reasons are not hard to find. First, at this level a considerable number of highly educated specialists are required, for example, in the fields of art, physics, industrial arts, and business and for the various vocational shops. Second, it is in the same fields that business, industry, and the colleges are also competing for qualified specialists. Consequently, the superior high school staff is frequently raided by these interests. Third, high school teachers are much more frequently moved to other roles within the school system, especially to counseling and to administration. Fourth, the high school teacher is, on the average, permanently lost to the profession at an earlier age and at a lower level of experience than is the elementary teacher. This is because he is much more often male, and the male teacher exits earlier, both because he is more frequently enticed elsewhere and because his economic responsibilities press him to earn more. These analyses are supported by documentation below.

Statistics gathered by the National Education Association have been consistent through the years in showing the median female teacher to be both older and more experienced. The March 1961 experience figure showed a ratio of two to one, the median experience for women being 14.2 years, for men, 7.1 years.[1] The decline in the median experience of all teachers between 1956 and 1966 is so great as to appear almost unbelievable, considerably more than one-third.[2] That this notably less experienced character of the teaching force hits the high school harder than the elementary school is evident upon the face of the above statistics, along with the fact that female teachers constitute the overwhelming majority except in the high school.

Still another fact that supports the need for the kind of examination presented in this chapter, although one of which few students of the high school seem to be aware, is the relative decline of the high school teacher's educational level over the past forty years. This decline may be expressed in two ways.

---

[1] National Education Association, Research Monograph, *The American Public School Teacher, 1960–61* (Washington, D.C.: National Education Association, April 1963), p. 38.

[2] National Education Association, *Research Bulletin*, 45 (October 1967), p. 87.

First, the typical high school teacher of 1960 was educationally not nearly as far ahead of his average pupil's father and mother as he was in 1930. In other words, the expansion of the high school teacher's education has failed to keep pace with the expanded education of the population generally. That this is true is demonstrated by the following figures. The average American adult of 1930 had a median schooling of 8.4 years, whereas in 1960 the median was 10.5 years. The difference would be greater still, had we the figures for those parents still young enough to have children of their own in high school. A more marked measure of the difference is seen in the facts that the proportion of high school graduates among the adult population more than doubled in those same 30 years, from 19.1 to 41.1 percent; and the proportion of college graduates almost doubled, from 3.9 to 7.7 percent.[3] On the other hand, only 13 percent of the high school teachers of 1930 had less than four years of college,[4] and we know that quite a number, even then, held master's degrees. The rise in the average level of high school teacher education in the thirty-year period is obviously less than dramatic.

The second way in which the expansion of the high school teacher's education has failed to keep pace may be seen by comparing his education to that of the college teacher and to that of the elementary teacher. The Folger and Nam study, cited above, shows that 88 percent of the elementary teachers of 1930 had less than 4 years of college, that by 1960 this had shrunk to 29 percent, and that those with one year or more of graduate education had risen from 2 percent to 24 percent, a twelve-fold increase.[5]

What do the data on college and university teachers reveal? While wholly and precisely comparable data do not seem to be available, it is clear from the following figures that the improvement in the educational level of college and university teachers between 1930 and 1963 has been marked. A 1930 study of the

---

[3] John K. Folger and Charles B. Nam, *Education of the American Population*, A 1960 Census Monograph, U.S. Bureau of the Census (Washington, D.C.: U.S. Government Printing Office, 1967), p. 138.

[4] *Ibid.*, p. 84.

[5] *Ibid.*, pp. 84–85.

faculty members in the then 69 land-grant colleges and universities of the nation showed that 18.19 percent held the doctorate and almost 34 percent more held the master's degree.[6] By 1963, a survey of all college and university faculties, both public and private institutions, showed that at that time 51 percent of 138,200 faculty members polled held the doctorate.[7] To the extent that state land-grant college and university faculties may have been representative of all faculties in 1930—and the difference, plus or minus, can be assumed to be relatively slight—it appears that doctoral degrees were more than two and one-half times as numerous in 1963 as in 1930.

The failure of personnel policies is characterized by inability to attract and retain the quantity and quality of professional personnel needed. This condition has applied to the high school's teachers for a quarter century.

THE PROBLEM ANALYZED

Teacher personnel policies for America's public schools have never had the study and attention that so basic a matter deserves. Seldom has the question been subjected to long-range planning at the hands of any national, statewide, or large city group. It has been neglected, for the most part, by educational research. The National Education Association and its affiliate bodies, it must be noted, have worked rather consistently for the upgrading of teacher education and certification standards. Likewise, the accrediting associations have established minimum standards of preparation for teachers in their member schools. State departments of education, too, have in most states consistently sought to raise teacher certification standards.

Enforcement of teacher standards is another story. Failure

---

[6] U.S. Office of Education, *Survey of Land-Grant Colleges and Universities* (Bulletin 1930), p. 587.

[7] Ralph E. Dunham *et al.*, *Teaching Faculty in Universities and Four-Year Colleges, Spring 1963* (Washington, D.C.: U.S. Government Printing Office, Department of Health, Education and Welfare, Office of Education, 1966), p. 5.

to meet certification standards has not consistently denied the teacher an opportunity to practice, as in law and medicine. Enforcement has been especially lax and violations most frequent since the close of World War II, somewhat more than two decades. As in matters of money, Gresham's law also appears to work its havoc in the teaching profession; that is, the poorly qualified teachers tend to drive the well qualified out of the profession.

The so-called shortage of teachers has become a national byword. It has existed for so long as to be now taken for granted, like bad winter weather. Most of the American public, and many educators, do not realize that there is in America no shortage of teachers but actually a large surplus. There is a shortage of teachers teaching, and that is quite another matter. Furthermore, and contrary to general opinion, the surplus is more male than female. This is substantiated by the fact already mentioned, that the male teacher is lost by the schools much earlier than is the female teacher. Former teachers can at times be found running everything in the country, from the White House to the garbage truck. A final startling fact: If over the past quarter-century the schools had gotten an average of just two more years of service out of each teacher before losing him to other work, there would have been no shortage. This would have left qualified teachers to serve on the substitute list.

Instead of this situation, the nation has found an average of about 10 percent of its active teachers unqualified—more if qualification be rigorously defined—for each of the past twenty years, with the problem worsening last in 1966 and 1967. In addition, there are many teachers who are each year assigned outside their areas of preparation. This situation prevails despite the fact that there are probably at least two certified teachers in our society for every teacher the schools need. True, some of the certificates may have expired for lack of use, but in most cases these are subject to renewal with a minimum of additional college work, which might be acquired in a generally available part-time or evening program. One evidence of the great numbers of non-teaching teachers is found in the thousands of former teachers who have not withdrawn their funds from retirement treasuries in the state capitols.

STATUS OF THE TEACHER

By comparison with the other professional people he knows, often former college classmates, the high school teacher suffers not only in terms of earnings but also in terms of other marks of status. He seldom dictates letters and other documents that his work demands to a secretary, either live or electronic. Few high school buildings provide him with a private office, where he may confer in dignity with his clientele, the pupils and their parents. He has no access to a telephone of his own. Unlike other professionals, he usually gives orders to no assistants of any kind, only to his students. He normally does his own typing and keeps his own records, with whatever help he can persuade students or spouse to donate.

In many schools the teacher's autonomy is uncomfortably limited in dealing with his own pupils and his own subject, the area where he is the specialist. To make a field trip or add a paperback to required student reading, he must often cut red tape or justify his plans to one who has limited understanding of his purposes. Sometimes he finds that the curricular plans dispatched from the school's central office are rigid and oppressive to the point of dampening his initiative. In too many ways he is put on notice that his teacher judgment is not trusted. He often tends to be regarded as an apprentice so long as he remains a classroom teacher. This may be one of the reasons why so many teachers leave after only an apprenticeship service.

Anne Mitchell, a former teacher and a California educational consultant, wrote perceptively when she said:

> Education in America will never be as good as it should be until we do something about the role of the teacher. . . . Yet what is the role of the teacher in American education today? In the educational hierarchy, he is low man on the totem pole. In the power structure, he is the one without power. In the line of order, he is the one who takes orders from everyone else. The educational system in America today is a vertical hierarchy and the teacher is at the bottom. There is something terribly wrong here. . . . If one is at the bottom of the heap, then that is the

way one sees oneself, not as someone who is going to create a
society of free, intelligent, democratic individuals.[8]

How teachers view themselves and their work is a matter of
great consequence. First-rate professional service is unlikely to
be found in any group in America that lacks strong belief in the
cause in which it labors, that lacks high respect for the profession
as a whole, and in which members of the group lack high respect
for themselves. That teacher morale across the nation is today as
favorable as one might hope, that teachers are satisfied with the
autonomy and respect they enjoy—these are positions that few
informed persons will uphold. To the contrary, all signs point to a
more restive teaching corps than the nation has ever previously
had. Again, this unrest strikes the high school hardest, for almost
83 percent of the male teachers are in the secondary school, and
male teachers are more sensitive to the unfavorable ways in which
they compare, for reasons earlier explained, with practitioners in
other professions.

Experience of High School Teachers

The median experience of all teachers moved downward between
1956 and 1966 from 13.1 years to 8 years. For male teachers in
1966 it was 6.5 years.[9] The measure of median experience, it must
be borne in mind, does not give a clear picture of the degree to
which the schools are in the hands of neophytes, for it gives no
clue to the thousands of first-year teachers this year who will be
replaced by thousands of other first-year teachers next year. The
relatively inexperienced teacher phenomenon has struck the high
school harder than the elementary over the past ten years for
two reasons. First, most of the men are in the high school, where
they constitute the majority. Second, the great period of high
school expansion lies within those ten years, the 1947 postwar

---

[8] Anne Mitchell, "The Crux of the Matter," *Saturday Review,* January 15,
1966, p. 66.

[9] National Education Association, *Research Bulletin,* 45 (October 1967),
p. 88.

babies being ready for the ninth grade in 1961. During this expansion faculty recruiters most often found the needed additional teachers among beginners.

Some school administrators, including high school principals, are prone to argue spuriously that the inexperienced teacher is more effective than the mature teacher. If this is true, a matter of some doubt, it is indeed most damning of current teacher personnel practices. A thriving church seldom seeks the inexperienced minister. He who needs legal services does not normally seek out the lawyer who has not yet had time to get his diploma framed. A man whose middle pains him desperately seldom calls the physician who first began to practice yesterday. If teaching in a given school permits teachers to deteriorate, something is terribly wrong with that school and with that school system.

All professionals who work in stimulating situations and who are appropriately rewarded for superior service tend to grow in their capacity to serve, in their insights and usefulness to the organization and to the people involved. The administrator who contends otherwise is probably thinking of the teacher who should not have been given a permanent contract fifteen or twenty years ago, for he was not then a good teacher and did not possess good potential. It is too often regretfully true, also, that the school leadership has neglected to encourage and reward professional growth, has discouraged or placed obstacles in the way of initiative and experimentation, and has thereby become a party to the teacher's actual deterioration or failure to develop something near full potential.

Education of High School Teachers

The adequacy and appropriateness of the teacher's education is among the most useful and the most objective of the factors constituting a teacher's fitness for his job. What is happening to the high school teacher in this regard? How well has he been prepared to know his field and how well to teach it? Is the median preparation of high school teachers declining or advancing? Are master's degrees more or less abundant than a few years ago? Finally, to what extent have the master's degrees held been designed to make the teacher a better teacher in his chosen field?

At what level should the education of the teacher first be appraised? A good case can be made for examining the teacher's education at the high school level, where choices are typically first open to the student. The reason is that the teacher of almost any subject is better qualified, other factors being equal, if he has a good general education. The teacher of industrial arts is better for exposure to the sciences. Likewise, the teacher of science is more effective for exposure to industrial arts. The teacher of English or social studies is handicapped if he lacks introduction to the domains of art and music. The art or music teacher without literature, history, and foreign language is without background for his work. How strong the general education background of secondary school teachers is we do not know. We do know that most teacher-training institutions require from one-fourth to one-third of the college degree work to be done in general education areas, although the nature of the high school course laid under this may vary greatly, often meeting only minimum state standards for graduation. This matter calls for further study and consideration by secondary school leadership, state departments of education, and by teacher-training institutions.

How adequate is the teacher's subject-matter preparation? In general it is probably true that standards of subject-matter preparation for high school teachers are the highest they have ever been. There are, however, disparities worth noting. The first of these is seen in the temporary certificate, which carries with it no greater guarantee of appropriate subject-matter preparation than of adequate professional preparation. Arts and science majors often fall short of teaching-subject majors in quantity and more often fail to include specific subject-matter courses needed by the young person who is to attempt instruction in the field.

The teacher may be well and appropriately qualified to teach in a given field but too frequently assigned to teach in another. A study of beginning teachers in the fall of 1961, sponsored by the Ohio Education Association, showed that beginning teachers in the basic academic fields of English, mathematics, sciences, social studies, and foreign languages, collectively, were college majors in their respective teaching fields in only 49.1 percent of the cases. The nonmajors ranged from a high of 64 percent in English to a low of 36 percent in foreign languages.[10] What is true of Ohio is not unlikely to be fairly typical of the nation generally, since in most national studies of public education Ohio ranks not far from the median.

It is interesting and a little disappointing to note that secondary teachers in the traditional academic fields are less well prepared in their subject areas than are the teachers in fields such as art, music, home economics, business, industrial arts, and health and physical education. The writer's own recent study of the 150 secondary teachers in a Midwestern factory-college town of 30,000 people showed that teachers in the latter category had an average of twenty-six semester hours more in their teaching fields than had the academic teachers. In fact, such special teachers had on the average more than twice as much work in their fields as had the English and mathematics teachers.[11] There is no reason to suppose that this situation is notably atypical.

In professional preparation the teacher's qualifications are seldom very much above the minimum state requirements for certification. The range is eighteen to twenty-four semester hours in most parts of the country, with one-third to two-fifths of that credit assigned to student teaching. The prospective teacher has usually had little or no introduction to audiovisual aids, no work in developmental or remedial reading, an inadequate introduction to the understanding of the adolescent, and only one course (often a weak one) in the philosophical and social foundations of education. The beginning teacher is, consequently, inadequately prepared professionally, both from the standpoint of appreciation and technique, to deal with the socially disadvantaged or low-motivation learner. This is by no means the least of the reasons why the nation is slow in making universal education universally effective, a matter now so necessary to our kind of civilization and society.

---

[10] W. R. Flesher *et al., Public Education in Ohio* (Columbus: Cooperative Educational Enterprises, 1962), p. 139.

[11] School Survey Service of Kent State University, *A Study of the Alliance School System* (Kent, Ohio: Kent State University, 1964), p. 28.

Graduate Study of High School Teachers

How extensive and how appropriate is the graduate study that secondary teachers have done? The doctoral degree, while not uncommon in a few select high schools, is so infrequent generally as to make it scarcely worthy of note. The master's, however, has been common among high school faculties for about fifty years. NEA statistics of March 1956 showed that 43.7 percent of the nation's secondary school teachers held the master's degree.[12] The comparable figure for March, 1963, just seven years later, was 31.4 percent.[13] During this same period the number of master's degrees held by elementary teachers advanced 2.9 percent. It must be noted that a May 1970 study shows that the master's degrees held by secondary teachers had by the school year 1968–1969 climbed back up to 40 percent, still short of the 1956 figure.[14] It is only in recent years, of course, that a sizable majority of elementary teachers have reached the point of holding the baccalaureate degree. These figures further substantiate the point made earlier in the chapter; namely, that the high school teacher's level of education is not keeping pace.

How appropriate is the high school teacher's master's degree? That is, to what extent is it designed primarily to make him a better teacher? Unfortunately it is often only remotely or incidentally designed to make a better teacher. In many cases it is directly structured to make a counselor or an administrator. Here the fault must be shared by the universities and the employing school systems.

Many universities have no master's programs designed with the high school teacher in mind in either their academic departments or their colleges of education. The subject-matter departments tend to gear their graduate programs to the production of researchers and college teachers. The colleges of education tend to point theirs toward the production of administrators, ignoring the crying need for better-prepared teachers.

[12] National Education Association, *Research Bulletin*, 35 (February 1957), p. 13.

[13] National Education Association, *Research Bulletin*, 41 (December 1963), p. 104.

[14] National Education Association, *Research Bulletin*, 48 (May 1970), p. 36.

Public school personnel policies and salary schedules, with few exceptions, have appeared to pretend that this problem does not exist. All too typically the English teacher is rewarded just as highly for a master's degree in ichthyology as in either English or in education, even though the emphasis in the latter is upon the learner and learner problems. The social studies teacher is paid just as well for a master's degree in school business management as for one in history or in social studies education.

The master's degree market for high school classroom teachers is large. Neither the schools' personnel policies nor the practices of the universities make sense. It is time for the high schools to demand and for universities to provide graduate programs that are appropriate to high school teachers' needs. It is time for school personnel policies to stop saying, in effect, that one master's degree, whatever its content, is as good as any other for any teacher of any subject.

Teachers' Intellectual and Cultural Interests

Whatever else the adolescent sees in his teacher, he sees a mind at work. Imitation is a powerful force in education. It is important, then, that the adolescent see in his teacher a mind that is alert, probing, examining, exploring, constantly learning. An increasing number of teachers continue to read and study widely. Many others do not.

What do today's high school teachers read? The writer has carried this question to the academic teachers of more than thirty high schools over the past dozen years. With few exceptions the lay journals read by such teachers have been found in the following list: *Reader's Digest, Saturday Evening Post, Look, Life, Time, Newsweek,* and *U.S. News and World Report.* Seldom have their interests led them to such journals as *Harper's, Atlantic Monthly, Saturday Review, Fortune, American Heritage,* or the *Sunday New York Times.* A good 40 percent reported that they had read no new (to them) book that had a significant bearing upon their respective teaching assignments within the previous six months. One who neglects reading for six months has neither well-fixed nor widely ranging reading habits.

Today's world is a rapidly changing world. It is indeed difficult to be accurate and truthful in what one teaches about Russia, Africa, nuclear energy, or even about the chemistry of cooking. Teachers who are themselves reluctant learners are in a feeble position to encourage their pupils to behave otherwise. All teachers must be led constantly, through every possible means available to the school's leadership, to continue to grow in their understanding of both subject and learner, to expand their social and mental horizons. A considerable part of the school's in-service education program for teachers should be directed toward this end, an expansion of the teacher's sphere of inquiry, reading, and concern. Teachers are like other human beings. They will remain asleep when there is nothing to wake them up and little reward for waking.

The Professionalism of Teachers

Ask a dozen school superintendents and a dozen high school principals the question, Do you encourage the teachers in your high school to be professional? Will any one of them give a negative answer? Follow this question with inquiry as to the specific ways in which professionalism is encouraged. What happens now? Most leaders quickly run out of illustrations. Some will be equivocal or embarrassed. How many, for example, assist the teacher with travel money for occasional attendance at professional meetings that look toward improvement in his teaching field? In many areas, as long as fifty or more years ago, teachers received an additional day's salary for attendance at each of the county institute's Saturday sessions, professional meetings that were scheduled two to four times a year. This represented perhaps 2 percent of the teacher salary budget. Relatively few schools are doing so well today.

What organization offers most to professionalization of the high school teacher? With few exceptions it is his national subject-area classroom teachers' organization. The National Council of English Teachers offers the English teacher much help toward professionalization, but a casual examination of the situation among Ohio high school teachers of the subject reveals that only about 10 percent of the appropriate teachers are members.

The National Council for Social Studies reported in early 1966 that its 11,000 secondary teacher members represented an estimated 11.4 percent of the potential membership.[15] Among science and mathematics teachers, membership in such organizations is a little more common, but in only one school system that he examined did the author find as many as 40 percent of the mathematics teachers carrying membership in their national council. No other group inventoried approached this level. Obviously, there is much room among high school teachers for growth in professionalism as expressed in membership in their appropriate teacher organizations.

An unpublished study made by the writer and David E. Koontz in the school year 1965–1966, which reached highly rated school systems in all fifty states, revealed that most such systems do not gather precise data on membership in such organizations. The degree of concern for professionalism is almost too clear.

It is here assumed that the teacher who belongs to the National Council of English Teachers, who receives and reads the *English Journal* regularly, cannot avoid being a more professional and a more effective teacher of English as a result of this affiliation and this interest. If he is helped by the school to attend the national conference of this organization, at least once every four or five years, he will feel more professional and behave more professionally. The same is assumed to apply to his colleagues in science, mathematics, social studies, foreign language, and other fields.

PROFESSIONAL HELP FOR THE TEACHER

How much and what kind of help does the high school teacher get in developing his teaching capacity and professional power to its fullest? Emphasis here will be given to three measures of such help: first, the orientation program and special attention or consideration the beginning teacher gets; second, the continuing inservice education plan and program for the teacher; and third,

---

[15] T. M. Gillespie, Assistant Secretary, National Council for Social Studies, January 26, 1966 (letter to the writer).

the opportunities that are provided the mature or established teacher to gain the satisfactions and status that accrue to the exercise of initiative and leadership in the shaping of curriculum and policy.

Orientation policies and programs for new teachers are in most schools relatively raw and undeveloped. Most high school principals confess that the lack of adequate administrative and secretarial help and the press of other duties combine to prevent them from assigning the time to the orientation of new teachers which they realize the task demands. Too often the new teacher's help is limited to a single day before school starts in the fall, and the counsel he gets emphasizes routine procedures. Too often, also, the beginning teacher gets the classes that are the least desirable or hardest to teach—he gets what is left after senior staff members have taken their choices. In a sense he is faced with a situation that dares him to make good. That so many beginners do survive is a testimony to their unusual fibre and determination rather than to the consideration they get and the help they receive.

There is a great deal of naiveté among both administrators and older teachers about what the beginning teacher knows and what he does not know, about what he is able to do and what he is unable to do. This is due in part to the teacher's desire to forget as soon as possible those fears and anxieties that characterized his own early days of teaching. It is due also to the fact that schools, like other organizations in recent years, have become gradually but steadily more complex organizations, their expectations today greater than those in which the principal and the senior teachers received their initiation. They have had an opportunity to get acquainted with these added and complicating factors one at a time. Nine to eleven weeks of student teaching, sometimes under an indifferent critic teacher, cannot be expected to turn out a polished teacher who knows all the answers.

This situation will very probably get little better until the day arrives when all beginning teachers have been prepared through at least a full year's paid and supervised internship, in which the intern carries not more than 60 percent of a normal teaching load. Until that day arrives, however, the principal who wants a first-rate teaching staff will have to assume a larger role in teacher education than he typically now plays. A recommended orientation program or on-the-job internship is described in Chapter 8.

The in-service education of the high school teacher today is with rare exception no more particularized, no more tailored to meet specific expectations, than it was a half or three-quarters of a century ago. For the most part the old institute pattern is followed. The pupils are sent home for a day, and the teachers listen to imported lecturers who usually deal with general and more or less philosophical subjects in the area of education.

How many modern mathematics programs have been launched in high schools since 1954 without qualified and ongoing professional help over a period of at least weeks or months? This is one of the main reasons why many such programs have been abortive or have fallen so far short of their potential. The general supervisor's usefulness to the specialized twentieth-century teacher is sharply limited, whether he is called a principal, consultant, director of audiovisual aids, or some other title.

Only in the largest school districts are subject-area specialists employed as directors, consultants, or supervisors in their field. Even in such cases the supervisor often gets involved with administrative routine and the machinery of organization to such an extent that his expertise is directly and personally available to very few teachers. In brief, today's high school teacher seldom finds one to whom he can look with confidence as a leader in his chosen teaching field and whose recurring help will be available to him as he seeks to develop his own full potential as a teacher. Well-qualified department heads with sufficient relief from teaching have been useful to many teachers, but their availability has been the exception rather than the rule.

OTHER HELP FOR TODAY'S HIGH SCHOOL TEACHER

One need not go too far back into the history of American education to find the teacher building the fire and sweeping out his own classroom. Finally, the teacher was given janitorial or custodial assistance. Clerical, monitorial, and technical assistance have been slower to come. Here and there this matter is beginning to get attention, but as yet only a small minority of high school teachers have aides in these areas. Rather, the high school teacher probably takes orders from more people and gives orders to fewer than does any other professional in America who is educated to his level.

Some progress is being made in relieving teachers from the monitoring of the lunchroom, from the patroling of the study hall, and from numerous clerical and bookkeeping tasks. The relief comes sometimes from the employment of off-duty firemen, of housewives, of college students, or occasionally of high school students themselves. Strangely, resistance to a broadening of such practices sometimes comes from teachers themselves. Surely this view must be credited either to a lack of long-range vision, an inadequate view of the teacher's role, or to a sense of security that the teacher finds in his current clerical or custodial duties. In these latter he can clearly see how well he is getting along. The results of his labor are more measurable.

Lackey Chores

It may be that teachers have become so accustomed to perform-ing themselves all the odd jobs that go along with the operation of the school that they often feel neglectful, perhaps even a bit frustrated, if denied the opportunity to do so. At any rate, they are still doing most of these odd jobs in most high schools today. Less than a decade ago one midwestern state's legislature passed a law requiring school boards to grant teachers at least thirty minutes' freedom from pupil supervision in order that they might peacefully eat their own lunches. Compliance with the law is undoubtedly less than universal at this writing. In how many states and in how many communities does no such humane con-sideration prevail even at the present time? The implications for dignity, status, and professionalism are all too clear.

TEACHER'S SELF-ESTEEM

A prominent element in the morale, in the dignity and status of any calling, is found in the way the practitioner views his work. What does he see as his social role? Where, in the hierarchy of values, does he place his service to society? How significant does he think he is? This is the question that Anne Mitchell, quoted earlier in this chapter, asked. It is of even greater consequence to the teacher than to those of many other occupations because the teacher's chief impact is often exerted upon intangibles.

The way one views himself is conditioned by the way in which he thinks others view him. What is his role in the decision-making process? What power does he have? What influence does he wield? With what financial rewards is he recognized?

A hypothetical example may serve to make the importance of this issue clear. The example might be found in any field. The counterpart of such an imaginary person is indeed found in all secondary teaching fields and all over America. He is real and alive. He is almost as often female as male. Let it be supposed that he is an English teacher in a superior high school of 1,500 students, where he is one of seventy-five teachers. He is thirty-five years old, has taught twelve years prior to the present, and he holds a master's degree, with eighteen semester hours of the master's work having been taken in graduate courses in English. He is one of the high school teachers who wrote a master's thesis, although it cost him a full year of delay in getting on the master's degree salary schedule. Furthermore, at his insistence his thesis topic was one of high school application. His scholarship throughout, though less than *cum laude,* was definitely above average. Since attaining the master's degree, this teacher has attended a John Hay Institute on the humanities. From the beginning he has maintained membership in the National Council of English Teachers. Twice at his own expense he has attended national conferences of the organization, these being the times when it was held near enough to prevent the expense from being prohibitive.

In addition to these superior professional credentials, this teacher has thoroughly demonstrated superiority as a teacher of adolescents. Parents, students, and colleagues recognize him as a superior teacher. He teaches English composition as a discipline of clear thought, literature as an interpretation of life. Each issue of the school's student magazine of creative writing carries more contributions from the students of his classes than from those of any other teacher in the school.

It is important to make clear what this teacher is not. He is no kind of administrator or quasi-administrator. To use an inappropriate but thoroughly understood phrase, he is just a teacher.

What power, what influence does this man wield? Where does his role as a decision-maker begin and end? Obviously, he influences his students greatly and positively. Returning from college or the armed services, they visit his classroom to tell him how much his classes have meant to them. Has he played a prominent role in revising the English or language arts curriculum for the entire school system or for the high school? No. What effort has been made to spread among his immediate colleagues or among junior high and elementary teachers his stimulating influence, his vision about what is important in his field or about attaining the positive reaction of young people? Nothing specific that one can name. Has he ever been salaried for a summer or part of a summer to work on a curriculum or upon plans for an experiment that he had in mind for the ensuing year? No. Has the school system offered expense money for attendance at a national conference? Only in rare communities. The possibility apparently has never crossed the mind of anyone in authority, despite the fact that a few dozen school corporations across the land have been doing such things for many years.

In any appraisal of situations like the one under consideration here, it is important to recognize that the individual knows that he is highly regarded as a teacher. The signs are usually quite clear. It is only the tangible evidence that is lacking.

Finally, as this potentially promising and distinctly superior teacher looks about him, as he surveys the financial status of the other seventy-four professional members of the staff of his high school, what does he find? Starting with the principal and his two assistants, and continuing through the range of deans, counselors, and head coaches, he is able to count fifteen people, 20 percent of the staff, who receive better salaries than he does. As this bears upon his mind—and it is certain to do so—what conclusion is forced upon him? He is forced to conclude that this school, this school administration, this school board, this community does not value superior teaching—despite all its talk to the contrary.

This situation is in sharp contrast to the relative status of the professor in the university. Almost every university staff contains a number of faculty members who not only earn more than any dean the institution employs, but who are far more widely known and whose power is more widely felt through their writing, lecturing, and consulting services.

Letting his mind nurse on this injustice, what does the hypothetical teacher do? The following are perhaps the most popular options. First, he may turn to college teaching, where he finds his teaching time preempted for only ten to fifteen hours a week, but where his earnings are increased little, not at all, or are actually reduced, since he lacks the recognized college union card, the doctorate. Second, he may return to the university for evening and summer classes, taking the courses that qualify him for the principal's certificate, so that he may join the army of hopefuls whose preparation for school administration is less than first-rate. He has no genuine interest in school administration, and perhaps this contributes to his becoming a frustrated administrator, which usually means a less effective teacher. Third, he may leave teaching for higher earnings in one of a variety of positions in business or industry. Fourth, he may supplement his teacher income with a second job or interest, in which he sometimes finds the status teaching has failed to provide. More often, however, this route leads to further deterioration of status, for he turns to relief driver of bread or milk routes, to selling shoes, to painting houses, to tending bar, to any of a large number of pursuits in which his more than five years of collegiate education mean little. Fifth, instead of any of these alternatives, or in combination with one of them, he turns sour, feels put upon; his consuming passion for reading in his field declines, as do his professional interests; and the quality of his teaching goes down. By hanging on until retirement he may do the school more harm than had he left teaching at the height of his teaching power.

Such a teacher often represents the backbone of a potentially superior high school, although too often he in time becomes disaffected and disgruntled. Possible remedies for this, among the gravest of the dilemmas facing the high school, have here only been inferred. In the following chapter they will be given more careful attention.

SUMMARY

An effort has been made in this chapter to show that the policies applied to high school teacher preparation, recruitment, orientation to the task, upgrading, status, dignity, and participation in policy making have failed to attract and retain the quantity and quality of teachers that first-class secondary education requires. This state of affairs seems to be substantiated by the following.

1. The typical or average educational preparation of the high school teacher has not moved upward over the past forty years in proportion to that of either the elementary or the college or university teacher. In some respects the median education of the high school teacher has in recent years actually regressed, the number of master's degree holders having reached in 1956 a pinnacle from which it has declined considerably.

2. A needed concern for teacher personnel problems, especially marked from the beginning of World War II, has been neglected by both school systems and by university research.

3. The problem of retention of the well-qualified teacher, especially the male teacher, has been characterized by pronounced neglect.

4. The past four decades have witnessed a neglect of attention to the status and dignity of the high school teacher. He needs larger opportunities to feel the flush of influence, worth, and professional recognition.

5. The median experience of all public-school teachers has moved downward sharply over a decade, falling to 8 years in 1966. For high school teachers it is even lower, the median for men teachers being 6.5 years.

6. Too many teachers are still teaching outside their college majors, and teachers in the special fields are notably better prepared in their respective fields than are academic teachers.

7. Salary schedules are often undiscriminating in rewarding master's degrees; that is, little attention is given to the appropriateness of the degree content to the teacher's

assignment. School systems and universities share the responsibility for improving this situation.

8.   The cultural and reading interests of high school teachers are often less broad and less pronounced than might be hoped.

9.   Only a minority of high school teachers are actively affiliated with the professional organizations that have the most to offer to their teaching. Encouragements in this direction by the employing school system are rare and limited in nature.

10.   The in-service professional development of the teacher, from a well-developed orientation to the regular and ready availability of highly qualified consultants is generally far below the level required to develop the teacher's full potential.

11.   Teacher aides, or paraprofessionals, giving support and dignity to the teacher's role, are still the exception rather than the rule, and their potential functions in behalf of a better education are relatively undeveloped.

12.   The belittling phrase "just a teacher" seems to have justification when the highly qualified and highly successful teacher measures either his financial reward or his influence in policy against that of similarly qualified and experienced administrators, coaches, counselors, deans, and other quasi-administrative personnel serving the school. Consequently, either his enthusiasm is replaced with disgruntlement or he takes one of various routes out of teaching.

8

Quality Teachers: Development and Retention

> There is one innovation for which I have fought,
> in season and out of season, namely, the innova-
> tion that would put a competent and cultured
> teacher into every American classroom.
>
> *William Chandler Bagley*

The nation cannot have notably better high schools than it now has without first making sure that the high schools have, on the average, notably better teachers. Gadgetry and supervision, some aspects of which teachers are increasingly rebelling against, will never provide a first-quality education. The teacher is the great curriculum maker, and he is insisting upon playing this role ever more fully. It is the teacher who is there in the flesh who most influences the student, rather than the one who is there as text author, curriculum-guide maker, state high school standards supervisor, principal, superintendent, or whatever.

Many Americans have made the mistake of equating the school with the building. Actually, the school cannot be equated with any single element of its makeup, but the element that weighs more than any of the others—than all the others combined —is the faculty.

179

THE BASES OF QUALITY

What factors must a teacher personnel policy take into account to attract and retain high-quality teachers in a high school? What elements are basic to such a policy? The elements of job satisfaction in a profession are up to a point somewhat similar to the elements of job satisfaction generally. These include such considerations as the comfort and cleanliness of the working environment, the congeniality of supervisors and fellow workers, the hours of work, the definition of a work load, the pay, and the fringe benefits. For the most part, with the exception of perhaps work load and pay, it is not these elements that concern the high school teacher. Teacher pension plans, sick leave, hospitalization, and insurance provisions have been relatively easy to acquire. Teacher organizations have effectively promoted them, and school board members have been sympathetic because they work for organizations that provide them. Progress in attaining such provisions is easily measured. These are the tangibles.

It is in the intangibles, the less easily measured matters, those more characteristic of a profession, that high school teaching fails in the eyes of many to measure up. No small part of the educational revolution now in progress is the change that is taking place in the way the teacher views himself. He is in the process of lifting himself a long rung, possibly several rungs, on the ladder of professionalism. Because the goals sought lie largely in the realm of the intangible, the process is slow and agonizing. Teacher groups have a hard time conveying to boards and administrators what they want. At times their goals are not clear in their own minds. Of significance, however, is the fact that there is mass action, sometimes indirect, but action, nevertheless, toward greater professionalization. This is the first component of progress for the administrator and the board member to understand. Today's needed gains for the teacher are more subtle, more difficult to acquire. To a degree this is what the present shouting and action is all about.

The first sentence of Myron Lieberman's book on *Education as a Profession* notes that "the experience of the established professions clearly indicates that occupational groups do not achieve professional status until the members of the groups concerned participate *en masse* in the movement to achieve professional status."[1] That there is among American teachers today activity *en masse*, at least sometimes, toward professional goals is most obvious.

Some of the added stature that the teaching profession needs will have to be provided by the profession itself. Here the concern is only indirectly with elements that fall into that classification. Our interest centers upon the teacher qualities necessary to place in efficient operation the kind of school described in Chapters 5 and 6. Toward the development and sustenance of such qualities, the school's leadership and personnel policies, as well as individual teachers, quite apart from their professional organizations, can make substantial contributions.

CONDITIONS SOUGHT BY QUALITY TEACHERS

Leadership must think in terms of the elements that will enable the school to attract and retain in the classroom more high-quality teachers. Such persons have both an insatiable intellectual curiosity and a combination of social concern and psychological appeal that enable them to lead young people toward broadly conceived goals that are good for them and for society. What kind of personnel policy will tend to assure such teachers? In seeking terms to define the conditions that may be expected to attract and retain such teachers, one comes up against the problem that such terms have different meanings to different people. There is the question, too, of the degree to which a condition may be in part cause and in part result. Certainly such conditions are not mutually exclusive; they tend to support one another. Any list of them will be incomplete, but the ones discussed here are the most important.

Teachers seek and need more autonomy and more power. As his fourth characteristic of professions, Lieberman lists "a broad range of autonomy for both the individual practitioners and for the occupational group as a whole."[2] Positions of dignity and status, too, tend to attract able people. These characteristics may be ascribed only in part to the possession of autonomy and

---

[1] Myron Lieberman, *Education as a Profession* (Englewood Cliffs, N.J.: Prentice-Hall, 1956), p. vii.

[2] *Ibid.*, p. 3.

power, but the role of the high school teacher needs to be managed in such a way that such terms are more characteristic of him. Finally, an able person will remain in an occupation that is giving him the recognition and the reward that he thinks his effort deserves. These factors will reappear throughout the discussions of this chapter.

TEACHER EDUCATION

Every high school teacher should have a strong undergraduate major in the subject he teaches, and eventually he should have some graduate work in it, if for no other reason than as a manifestation of the depth of his interest in the field. It is difficult enough to teach skillfully a subject such as English or social studies even when one has made a lifetime study of it. Without such a background and feeling for the subject, it is nearly impossible. One must believe in the product he peddles; the adage applies with double force to learning. The teacher is the true specialist in any school situation, and he should give evidence of his specialist background.

Chapter 7 called attention to the fact that academic teachers ordinarily present fewer credits in their respective teaching majors than is characteristic of teachers in such subjects as art, music, industrial arts, and home economics. In assembling and developing a first-class high school faculty it would appear that a minimum of fifty semester hours or seventy-five quarter hours of credit in the teaching field might be expected, at least eventually, of all academic teachers, with foreign language teachers highly encouraged to take appropriate foreign study rather than graduate credits in an American institution. This amounts to a little less than one and two-thirds years of college work and would not seem to be expecting too much.

Alternative Qualifications

Rules of thumb all have their limitations, and it is recognized that there would be many exceptions and variations for the requirement just suggested. For example, a most effective teacher of English might present fewer credits in literature but might have a minor in journalism or perhaps some substantial working experience, summer or otherwise, in the field of journalism. Standards of performance are often more reliable than the college registrar's record. Again turning to the field of foreign language as an example, the ability to converse fluently in the language represents an acid test, one that only a minority of today's high school foreign language teachers can meet. Here this should be sought above certain other considerations.

As a measure of the reasonableness, however, of the recommended standard, Table 7 shows a number of the subject-matter requirements for initial certification in a large, well-known Midwestern university's college of education.

TABLE 7
High School Teacher Certification Requirements
in Selected Teaching Fields

Teaching Field	Quarter Hours for Teaching Major°	Quarter Hours for Teaching Minor°
Art	99	52
Business education	62 to 103†	37
Health and physical education	72 to 90†	37
Home economics	69	52
Industrial arts	68 to 87†	41
Music	109	36–39†
Biology	55	42
English	53	44
French	50	35
History and government	59	52
Comprehensive social studies	103	no minor
Mathematics	50	35

Source: Kent State University General Catalog, 1967–1969, pp. 142–145.
°Requirement for degree is 192 quarter hours; for the semester-hour equivalent, multiply by ⅔.
†The student has two or more options in these fields.

The highest ranks of recognition and reward should with rare exception be open only to the teacher who has acquired a master's degree, preferably one that has expanded his professional as well as his subject-matter qualifications. He should understand on a rather sophisticated level what schooling is all about, how the problems of both society and education have changed in recent years, and what both the psychological and sociological holdbacks are.

ORIENTATION TO THE JOB

Eventually the professional preparation of the high school teacher is destined to be placed at the graduate level, but perhaps not until present staffing problems have found relief. In the meantime, the high school that is to build a superior staff will find it necessary to construct a kind of internship of its own. The present limited experience in student teaching and the few professional courses that the student gets while earning his baccalaureate degree cannot be expected to turn out a polished teacher who is ready to take the responsibility of a full teaching load and handle it with assurance, especially when there is no solid provision for regular counsel and help. Almost nowhere else in America's professional life is such sophisticated genius expected of the neophyte.

The National Association of Secondary School Principals has recognized this problem and has undertaken to sponsor an experimental teacher-induction project under the direction of Douglas W. Hunt.[3] In its first two and a half years of operation, the project, supported in part by the Carnegie Foundation, reached into five states and involved five cities and two county school systems. It worked with three hundred fifty beginning teachers. The cooperating teacher, who is released from some of his other duties to work with the beginners in each school, starts his work with them as soon as their contracts are signed in the spring and continues to meet with them at intervals through the summer. The induction program continues throughout the first school year, intensified in the first semester. Participating schools report

[3] Douglas Hunt *et al.*, "Teacher Induction: A Key to Excellence," National Association of Secondary School Principals, Bulletin 328 (May 1968), pp. 68–78.

favorable results, the minimizing of early discouragement, and the strengthening of commitment to the profession.

First-Year Experiences

The teacher's first year of service, even the first few weeks, represents a crucial time. The beginning teacher needs professional help in shouldering his job that lies far beyond the scope of how to complete attendance reports, how to fill out report cards, and how the accounting office arrives at the figure on his pay check. It is at this time that many teachers who are later lost to the profession make the decision to depart as soon as it can be done gracefully. David Koontz' study of seventy-six first-year high school teachers in thirty-six Northeast Ohio high schools showed that twenty-one of the teachers, or 27.6 percent, had made the decision to leave the profession before their first year was finished. Of further interest was the Koontz finding that the mean annual teacher turnover for a five-year period (1962–1967) in high schools with over 500 students was less than 10 percent in only two of the thirty-six schools and 25 percent or more (ranging up to 42.7 percent) in seventeen of the thirty-six schools. Koontz concluded that adequate induction programs favorably influence the determination of the beginning teacher to remain in teaching and that genuine involvement in the overall problems of the school appears to have a strikingly favorable influence in this direction.[4] His study tends to reaffirm the findings, especially with respect to male teachers, of earlier and somewhat similar studies.

The high school that would develop and retain a superior staff of teachers should do no less by way of induction than the equivalent of the program sponsored by NASSP. In the kind of high school recommended by this book, the beginner should never have a full teaching load. If the beginner, in addition to getting help from a senior staff member as in an induction program, could be assigned full responsibility for only two classes

---

[4] David E. Koontz, "Professional Attitudes of Beginning Teachers and Their School's Personnel Policies," (unpublished Ph.D. dissertation, Kent State University, 1967), pp. 70–71, 152.

and then placed in charge of a work-study laboratory in his teaching field for half of each day, he would get an ideal induction. Not only would he be very useful to the students in the work-study laboratory, but he would also have a chance to learn what the students' learning problems are and how they think and feel. More important than anything else would be his opportunity to learn something about other means of teaching than the method of standing in front of young people and talking to them. Such a year might be regarded as the internship, with continuing help and overseeing from the campus of the teacher education institution.

EXPERIENCE, TURNOVER, AND COMMITMENT

The experience of any group of teachers, assuming that they work under conditions conducive to professional growth, is not only a tangible measure of know-how or fitness to teach. It is also an index to teacher turnover and to teacher commitment. A faculty that is heavily weighted with teachers who are teaching because they cannot make a more favorable connection at the moment is not likely to be a superior faculty. Teachers who look upon teaching as a temporary commitment are seldom among the school's most positive human assets.

A high turnover of teachers adversely affects school quality in other ways. First, it drains off leadership energy that might otherwise be turned toward school improvement. New teachers and beginning teachers require more help; they ask more questions; their inexperience gets them into more problems. A school where teacher turnover is consistently high is hard pressed just to hold its own. Forward motion is almost out of the question. If a school is in such a position that it must depend upon the new teacher to bring the innovation or invention, this is merely testimony to the degree of stultification that has taken place.

If the reader is inclined to think that the figure cited in the Koontz study is extreme or unrepresentative—that is, 27.6 percent of the beginning teachers having made up their minds to leave after just eight months of teaching—here is further evidence: Douglas Hunt, of the NASSP Induction Project, predicted

that of the beginning teachers who started work in 1965, 31 percent would not report in 1967.[5] The seriousness and proportions
of the problem can be seen better when it is realized that the
annual number of beginning secondary teachers in the nation
now amounts to almost a hundred thousand, or about one-eighth
of the total force.

Effect of High Teacher Turnover on Morale

The effect of high teacher turnover upon those who regard
themselves as more or less permanently committed can hardly be
other than demoralizing. They see that the young man who
taught business courses with them just a few years ago has
become vice-president of the bank. Then they think of their
former mathematics department chairman, a highly respected
teacher. He left to become executive secretary of a local savings
and loan association. They think of the numerous apparently
promising young people who stayed only a year or two, and
they ask, "Why? Is our job that uninspiring? Is it without
promise? Could it be that we are the foolish ones?"

Minimizing Teacher Turnover

The would-be superior high school must do a number of things
to minimize teacher turnover. Is it possible that teaching is too
attractive to the first-year teacher and too unattractive to the
teacher in his third, fourth, and fifth years of experience? Might
a real internship help? This might be handled as described in the
discussion of orientation, with the first-year salary 10 to 15 percent lower than current starting salaries, but with a 25 percent
advance for the second year. This would tend to discourage the
adventurer, the person who is merely marking time. It would
also call upon the school to select its teachers with more care and
with heavier emphasis upon future service, since the school

---

[5] Douglas Hunt *et al.*, "Preparation for Reality: Induction of Beginning
Teachers," National Association of Secondary School Principals, Bulletin
319, p. 64.

would have a considerable investment in each before he became fully operative.

The point made here is that it is both difficult and improbable for any high school to provide high-quality educational service when it has a 25 percent turnover of staff each year. In fact, any school that annually employs more than one new teacher for each seven on the staff is endangering its educational quality, and every effort should be made to drive the ratio down to no more than one for each ten. To develop the kind of school in which it is exciting to teach will help greatly. Other suggestions will be found in the remainder of this chapter.

GREATEST NEEDS OF TEACHERS

In the world of work, whether the calling is one of high or low estate, whether the output or product is relatively unimportant or of great consequence, the elements of human motivation must be sought and harnessed. Douglas McGregor, an authority in the field of management, lists a hierarchy of worker needs that must be met: (1) physiological needs, such as food, shelter and clothing; (2) safety needs, such as guards against danger, threat, and unfair treatment or consideration; (3) social needs, such as a sense of belonging, acceptance, and congenial relations with one's fellow workers; and (4) egoistic needs.[6] Because these egoistic needs are so relevant to the ensuing discussion, McGregor's definition is useful. He lists two kinds as follows:

> 1. Those that relate to one's *self-esteem*: needs for *self-respect* and *self-confidence,* for *autonomy,* for *achievement,* for *competence,* for *knowledge.*
> 2. Those that relate to *one's reputation*: needs for *status,* for *recognition,* for *appreciation,* for the *deserved respect* of one's fellows.[7]

Laid on top of this hierarchy of needs, embodying elements of the others, and extending them to their complete human dimen-

---

[6] Douglas McGregor, *The Human Side of Enterprise* (New York: McGraw-Hill, 1960), pp. 35–39.

[7] *Ibid.,* p. 38 (italics added).

sion, McGregor says, "there are the needs for *self-fulfillment,* for *realizing one's own potentialities,* for continued *self-development,* for *being creative in the broadest sense* of that term."[8]

At the lower end of this hierarchy of needs, teachers have generally won most of the victories. At the top end they have most of them yet to win. Today the egoistic and the self-fulfillment elements are the ones most in need of attention. There are still too many schools where teachers are regarded merely as workers, subject in some cases to the same rules as janitors. There are still schools where teachers "sign in" or punch a time clock. Can self-esteem be high or can autonomy be great when such conditions prevail? The conditions under which high school teachers attempt to render their service must be shorn of as many of the frustrations as possible. Teachers are guilty of neglect, of course, when they fail before accepting a position to ask what efforts are made to smooth the way for their becoming truly creative teachers.

RECOGNITION

As indicated in the McGregor quotation, recognition is a term that carries a number of implications. Status, reputation, appreciation, and deserved respect are all involved. Out of these come the incentive to do still more or still better. Random House dictionary definitions that apply include: "the acknowledgment of achievement, service, merit; the expression of this in the form of some token of appreciation; formal acknowledgment conveying approval or sanction;" and finally and importantly, "acknowledgment of right to be heard or given attention."[9]

Recognition in Industry and Business

As a high school principal in a defense-factory town during World War II, I recall being pointedly reminded by a most able department chairman that the counterpart of ceremonious recog-

[8] *Ibid.,* p. 39 (italics added).
[9] *Random House Dictionary of the English Language,* unabridged ed. (New York: Random House, 1967).

nition programs for manufacturing employees held regularly in the school gymnasium was nowhere in evidence for teachers. The silver pins for fifteen, the gold pins for twenty-five, the diamond-studded pins for thirty-five years of faithful service: this kind of recognition in some variation has long been common to industrial practice. A number of industrial and marketing organizations recognize extraordinary employee contributions in more tangible terms. The largest manufacturer of rubber products in the world, for example, has had an employee suggestion plan since 1912. This may be one of the reasons why it is the largest. All employees are eligible, and the cash awards for usable suggestions range from $10 to $10,000. The effectiveness of the plan is indicated by the fact that in one recent ten-year period, suggestion awards averaged $70,000 a year.[10]

It is not here suggested that industrial plans for employee recognition be bodily transplanted into the high school. It is suggested that the universal human need for appropriate recognition applies to the high school teacher, too.

Recognition for the College Teacher

Turning to a more directly comparable and more professional field of employment, that of the college and university teacher, we find a different approach to recognition in the choice of ranks to which one may be assigned and through which he may advance. The device of rank has an ancient history in the church and in the army. Collectively, American colleges and universities employ at least eight different ranks among those who have more or less teaching responsibility. These are applied—and this is an important distinction—without regard for any administrative responsibility the individual may carry. For example, a man may be a chairman of a department of instruction and at the same time hold lower rank and receive a lower salary than another professor who carries no administrative responsibility. Though the terms by which some of the ranks may be designated vary widely, the eight college teacher ranks shown in the table below

[10] Goodyear Tire and Rubber Company, "Goodyear Suggestion Plan" (September 1967).

are fairly representative. In general, the higher ranks carry the higher salaries, although there is usually salary overlap. Variation in practice is greatest at the apprentice and superior levels.

TABLE 8
Ranks Employed in College Teaching Staffs

Apprentice Levels	Regular Levels	Superior Levels
Graduate Assistant	Instructor	Senior Professor
Teaching Fellow	Assistant Professor	University Professor
	Associate Professor	Distinguished Service
	Full Professor	Professor

Experimentation with Rank

Professional rank holds before the college teacher throughout his professional life a goal he can strive for, something above and beyond the level on which he finds himself at the moment. Traditionally the high school teacher has not had the incentive of advancement in rank held before him. Recently, however, a California professor proposed a teacher personnel policy that recognizes four levels of service. At least one California school system has placed in operation some of the plan's basic elements.

Professor Allen espoused the need for what he termed a "differentiated teaching staff," and he suggested that four levels of teacher service be recognized, stressing that he thought the titles applied were of little importance. His idea is presented here

TABLE 9
Proposed Levels of Teacher Rank and Function

Rank	Function	Salary Index
Professor	Anticipate future needs	2.4 to 3.6*
	Make long-range plans	
Senior teacher	Shape curricular concepts	1.8 to 2.4
Staff teacher	Illustrate methods	1.4 to 1.8
Associate teacher	Carry out assignments	1 to 1.4

*Figures represent a ratio of the starting salary of the associate.

in tabular form (Table 9), with Allen's salary proposals converted to an index figure, the lowest rank at the bottom.[11] No brief is held here for Mr. Allen's descriptions of differentiation in function. The categories are probably too rigid and too limiting. The idea is suggestive of one possible way to get the teaching profession out of the doldrums, however.

Max Goodson proposed in 1958 that public school teaching on four levels of service be recognized. He advanced the thought that the relatively low social status of teaching might be connected with the fact that its ranks are not stratified. He proposed four ranks, topped by that of the *career teacher,* he whose qualifications are clearly superb and beyond those of any certification requirement and who has showed a permanent dedication to the profession. Below him is the standardly qualified *teacher,* whose credentials are reviewed periodically for possible promotion to career status. Third is the *associate teacher,* the rank of most younger and beginning teachers. The fourth rank is the *amateur teacher,* who might be comparable to the paraprofessional or teacher aide.[12] Goodson's terms might be improved upon, but his view is worthy of consideration. The California terminology, with *teacher aide* added at the bottom, seems to be better.

Merit Rating

Through the years there have been other proposals for recognizing that not all teaching should be presumed to represent a single level of performance. Most school systems and most high schools have not seen fit to heed them. All such proposals seem to get embroiled in the issues of merit rating and merit pay, although the principle of merit pay has a long history in many of the nation's more favorably regarded colleges and universities, where young but eminent professors earn more than senior colleagues of less repute. Practices in industry, business, and higher education

---

[11] Dwight W. Allen, "A Differentiated Teaching Staff," *California Education* (Calif. State Department of Education, 3: June 1966), pp. 12–15.

[12] Max R. Goodson, "Differentiating the Profession of Teaching," *School and Society,* 86 (May 24, 1958), pp. 239–240.

support the idea that appropriate recognition of the superior high school teacher is needed. Administrators and school boards may eventually have to make a choice as to whose morale will concern them. Is it to be the morale of the superior teacher or the morale of the inferior teacher? The choice may eventually determine which kind is to be in greatest abundance in the school.

A newspaper account of a few years ago comes to mind. Between halves of the football game, alumni and former students of a rather small high school in Iowa presented a new car, not to the coach, but to a lady who had for twenty-five years taught her students and her mathematics with obvious respect for and devotion to both. This was a fine bit of recognition for this teacher, but how many thousands of teachers across the land have given great dedication, generated high enthusiasm, provided deep understanding and inspiration, yet have gone to their retirement with no more formal recognition than a dinner arranged by their teacher colleagues?

Inappropriate Recognition

One teacher, fresh from a quite affluent suburb, reported that its influential ladies made a compact to keep their Christmas giving within bounds. Their thoroughly businesslike list included two dollars for the trash man—and two dollars for the child's teacher. How long will it take the status needs of teachers in that community to recover from such an ill-considered judgment? The teacher seeks no present, but he seeks due respect and appreciates an occasional thank you. In many communities it may be necessary to alter attitudes through quite subtle approaches. The most respected industrial executive, lawyer, architect, or physician may be able to present the case with more effectiveness than any school administrator.

There are many paths to appropriate and useful recognition for teachers. One is appointment or election by one's colleagues to committees that hold the power to bring changes, to make oneself felt. A recent National Education Association study on teacher satisfactions determined that salary was not the single most important factor, and concluded: "Most people want to feel that they are an essential and recognized part of an important enterprise. Teachers seem to be no exception."[13]

Teacher Participation in Recruitment and Policy

One place where the teacher's judgment is most useful but where it is only rarely consulted, is in the recruiting, interviewing, screening, and nomination of new colleagues. It is a practice that has added professionalism and status to the college teacher's job for generations. It is almost universal among physicians on hospital staffs and among the nation's great law firms. Such a practice will build morale and team play as few other practices might. It will strengthen teacher capacity to carry responsibility. How can a teacher fail to help a new and younger colleague succeed when he had a part in selecting him? Teachers in any department know better than others the strengths needed to supplement their own. They do not wish to see themselves and their department downgraded by the introduction of inferior personnel. Pride can be put to work in recruiting the best possible staff. What a mockery of professionalism to have a new teacher introduced at the first high school faculty meeting in the fall and find that he has not previously met a single person there, not even the principal. Some school superintendents and some school boards will argue that teacher personnel selection cannot be decentralized, that the legal authority resides with the superintendent's office, although in the high schools of one Midwestern city of half a million people, teacher appointment nominations have originated in the buildings for half a century.

Some administrators, in their overzealous protection of the status quo, appear to have a limited view of responsibility. They overlook the concept that he who generates in others the capacity to carry responsibility is thereby best carrying his own. Legal authority for recommendation of the new teacher appointment surely does reside with the superintendent, but he may receive nominations from anywhere. The principal who wants to build a superior high school will insist upon teacher appointment nomi-

[13] National Education Association, *Research Bulletin,* 46 (May 1968), p. 41.

nations originating in the building, and he will share the recruiting and screening responsibilities with the appropriate staff members. He will realize that when a teacher weighs the qualifications of a prospective colleague, he unconsciously reevaluates himself, an exercise from which the school can scarcely fail to profit. A strong faculty is built by cultivating a general staff concern for quality instruction, and the more often the teacher is involved in decisions capable of increasing quality, the more readily will it come to pass.

Numerous ways of recognizing professional merit in the teacher commend themselves to examination and experiment. Almost any high school of 500 students or more could profit from the establishment of a faculty senate or advisory faculty body, a part or all of whose members might be elected by their colleagues. This might consist of five or more teachers, depending upon the size of the school. It should meet regularly, be presided over by one of its elected members, and should be consulted by the principal on all matters of school policy and most major problems. It should not, however, have the power to overrule the principal, although regular disagreement might indicate the wrong principal, the wrong council, or both.

Many of us, as principals, have complained about the lack of teacher interest in the progress and image of the school as a whole. Such complaints neglect the pertinent questions. What reasons have the teachers to show such concern? To what extent have they been involved in consideration of the problems and of potential solutions? Teachers will respond with interest in the total school, with a broad spiritual attachment to it, wherever they are given reason to feel that their opinions are sought and are highly regarded.

REWARD

Reward is closely linked with recognition. It is, in fact, recognition with a tangible dimension. Its most useful form is salary, or more accurately, total annual earnings. Again it must be remembered that a strong high school faculty is characterized by such manifestations as firm commitment, long-term commitment. The short-term teacher is gone before he has time to assess carefully the learning potential of either the environment or the students. The consequence is that leadership time which should be invested in teacher development is given to recruitment and orientation, which eventually becomes so discouraging and frustrating that the leadership tends to give up.

Greater Use of the Quality Teacher's Time

Aside from the possibility of differences in teacher rank, which might have their effects upon salary, there are ways in which the alert, the thinking, the working, the inventive teacher can be encouraged and rewarded. One way to encourage such a teacher is simply to buy more of his time. Assuming that the school cannot afford to buy more of the time of all teachers—and perhaps it should not do so even if it could—then the extra jobs, such as summer school teaching, should be distributed solely among the better-qualified teachers. Likewise, the teacher who is employed for summer weeks to revise a curriculum or to do curricular research should be the teacher who has shown initiative in curriculum, the one who has got something started on his own, who has shown the interest to invest his own time. The operative rule might be: The Lord and the school board help those who help themselves.

Such a policy is just as important to the teacher who is less than fully qualified as to the better-qualified. It will encourage the former to get himself fully qualified in a minimum number of years.

Something quite close to the policy recommended here prevailed at Glencoe, Illinois, for about twenty years, 1946–1966. There the teachers were offered an extended contract (for eleven months instead of nine and a half) on one of four bases: (1) summer school teaching, (2) curriculum research and development for the school, (3) approved further schooling, or (4) approved professionally developmental travel. It was abandoned for financial reasons. The plan recommended here is more economical than the Glencoe plan because it calls upon the teacher to get himself fully qualified, while the Glencoe plan helped to finance the teacher's higher qualifications. The plan proposed here emphasizes the rewarding of the highly qualified and polished teacher, and it notifies others as to what they must do if they are to be so rewarded.

The total annual earnings are especially important to the married male teacher, although it is not suggested that any preference should be bestowed on that basis. Preference should rest upon qualification and performance, and this should be made clear to the teacher before he is employed. Such a policy places the emphasis upon the long-range results, quite a turnabout from the policies of expedience that have been so common for twenty years or more. Along with other changes in teacher personnel policy discussed here, it may mean somewhat rougher going for a short while. When one is in a hole, however, he sometimes finds that he must dig the hole wider in order to get out. A patiently developed long-range teacher personnel policy and salary schedule that are designed to reward the superior teacher will go far to reduce teacher turnover, to retain and make the able teacher more able, and to enhance the learning environment.

In most communities this cannot be done without spending more money. If teachers are retained longer, the school will soon have more teachers near the top of the salary scale. If only the better-qualified are put to work in the summer school and on curricular studies, this will add some cost to the summer operations.

Salary Policies

The pay scales for teachers are in many communities so inadequate as to be unattractive no matter what manipulations are effected. Not all school systems will be able to go as far as the California school system cited earlier. Any high school, however, that reaches for superior teachers and superior results must be prepared to find at least $2.50 for its best teacher every time it finds $1.00 for the beginner. If it remains more impoverished than this, it can expect to provide only an impoverished education.[14] Further, potential annual earnings for the teacher must

[14] See Burton W. Gorman, "The Teaching Profession Tomorrow," *School and Society*, 82, (October 29, 1955), in which the writer pointed to the necessity for some such policy.

equal or surpass those of any coach, any dean or counselor, any assistant principal, and must approach nearer to those of the principal himself. Only by such a salary policy can the community, the school board, and the administrators convince the kind of teacher they especially wish to retain that they prize his services.

HELP FOR THE TEACHER

The superior high school of the future will arrange for the teacher three kinds of help that have often been missing in the past. One of these is physical. It involves such matters as space, privacy, and access to a telephone. Its cost is not high. Second, the teacher needs human help that represents a higher level in the educational echelon. He needs direct and more or less constant access to a consultant in his field who knows more about it than does he. Third, he needs a variety of human help from below his rank in the educational echelon. He needs the service of technical, illustrative, monitorial, secretarial, and educational aides. He needs the help that will stretch his services, thus making them more useful to a larger number of students.

Physical Aids to Efficiency and Status

Aside from its favorable influence upon status, the high school teacher must have a more or less private and appropriate office, a place where he can talk with his colleague or his client, the student, simply because this will increase his teacher efficiency. The teacher who reads these lines may remember being called from his class by the principal or the secretary to talk with a visiting parent. Where was the conference held? In the corridor, outside the teacher's classroom door, unless the principal elected to surrender his office for the purpose. The teacher must have a telephone, not necessarily his alone, but one that is accessible and convenient, for he must be equipped with every encouragement to utilize local resources in learning, to talk with students, parents, and citizens whenever and wherever education may be better served. He should also have a full-size office desk of his own, bookshelves, and filing cabinets—minimum equipment for a professional. He should be provided with a typewriter if he wants one.

Need for Highly Qualified Consultants

Consultant service from a highly qualified specialist, one who is both a subject-matter expert and an educator, is a must for the modern high school. Developments in all fields move too fast for the generalist to hope to be more than superficially acquainted with them. For this reason the real usefulness of the general supervisor at the secondary level is nearing an end. The mathematics consultant, for example, should hold or be well along toward the doctorate in mathematics education. He should be a mathematician and an expert in the teaching of mathematics. If the school system is too poor or too small to make practical the employment of such a person for the one school organization, it might join with other school corporations in employing such persons. In sparsely settled regions one such person might be held accountable for leadership in his field in several counties. Failing to effect such an arrangement, the high school might contract for at least a few days a year of the time of such an individual whose regular work serves a nearby university or teacher education institution. This is not meant to imply that just any college teacher of mathematics or English or science might be of ongoing usefulness to high school teachers in his field. He would have to meet the criteria set out here. He would be selected for his special qualifications.

Teachers are like other people, especially like others who work in areas where the intangible elements bulk so large. They need occasional reassurance, from someone who they feel knows his business thoroughly, that they are doing well. And when they are not doing well, they need the expert to help them discover what is going wrong. Probably nothing else could be done to the high school—that is, nothing else that might represent a commensurate cost—which would lift the quality of instruction so much. An expenditure of $5 a pupil for such consultant services, generous as a starter, would increase the budget of a $700 per capita high school about seven-tenths of 1 percent.

Teacher Aides

The teacher aide concept has taken slow but steady steps in the past dozen years. A number of high schools have, through aides, relieved their teachers of practically all monitorial and policing responsibilities. Such tasks as study hall and cafeteria supervision will be sharply reduced in the kind of high school described in this volume, for the study hall disappears and students are taught to accept more responsibility for themselves generally. The lay reader of English themes has been the only kind of academic aide with which any large number of high schools have experimented, although interest in it does not appear to be as thriving as just a few years ago. This is perhaps because many high schools have reduced English teacher loads. The high school has never had on any extensive scale the counterpart of the college laboratory assistant.

The modern high school needs to find electromechanical skills in another type of aide, one who will look after and set up, with student help, movie projectors, tape recorders, record players, and other such devices that will be used with increasing frequency in instruction. These electronic gadgets are far from foolproof, and the teacher typically has neither the time nor the inclination to become a mechanic. His function is to think of purpose and to determine, for example, what film is to be shown when and where. The teacher should always be the director of the operation, but the mechanical operation itself should be in the hands of an assistant.

The teacher must have at his command all the secretarial service he can intelligently use, although the secretarial service for students and student groups should with rare exception be handled by students themselves.

Every high school should have at least one aide who possesses graphic art skills. This aide will frequently work directly with a student or student group on a project, helping to picture it more vividly. Just as often he will work with the teacher, preparing for him distinctive graphs, charts, and illustrations designed to make his teaching more vivid.

The most important aide of all in the high school portrayed in Chapters 5 and 6 is the academic aide, or apprentice teacher, who works with students in the work-study laboratory devoted to a particular subject area. This aide will at times be able to double in one or more of the services mentioned above, but the first demand upon his time will involve him with students. He will work, of course, under the direction of the teachers in his subject area.

Number and Cost of Aides

The kind of high school advocated here will require at least one aide for each five teachers. This represents, I believe, the chief difference in its cost over that of the traditional high school. Assuming that the average teacher aide is to cost 50 percent of the average teacher salary, and further assuming that present instructional costs of the school constitute about 75 percent of the total cost, then the total operating cost of the school will rise about 7.5 percent with the addition of such an allotment for aides.

Any high school that now has a certificated person-student ratio near the national average of about 1 to 20.5 should consider the addition of aides before further reducing teacher loads. Any school, however, that still has teachers meeting six classes a day should first reduce teacher loads.[15]

SUMMARY

The factors emphasized in this chapter will go far toward meeting the egoistic needs of today's high school teachers. They will enhance the dignity and the status of the high school teacher in numerous ways, some of which can at present be scarcely imagined. They will reduce teacher turnover and teacher frustra-

---

[15] In 1965, 29.7 percent of secondary teachers were teaching six classes or more per day. National Education Association, *Research Bulletin,* 43 (October 1965), p. 71.

tion. They will help the teacher to feel that he counts, that his services are prized. He will feel more like a professional and less like a hired hand. They will tend to sort teachers out on a different basis, to give the job more appeal to the imaginative and inventive, perhaps less appeal to the plodder who is chained to a textbook.

The very nature of the kind of high school proposed will make the teacher's work more exciting. There will be wider variety in the day's work, more team play among teachers, a better chance for them to find professional stimulation in their colleagues and in their students. The informal relationships promoted by the nature of the organization promises deeper satisfactions for all. The school promises to be a greater success as a social community. These changes will fill many voids in the egoistic needs of teachers. They will have a better chance to measure their failures and their successes. Their struggle for dignity and status will be more fully in their own hands. In turn, the school can expect to attract an increased number of highly qualified teachers. It can expect them to find their teaching more rewarding. It can expect educational quality to be enhanced.

9

Innovations:
Questions and Doubts

We are continually looking for ways to escape
the necessity of exercising our intelligence. This
is why we pant hotly after the formula, the
recipe, the magic answer, the all-embracing
solution.

Sydney J. Harris

The great push of progressive education, an earlier era of innovation bounded roughly by World War I and the Depression, made
its chief impact upon the elementary school. The passion for
innovation that has characterized the past fifteen years, although
there are exceptions, seems to have been far more widely felt in
the secondary school. There have been other differences. Progressivism was ideationally and socially inspired to a larger
degree than recent school reform has been. And progressivism
was the product of delayed action, a full generation having
elapsed between the time of Joseph M. Rice and the 1920s, when
progressivism became somewhat generally accepted. The Francis
Parker influences started still earlier than those of Rice. Recent
reforms, however, have been almost instantaneous, or there have
at least been attempts to make them so. This may explain why
acceptance of most recent innovations is as yet quite uneven. It
is in part this hurry that has made some of the changes superficial

or mechanical and that has tagged some of them for an early demise.

The high school has taken the brunt of the educational criticisms aimed at the nation's schools since World War II. Recent innovations have been responses, with few exceptions, to recent events. Of all of these, the shock the American people experienced in 1957 on the launching of the Russian satellite Sputnik is generally acknowledged as of greatest influence. Once the people began to feel that the schools could help more effectively with problems of international competition, they began to look to them to provide major help with widespread domestic problems, too. In a world that is intent on production, it is not surprising to find a large proportion of the recent innovations aimed at improved teaching and learning efficiency. Most seek to speed up learning, only a few to tone it up.

THE RECENT EMPHASIS OF INNOVATION

So much is innovation a hallmark of today's literature on secondary education that one dare not write a book in the field without treating popular components of reform, whatever his risks in so doing. So new are some of the innovations that education dictionaries do not list the terms applied. So busy are innovators espousing their own special restoratives that few have taken the trouble to attempt a listing, let alone a categorization and criticism. These tasks are undertaken in this chapter and the next, although the writer is fully aware that he may be criticized for some inclusions or omissions—or both.

Carter Good's *Dictionary of Education* gives no definition of "innovation," but the usual definition of the word is "something new." Many so-called innovations in education are not really new, though. They are reincarnations of earlier school phenomena or practices, now wearing different names. Some of the innovations overlap others. Some are designed to serve only very limited portions of the high school student body; others are interpreted or applied with this limited effect.

Some innovations are built on slogans. Those that were direct outgrowths of Sputnik have been aimed primarily at better education for the students thought to represent high potential in future leadership or service to society, although they usually affected all students either directly or indirectly. Interest in such innovations is fading because the events that inspired them have been overshadowed by other even more compelling events. All can be expected to leave some permanent residue with the schools, regardless of their longevity, but the results will include scars as well as gains. Experiences with any will tend to reveal previously unrecognized vacuums to be filled.

CLASSIFYING AND TESTING INNOVATIONS

In the listing and classification used here, some currently popular nomenclature is intentionally avoided, with the hope of avoiding or minimizing current confusions. A few of the widely discussed ideas, such as team teaching, are multiple and complex in nature; that is, they really involve a bundle or a package of ideas. As mentioned earlier, some so-called innovations are really only revised forms of earlier ideas or experimentations. Others are merely specialized extensions of long-accepted ideas. An example of the latter category is television teaching, simply another audiovisual aid. It is a variation of the sound motion picture, the chief difference being only the electromechanical processes by which it is placed before the student.

The usefulness of any innovation is dependent upon the purpose it is designed to serve. Some innovations have been designed to serve certain specialized interests or groups of students. An example is the advanced placement program, which services the ablest of the college-bound students, a quite limited portion of the high school student body, usually in a very limited number of subject areas.

Some innovations are designed to stimulate and intensify student interest and thereby to enhance the effectiveness of the learning experience. Others are designed to broaden the curriculum and give emphasis to life-related understandings. Such are the humanities courses. All that are worthwhile add variety to the learning experience and depth to the understanding. Some of the most significant do not directly concern themselves with method but have implications for method. Examples here are the reassessment of human potential which includes the concern for creativity and the new interest in the socially disadvantaged, and the use of paraprofessionals, or teacher aides.

Purpose and Innovation

The stress here is on the idea that any school or group of teachers launching into innovation should very carefully consider the purposes to be served and should place their emphases upon the realization of those purposes. No innovation is good in and of itself. Its goodness stems from what it achieves. One is led to doubt both the educational insight and the integrity of a principal who boasts that his school contains something of every innovation that can be found anywhere in the nation. This sounds very much like innovation for its own sake.

Two further observations must precede effort at classification and appraisal of recent innovations. First, innovations appraised here as among the less promising, at least in purpose, may later be subsumed under others that are more inclusive. Second, all attempts at evaluation have their limitations. Almost any change can lead to improvement if certain conditions prevail. So much depends upon how bad conditions were before and upon how much enthusiasm and genius is poured into the new. Where faith is great, the Hawthorn effect is felt, at least for a while. In general the three levels of potential below are listed in order of their expanding usefulness, that is, the third category is viewed as having the highest long-range potential for improvement.

  I. Those in need of further study, analysis, or alteration
     1. Ability, or homogeneous, grouping of classes
     2. Advanced placement classes
     3. Television as an in-school teaching tool
     4. Programmed and related self-teaching devices

 II. Those now appearing to hold promise
     1. Further development of audiovisual aids to learning

2. Extended use of local institutions, things, and persons in learning
3. Unified or closely allied studies
4. Humanities courses
5. Team teaching components
6. Individualized and varied scheduling

III. Those involving significant change in organization or structure
1. Extension of the ungraded idea
2. Paraprofessionals, or teacher aides
3. Independent study and design
4. Restructuring the subject matter taught
5. Reassessment of human intelligence or potential
   a. Concern for the disadvantaged
   b. Concern for creativity

ABILITY GROUPING

It is at once both strange and understandable that the practice that offers perhaps the least potential for improvement in educational quality is the most widely used of all. It is strange because it reveals the incompleteness with which the nature of learning is understood among school people. It is understandable because school leaders were under heavy pressure to take action in the years after Sputnik, and the ability grouping of classes is relatively easy to effect, especially if one's conscience does not require him to undergird it with consonant materials and instructional practices. It is anything but new in American education, this last wave of its use being at least its third trial in about a century. Evidence that its practice is again in decline mounts daily. Some of its strongest proponents of just a few years ago are now giving evidence of modifying their positions upon it.

What we apparently failed to realize, as we adopted ability grouping, was that although there may be mass teaching, there is no such thing as mass learning. Our aim was a proper one—We strove to adapt our program to individual differences. We went about it in what at first examination appeared to be a very logical manner. Effort was concentrated upon attempts to do a better job for the very bright student, although research on the subject indicates that the type of class grouping employed makes the least difference to the bright children.

The Uniqueness of the Learning Product

John Dewey and others have taught us that there is no such thing as passing an idea whole from one human mind to another. What the learner gets is novel. It may be likened to the chemical process. The currently introduced element is added to a variety of compounds (students). Since each compound to which the new is added is different, the result in each case must be different. It is important to understand, too, that the more complex, the more broadly or generally useful the new idea being taught, the greater the variations in individual results. The more limited in nature and application the idea or skill is, the more similar will the student responses be. Thus student responses in typewriting are more similar than in geometry. Never is it identical, for the individual student never reveals all of the image he gets. He sees even the simplest idea in a different context, a different setting, applied to or among different phenomena. What is learned is a mixture of the student's former self or experience (always unique) and the new. Hence the result can be nothing but new or different. The only way to tailor learning for the individual, the goal sought in ability grouping, is to make it different for each individual in the class, no matter what the basis of class organization.

False Assumptions and Distorted Emphases

Ability grouping not only fails to serve its avowed principal purpose, that of individualization of the instruction, but it also often acts as a delusion that gives the teacher a false sense of accomplishment. Having selected text materials, illustrations, readings, and a pace that he feels appropriate to the ability level of the group, he is tempted to feel that the job is done; there is no further need for individual adaptation. He thus falls into a denial of individual differences.

What is education? It is many things, among them an introduction to differences. This means, in part, that the more the problems of one's classmates differ, the more one can learn from them. The more similar the problems, the less one learns from his classmates. This phase of education has never been carefully assessed. How much and what kinds of learnings does a student pick up from his associates? From the Supreme Court down, many thoughtful and analytical observers agree that such educational gains are substantial.

Incentive often comes from a classmate. Our concern for the culturally disadvantaged has taught us that a child cannot strive for a goal he cannot envision. One of the best agencies of vision for any human being is the opportunity of witnessing a contemporary succeed with what one previously thought uncommon, unnatural, uninteresting, or unattainable. By his colleague, too, the student is often led to see how desirable is the element that he otherwise would not desire.

A student receives both incentive (usually indirectly) and help (often directly) in learning from his classmates. Furthermore, a pupil often sees the learning problem that besets a classmate more quickly and more clearly than the teacher, and he can frequently frame the answer in more immediately understandable terms than the teacher, simply because he is closer to the experiences of his struggling classmate. That the helping student benefits, along with the helped, there can be little doubt. All who have had experience with the "each one teach one" movement are agreed that the teaching pupil always gains substantially, even when there is doubt about the gains of the pupil taught.

That the bright student's chance to learn is depreciated by the presence of less perceptive students in the class has never been established. This is somewhat like saying that the ten-second dash man cannot run the dash in ten seconds if there is a 12-second man in the fourth lane. The comparison, however, overlooks some important components. Education is more than a matter of dashing ahead at full speed, although it has been too often limited to no more. Any education worthy of the name makes frequent stops for deliberate examination of phenomena along the way. Again, the more complex, the more generally applicable, the more genuinely useful the idea, the greater its impact. To be slowed and asked to take another look is often a favor to all.

Warnings Against Ability Grouping

The use of ability grouping involves American education in one of the most singular educational tragedies and inconsistencies of our time. While we fight on one front to eliminate a bedeviling and stubborn racial and social segregation, which usually turns out to be a type of ability segregation also, at the same time we take pains to set up within the walls of a single school building a segregation that perpetuates the disadvantages of the already disadvantaged. A British educator, a professor at Glasgow University, commented on this inconsistency in 1958. He urged America not to "smuggle in ... a new kind of segregation no less bedeviling" than the problem already in existence.[1] Americans appear not to see the inconsistency and seem to forget that the prime demand of the Supreme Court's Brown Case decision said: ". . . in the field of public education the doctrine of 'separate but equal' has no place. Separate educational facilities are inherently unequal."[2]

Quality Education for All Students

The literature on the teaching of the gifted is heavily weighted with emphasis upon the need for varied and creative approaches to learning, for a rich variety of sources and readings, for field trips and invention, for the deep involvement of students, and for the individualization of assignments. This is a good description of superior education for all classes, whatever the ability range. There can be no quality education for any group of students where enrichment and variety in both method and materials are not present.

[1] W. Kenneth Richmond, "A Britisher's View," *Nation*, 186 (May 10, 1958), p. 411.

[2] Brown v. Board of Education of Topeka, 347 U.S. 483 (1954).

Evidence Against Ability Grouping

One piece of research that supports the position of the last few pages is a 1959 New York City study that involved 192 young people, 48 from each of four types of public high schools. Each of the four groups represented similar and relatively high to quite high abilities. The aim was to discover whether the kind of grouping employed in the high school influenced collegiate success. The first high school randomly sectioned classes with no regard for ability; the second employed limited ability grouping; the third used all-out ability grouping; the fourth admitted only high-quality students by competitive examination. All four high schools, as do good high schools everywhere, used a variety of enrichment techniques. Finding the college grades of the four groups at the end of their sophomore year amazingly similar, the researcher concluded: "No superiority of preparation for college can be claimed for either the special high school or the honors class program as contrasted with the comprehensive high school which had grouped students heterogeneously, . . . as indicated by grade point averages and honors" in college.[3]

Swedish educators had faith in ability grouping. There in the late 1950s they ran a carefully designed experiment involving pupils of the fifth, sixth and seventh grades from different schools in Stockholm. The data in, they concluded that the view which saw in heterogeneous grouping damage to the abler pupils was unfounded. Furthermore, they concluded that no advantage was shown in grouping together average or below-average pupils. As they stated it, "homogenization brings little to children in minus-select classes."[4]

In 1966 Isobel Pfeiffer studied, with the aid of trained observers, the teaching of five eleventh-grade English teachers. She used Flanders' Interaction Analysis system, which records the sequence of verbal activities at three-second intervals. Each teacher taught on two of the three ability levels used in the large,

---

[3] David A. Abramson, "The Effectiveness of Grouping for Students of High Ability," Ohio State University, *Educational Research Bulletin,* 38 (October 14, 1959), p. 180.

[4] Torsten Husen and Nils-Eric Svenson, "Pedagogic Milieu and Development of Intellectual Skills," *The School Review,* 68 (Spring 1960), p. 50.

respected high school selected for the study. She found that "teachers did not differentiate their patterns of teacher-pupil verbal interaction in classes of different levels of ability."[5] Thus one of the presumed reasons for homogeneous grouping was ignored in practice.

Ability Grouping Found Unconstitutional

The Brown case in 1954 has not been the only one to call into question the constitutionality of ability grouping, streaming, tracking, or whatever it may be called. In a United States District Court case of 1967, *Hobson v. Hanson,* a case now under appeal, the decision cited the Fifth and Fourteenth Amendments to the Constitution and ruled as follows:

> The "track system," which in public schools in the District of Columbia was a form of ability grouping in which students were divided into separate tracks ranging from "basic" for the slow student to "honors" for gifted students, *violated constitutional rights of Negro and poor children,* because *ability grouping* as presently practiced in District of Columbia school system *is a denial of equal educational opportunity* to the poorer and the majority of the Negroes attending school in the District of Columbia.[6]

The Court, in support of its position, indicated that it understood that at least a part of the basis of assignment of a pupil to a given track was intelligence tests standardized mainly on middle-class white children. However, throughout the decision equality of opportunity, not race, was emphasized. Frequent reference was made to the children of the poor without reference to race. The fact that the Washington, D.C., public school population is about 90 percent Negro must not obscure the main issues and the far-reaching consequences of the case.

---

[5] Isobel L. Pfeiffer, "Teaching in Ability Grouped English Classes: A Study of Verbal Interaction and Cognitive Goals" (unpublished Ph.D. dissertation, Kent State University, 1966), p. 145.

[6] 269 Federal Supplement (Judicial Digest) 401 (1967) (italics added).

Judge J. Skelly Wright also observed in this case, at least by implication, that the more highly qualified teachers tended to be found in the schools where more honors track children were found, thus further interfering with equality of opportunity. By at least one newspaper columnist Judge Wright was dubbed a zealot. The American Association of School Administrators now has a special commission at work on the issue. To date it appears that the attitude of this group has been chiefly defensive. It appears that there is considerable reluctance to face the issue squarely.

The Nature of the Issue

The issue involved is a basic one. Simply stated, it asks, Is the prejudgment of a child or youth consistent with American principles? It asks, Who am I, as a teacher or principal, to say, with whatever devices and analytical tools I can summon to help me, that this youth is capable and that one is not? Are our sorting devices valid? Are they good enough to stake a human being's future upon them? While much of Europe still clings to the Platonic tradition, the Europeans themselves have failed to note that even Plato effected his first drastic sorting of humankind at the age of twenty. Modern Europe has been disposed to do it at "eleven plus" to age fifteen, although their educational thinkers have been working relentlessly to change this, with here and there a measure of success. It is interesting to note that in the United States the trend for twenty years has moved in the opposite direction, placing greater emphasis upon stratification of students.

Even more broadly stated, the principle is not only an American but a human one. It says: No child shall be minimized or belittled. Every child has a right to think well of himself and his possibilities. If we really believe this—and this writer fully believes that most teachers and principals do—then each of us must take a stance something like this. It is my job to believe in my student and to help him believe in himself. I shall place little emphasis upon any ways in which his earlier culture has short-changed him. Rather, I shall seek to discover whatever human talents and possibilities he has and help him develop them, that they may reflect favorably upon both him and me.

Especially in the light of studies such as *Pygmalion in the Classroom,* which reveals that the learner tends to respond favorably to the teacher's faith in him and which underscores the power of the self-fulfilling prophecy,[7] we should be most wary of any practice that tends to lower the teacher's estimate or the learner's estimate of himself.

The high school principal or teacher that is unshaken by constitutional, human, or educational considerations should take another look at ability grouping if only for the public relations reason. The franchise is ever more widely exercised by less affluent citizens. The successes of education have shown such citizens how to exercise and insist upon their American and human rights. They have learned how important self-image is to human motivation. There are more potential votes for school tax levies among the average and basic groups than among honors groups.

It is recognized that high schools were just a few years ago under tremendous pressures to move in directions that would at least appear to be movement toward higher quality. Perhaps expedience at times justifies the adoption of devices that serve as window dressing. This does not mean that we must live forever with what is recognized as window dressing. The school has a responsibility to demonstrate that its program and its practices reflect forthrightness and honesty of motive. When active pressures have subsided, when objectivity is again possible, the window dressing should be removed.

Necessary Grouping

Some sort of grouping is essential for instruction. In general, a sound principle for grouping may be to place together students that need or want to learn the same subject. Interest grouping is appropriate. Thus those who want to study French are placed

---

[7] Robert Rosenthal and Lenore Jacobson, *Pygmalion in the Classroom* (New York: Holt, Rinehart and Winston, 1968).

together; likewise, those who are to study chemistry. In some cases prerequisites must be considered. Even this, however, must be subject to variation. We have, for example, a young man who is interested in auto mechanics. He wishes to enroll in physics, although he has not had the usual prerequisite mathematics. The only sensible solution is to admit him to physics and let him get as much from the course as he can, even without working certain problems, for nothing that he could study, no matter what changes overtake the automobile, might be expected to serve him better in the future.

One kind of segregation appears to be justified in any school. That is the segregation of the incorrigibles. No student has a right repeatedly and deliberately to get in the way of the learning of other students. At the same time no school has a right to expect all its faculty members to qualify or to act as corrective officers. To the extent that the school has enrollees who, after every reasonable effort to help them, still find it impossible to fit into the school's regular program and procedures, then a special program and special arrangements for them are in order. The school, however, should never give up the desire or the hope for the full rehabilitation of each such student. The school is subject to the same demands as is any other well-regulated society.

Open Opportunities

No student should ever be denied admission to any class solely on the basis of his reputed ability or intellectual capacity. Human talent or potential is not yet that well understood, and judgment of it is too frequently in error. Among the thousands of contributive citizens whom the school has rejected or repeatedly misjudged in recent generations are such persons as Winston Churchill, Thomas Edison, and Albert Einstein. Walter Scott's biography indicates that he profited more from following his own reading fancies than from any classes he took. To what extent can anyone be sure that today's students who are identified as gifted will be tomorrow's giving citizens, that they will be the great leaders and servants of civilization? If errors are made even as much as 5 percent of the time, great injustice is committed, against both the individual and society.

The essence of this argument may be briefly stated. Self-image is at stake. There is so much more to be gained by a positive approach to self-image. To undermine it is to destroy the person. Every human being, especially in our kind of society, must have the right to discover and decide for himself how much and what kind of ability he has. The job of the school and the teacher is to help him move this expectation and this realization as far up the scale as possible.

ADVANCED PLACEMENT CLASSES

Advanced placement in college is anything but a new concept. It has existed since the inception of colleges and universities. The means of judging fitness for advanced standing have not changed very much, consisting usually of examination, more often than not of professor-constructed examination. In 1900, as indicated in an earlier chapter, the line of demarcation between the high school and the college was less clear. Many students were admitted to colleges without high school diplomas. Fewer, from quality high schools, were admitted with advanced standing, so much advanced standing in some cases that today's practices are paled by comparison.

Advanced placement classes serve only a very small percentage of high school enrollees and of college candidates. Here reference is made only to the advanced placement program and examinations sponsored by the College Entrance Examination Board, with the help of the Educational Testing Service. The Board reports that just over 38,000 students took examinations for 1,076 colleges in 1965–1966.[8] The students represented 2,518 secondary schools, about 10 percent of the nation's total number of schools. Examinations are available in American history, biology, chemistry, English, European history, French, German, Latin, mathematics, physics and Spanish.

[8] College Entrance Examination Board, *A Guide to the Advanced Placement Program* (Princeton: College Entrance Examination Board, 1966), p. 7.

At a most highly selective state university (with an average freshman SAT score in 1966 of 1,153) 94 students, almost 4 percent of the more than 2,300 entering freshmen in September, 1966, received CEEB advanced placement credit. Almost two-thirds of the 152 students taking the examinations for this institution were graduates of private preparatory schools. Credit went to 51 students in English, 23 in American history, and to 18 in mathematics, tapering out to 2 students each in physics and French. Individual student credit granted ranged from a low of 3 to a high of 31 semester hours.[9]

Self-Selection

There is certainly nothing wrong with the idea of advanced placement. The objection here is to the advanced placement class in the high school and to its being open only to selected students and closed to others. Any advanced high school class should hold the potential of advanced placement for any industrious and capable student enrolled in it. It is a relatively simple matter for the high school teacher whose own preparation has been characterized by depth and quality to have at hand a list of readings and problems that the ambitious student might be encouraged to explore. Such work might be accepted in lieu of more standard content pursued by the rest of the class. The teacher whose weekly formal class periods have been reduced, as suggested earlier in this work, should arrange occasional individual conferences with the student for further analyses and encouragement. The opportunity should always be available, and the encouragement should be provided for the student to extend appropriate interests, whether for advanced placement or not. Student motive, obvious interest, and persistence should be the sole determinants of advanced placement effort by any student. There is no need for machinery of selection and specially designed classes. Thus another fragment of reform is incorporated in the overall design laid out in this book.

A simple note, signed by the teacher involved, should be

[9] Data provided by Director of Admissions Charles Bernard, University of North Carolina, Chapel Hill, N.C., April 26, 1967.

appended to the record of the student judged to have explored an area in such depth as to justify his request for an advanced placement examination. This judgment will be honored by the college or university that is willing to carry its share of high school-college cooperation in the student's interest. For that matter, there is no legitimate reason why a student who requests it should not have an opportunity to demonstrate his acquaintance with any field at any educational level. Having demonstrated achievement and understanding, appropriate exemptions and installment at an advanced level is in order. In the last analysis, of course, the establishment of college standing is wholly in the hands of the collegiate institution concerned.

Equality of Opportunity

Doubt is raised about the legitimacy of advanced placement classes as presently administered for the following reason. Fewer than half of the nation's medium-size comprehensive high schools, according to James Bryant Conant, are adequately staffed with teachers and other professionals, based on a minimum standard of 1 teacher to 20.5 students. Fewer than one out of five are staffed with a really favorable ratio, that is, 1 teacher to 17.4 pupils or fewer.[10] How is this pertinent? Advanced placement classes usually affect teacher ratios in other classes adversely. It is not uncommon to find the advanced placement classes with fewer than 20 students in a school where other classes in the same academic area average 30 or more. This situation violates the concept of equal opportunity. The matter is somewhat different in the case of other small classes if they are not closed to a student solely because of his adjudged ability level.

Regardless of the adequacy of the professional staffing of a high school, its leadership has a responsibility to organize its services to assure to each student, so far as is humanly possible, equal accessibility to the human and material resources of that school. Simply put, this means that any student must have as good a chance as any other to find himself in the classes of the

[10] James B. Conant, *The Comprehensive High School: A Second Report* (New York: McGraw-Hill, 1967), pp. 14–15.

school's best teachers, to gain access to its finest equipment. Nowhere in recent years have slogans, in the service of expedience, so frequently done violence to the very ideals the school teaches as here.

If both the ablest teachers and the largest portion of teacher time are reserved to certain students and denied to others, the high school thereby reneges upon one of its greatest traditions. Students will always avail themselves of opportunity unequally. For this the school cannot be faulted. The responsibility to make that opportunity equally available, however, is always the school's.

TELEVISION TEACHING

Television, like other media, represents simply another form by which other persons or their work may be brought into the classroom to help the teacher who is there in the flesh. Education took a long stride in this direction when Johann Gutenberg invented movable type in 1454. How far the efforts of persons other than the teacher can be exploited in this way appears to depend upon three considerations: (1) the practicality and accessibility of the form in which the exploitation is packaged, (2) the relative cost of bringing the package to the student, and (3) the appropriateness and effectiveness of the package in the learning task confronting the student.

A Perspective on Learning Media

Books have been cheap enough to be generally available for more than 500 years, but books still reflect many imperfections as learning tools. John Amos Comenius produced the first illustrated textbook about 350 years ago; yet illustrations and pictures in texts even today are often unclear and serve their purposes imperfectly. The practical phonograph has been with us for 75 years, but the recorded holdings of learning materials centers in most secondary schools are still relatively meager. Practical radio came about half a century ago, but somehow the promised educational future of radio has at no time attained any considerable maturity. Practical television is in 1970 less than a quarter of a century old. Perhaps education has expected television to deliver too much, too fast.

Education has made faster progress in using another medium, the motion picture, now nearing the three-quarter century mark, with the sound track added about forty years ago. Since television is another means of producing the sound motion picture, it faces rather formidable competition. To date, the sound motion picture produces a larger and clearer picture, and has the advantage of being fitted more readily into its logical place in the schedule. Movie equipment is more compact, occupies less space, and is more portable. Economy also seems to be on the side of the motion picture, with rental films being available at university centers in most states.

Criteria for Educational TV

It appears that educational television must yet prove itself in terms of certain clear demands. First, it must demonstrate that it can serve important purposes that sound motion pictures do not serve. Second, school dollars always being smaller in number than they should be, it must compete with other media in terms of cost. The foundations will not finance it indefinitely. Third, when it comes into the classroom on a regular, lesson-presentation basis, there is the psychological problem of a highly rehearsed and expensively produced competition for the regular teacher, in whom the pupil must place his faith for the individual and personal help that he needs.

In this competition one tremendous advantage rests with the television. It is unaccompanied by the noise that characterizes the 16-millimeter moving picture projector. Incidentally, school officials could get better machines if they let it be known that they are selecting for minimum noise and the quality of the sound reproduction. These elements have been less than startlingly improved over the past three decades.

It must be remembered that here we are discussing the in-school use of television. How much improvement in television programs generally may result from government financed and managed programs, if they come, we do not know. That many presently produced commercial television programs have their educational values and are worthy of the teacher's encouragement there is little doubt. Home viewing by the pupil, wherever useful, should be educationally exploited by the teacher and the school.

The typical high school, however, would be ill advised to make much of an investment in educational television until such time as it already has at least an up-to-date library with 15,000 to 25,000 volumes, rich resources in laboratory equipment, realia, artifacts, and a clearly superior array of audiovisual aids for all fields.

The real hope of educational television eventually may prove to be found in the development of standardized, economical video tapes which may be played by the student himself on a low-cost machine. In this event we shall have simply a variation of the motion picture.

PROGRAMMED LEARNING AND TEACHING MACHINES

In some respects it is probably wrong to place programmed learning and teaching machines in the same category. The reasoning followed here is that both serve as means of self-instruction, at least as presently interpreted and commonly espoused. They are seen as means of increasing teacher efficiency, of relieving the teacher of the necessity of teaching at all those things that the pupil, with the aid of mechanical and printed devices, may be able to teach himself.

Self-instruction is as old as learning itself. First learnings in any field have always been self-taught, employing, incidentally, the discovery method. Correspondence school lessons of all kinds, from their earliest inception, have represented a form of programmed learning. Foreign language vocabulary cards, probably centuries old, with the vernacular on one side and the foreign equivalent on the other, constitute a simple teaching machine. The device obviously serves the purpose of giving the student an instant check upon his answer.

Earlier Examples of Programmed Learning

The Dalton Plan, installed by Helen Parkhurst in the high school at Dalton, Massachusetts, in 1920, had as one of its features the completion of individual pupil contracts by each pupil independently of the others.[11] This was programmed learning. During the 1920s and 1930s an avalanche of workbooks almost buried American schools and scholars. These provided units of work that typically followed the adopted textbook and that covered the entire course. Each unit consisted of a series of blanks to be filled and choices to be made by the student—programmed learning. The workbook came to be regarded as a great evil, one which encouraged students to copy answers from the quicker student or to get the answers into the book in the minimum of time, preferably without the necessity of having to think about them, which always slows one down.

The Dalton Plan, particularly the contract-plan phase of it, left no permanent reform with the schools, but it did contribute to causing two decades of American schooling to be deluged with workbooks, which often appealed to the teacher who was less than energetic. Variations of the Dalton Plan had been used earlier in California and contemporaneously in school systems like that of Carleton Washburne at Winnetka, Illinois. They failed to attract any large number of followers, although the models had been set up with a great deal of care and integrity. An effort to individualize instruction, especially with respect to pace, the contract plan failed to attract numerous disciples for the following reasons: (1) it was too mechanical; (2) it did not in truth individualize and personalize learning; it individualized only the pace, while overstructuring other phases of learning; and (3) it tended to make school life a dull process, taking a large share of the social element out of it.

Elementary teachers in the early twentieth century frequently used and were themselves a part of a teaching machine to teach the multiplication table. The device was cheap (even

---

[11] The Dalton Plan is treated sketchily in many sources. For the historical context, see Lawrence Cremin, *Transformation of the School* (New York: Knopf, 1961), pp. 296–299.

teacher time was inexpensive in those days) and it was readily altered. Typically, it was a circle about two feet in diameter, drawn on the chalkboard by the teacher, who then placed the figures *1* to *12* around the perimeter of this circle, simulating the face of a clock. In the center was placed the multiplier, with the multiplication sign following it thus: *6* ✕. The teacher and sometimes her rubber-tipped pointer became the rest of this machine. She became the immediate validating factor, with a second pupil becoming the correcting device.

Personal and Social Elements

The importance of the teacher's personal and constant help and of the incentive one draws from classmates is clearly reflected in the drop-out rate of correspondence school course enrollees. With the exceptions of highly motivated adults of considerable student experience, such as teachers meeting requirements for upgrading or renewing teaching certificates, only small fractions of those enrolling for correspondence courses ordinarily complete them. In some cases the completions have been fewer than one out of ten. Programmed learning tends to resemble correspondence school study, although the student delivers his completed lesson in person rather than through the mail.

In a very real sense every textbook that the student studies on his own is an example of programmed learning. If it is well done, it leads him through logical steps from the simplest and most evident manifestations of the subject to its most complex applications.

Criticisms of Programmed Learning

Programmed learning and machine teaching are seen as innovations of limited promise for the reasons listed below. This position is substantiated in the discussion that follows the list.

1. The materials tend to be highly structured and tedious and often labor the obvious.
2. The intimate and immediate reactions of both teacher

and classmates, be they enlightening, humorous or frivolous, are missing.

3. Such materials are usually most effective with those aspects of learning that are most readily and easily acquired.

4. They tend to be most fully utilized by the students who are the most persistent but not necessarily the most creative.

5. They fail to meet the demands of individualization and personalization of instruction, individualizing only the pace at which the student proceeds through learning materials of a necessarily limited range.

To what extent are programmed learning materials rigidly structured and tedious? Do they tend to labor the obvious? A programmed approach to basic understandings in music introduces the learner, on the first page, to the word "beat," as a synonym for "pulse." Although the section is headed "rhythm," there is no mention of the meaning of that word at this point. Another book designed to teach the same material nowhere stresses the word "beat" under its discussion of rhythm. The point here is that programmed materials tend to encourage a single pattern of thought and to discourage others. In this way its structure is restrictive. The kind of intuitive learning advocated by Jerome Bruner[12] and others is discouraged by programmed materials, which are to be followed step by step. A courageous leap now to a conclusion reached six pages later is discouraged. The learning tends to be a single-track affair. Ancillary ideas and one's own notions about other possible routes to the goal are no part of it. One is invited to think, but only in the prescribed pattern, which is not education in its best sense.

Routine, especially prescribed and unalterable routine, is always dull. One wonders how creative and original might be a mind that could in patience and meaningful persistence follow some of the programmed materials for more than a few minutes at a time. Needless repetition of the obvious surely bores many

[12] Jerome Bruner, *The Process of Education* (Cambridge: Harvard University Press, 1960), pp. 14, 55–68.

students. For example, one programmed text in geometry labors the procedural device of designating the points of polygons with capital letters, never once indicating that any other simple designations consistently used might serve just as well.

The absence of the social element from programmed learning requires little elaboration. Because it must provide individual pace, the programmed material is handled in loneliness. How much and how meaningful is the learning one gets from his fellow students we do not yet know. The significance of such learning is recognized as substantial, however, by all thoughtful persons who have contemplated the learning environment, from the Supreme Court to the humblest teacher. Is the individualization of pace worth this price?

Simple, direct learnings are best served by programmed materials, although entire courses may be programmed. If material is to be self-taught, it obviously must be learned without teacher assistance, or at best with only occasional assistance. The programmed material itself becomes the drill sergeant. A question as yet unanswered in education asks to what extent we can plunge the student into a large problem or issue, permitting him as he moves in upon it to pick up the incidental and basic understandings that he needs to wrestle with it. Mounting evidence over at least two generations tends to indicate that learnings acquired in this more genuine context appear to be more permanent and to require little or no review.

Routine skills rather than the creative or inventive do not appear to make up the capacities of which our society today stands most in need. Increasingly our technology produces machines that are capable of handling the routine chores with a minimum of human assistance. Such assistance as they require emphasizes talent for analysis, resourcefulness, and judgment. Do routine learnings, routinely arrived at, meet this need?

Individualization is not achieved, for it never is in the highly structured, highly routinized advance upon the learning task. To equate variations in pace through such material with individualization of instruction is to do violence to the real meanings of both individualization and instruction. One will find both slow readers and fast readers holding full professorships of equal stature and remuneration on every university faculty in the

nation. Among the elements of individual difference of consequence in education, that of pace is well down the line.[13] Desire
or motive, intensity of interest, firmness and preciseness of goal,
the capacity to make novel inferences from learnings, an interest
in making analyses and continuing to think about relationships:
these are among the factors that must be served if education is
to be meaningfully individualized.

The Place of Programmed Learning

All of the above, disparaging though it may seem, does not mean
to imply that programmed learning has no place. Its place is
similar to that long filled by correspondence study; it has merit
in meeting certain legitimate needs. Student interests and student needs often are highly particularized or specialized. The
school cannot legitimately provide a class for a single student, or
for two or three. This indicates one place to put the programmed
course to work.

An instance of this principle in operation is found in a long-
continued operation at Benton Harbor, Michigan, where the high
school many years ago set up a correspondence study department.
The superintendent, in showing the writer and others how it
worked, said: "We believe that if the school has only one student
who wants a course in filling station management, for example,
the school should meet that need, if possible." Consequently,
Superintendent Mitchell had arranged with reputable correspondence schools to provide a wide range of courses for Benton
Harbor High School students, at school expense. The work was
performed under the supervision of a teacher of broad interests,
in a study laboratory equipped with apparatuses of an indescrib-
ably wide variety. This bit of secondary school history gives a
clue to one profitable application of programmed materials. They
constitute a means of broadening the curricular offerings. Assistance in evaluating student results might in some cases be found
outside the regularly employed faculty.

[13] See Chapter IV by Fred T. Wilhelms, "Individualizing Instruction,"
National Society for Study of Education Yearbook, LXI, Part I, 1962,
pp. 62–74.

Programmed and machine teaching might also be used with individual students who have short-range needs in connection with projects that deeply interest them. The student may need to fortify himself in a given area or to review what has slipped out of mind. The programmed or machined device thus is used in the same way that a book or any other learning resource is employed.

Perhaps programmed materials will some day reach a level of sophistication that will enable them to employ the individual idiosyncrasies, the unique experiences, of the learner. Perhaps recent transgressions of the too anxious publishers can eventually be overcome. For the moment the educational millenium of the programmed or machined lesson does not seem to be at hand.

SUMMARY

This chapter has examined the nature and limitations of four innovative practices that have been found in secondary schools in recent years. These are ability grouping, advanced placement, television teaching, and programmed learning. All have been found faulty and of limited usefulness. The first two are faulted for similar reasons: Advantages have not been proved; the grounds for selection are less than foolproof; violence is done to equality of opportunity; and the self-image, hence the incentive, of many learners is damaged.

Television teaching is seen as a variation of the sound motion picture, but with less flexibility, although its cost is somewhat greater. It must be viewed against the historical background of other educational media, starting with cheap printing in the fifteenth century. The school should possess an extensive, rich library and many other resources for learning before investing in television.

Programmed learning is viewed as failing to meet the most important needs of individualized instruction. It tends to emphasize pace and reinforcement through a limited pattern of learning that is precisely the same for all learners. It is most useful in the tasks of learning that are easiest for the learner. It often labors the obvious, in a lonesome and tedious process. Its most useful possibility is seen in the kind of flexibility of offerings that might let a given student take a course even though no other student in the school is taking that course.

The chief challenges facing today's high school are how to make secondary education universally effective and how to personalize or individually tailor the curriculum. The innovations treated in this chapter appear to offer relatively little to such demands. At least some of those discussed in the next chapter offer more.

10

Innovations of Substantial Promise

> When other men gorged themselves on the pro-
> ceeds of a successful hunt and vegetated in dull
> stupor for many hours thereafter, New-Fist ate a
> little less heartily, slept a little less stupidly, and
> arose a little earlier than his comrades to sit by
> the fire and think.
>
> *J. Abner Peddiwell, The Saber-Tooth Curriculum*

All innovations treated in this chapter are regarded as having substantial promise. This does not mean that each has equal promise. Nor does it mean that the continuation of any one of them in presently prevailing forms is advocated. Such would deny the distillation and unification of innovative practices urged by this work.

It must again be emphasized that this chapter and the one preceding it make no claim to being an exhaustive treatment of innovations in the secondary school. The aim is that of helping the reader to get a perspective on innovation, to call attention to related principles and antecedents, to emphasize interrelationships, to get a view of what each may contribute to the redesigned high school, to form a basis of judgment.

Although nothing is viewed as wholly new, the importance of continuing the search for means of cultivating the full potential of each individual must not be abandoned. The new age places new demands upon education. The educational philosopher Harry Broudy reminds us that "we have yet to evolve the teaching method and style appropriate to the new age."[1]

Modern man is still in the early dawn of understanding human potential and its optimum development. Science has just begun to make discoveries that are of use to educators. As Bertrand Russell suggested many years ago, the man in the street is just beginning to believe when the man in the laboratory is finding out that it is not so. Psychologists are today very doubtful about many matters on which there was broad consensus just a few years ago. Our educational philosophers change their opinions about what elements or combination of elements from the past are capable of serving the complex problems of today. For these reasons it is best to continue to question established practices, to experiment, to innovate, to take risks, to cut and try. Experiment is especially needed in those areas where the problems relate to making secondary education a reality for all. (See the discussion of Hutchins' *The Learning Society* in Chapter 12.)

The innovations discussed here, as listed at the beginning of Chapter 9, are each seen as having usefulness, in some form, to the philosophy and design of secondary education proposed in this volume. The only kinship claimed for the widely diverse ideas and school practices discussed in this chapter is found in their potential contribution to a better education for the American adolescent.

FURTHER EMPLOYMENT OF AUDIOVISUAL AIDS

Among the more recent and rather generally employed of audiovisual devices, none appears to outrank the foreign language laboratory and the overhead projector. Some might wish, with sound reasons, to classify the language laboratory as a type of teaching machine. Here there is no quarrel with any classification; the emphasis is upon function. The overhead projector is

---

[1] Harry S. Broudy and John R. Palmer, *Exemplars of Teaching Method* (Chicago: Rand McNally, 1965), p. 161.

frequently associated with team teaching, perhaps because its usefulness has been espoused often by those who are among the most vigorous promoters of team teaching. It is, however, useful whenever demonstration and illustration are pertinent.

The language laboratory, under reasonably competent direction, holds great potential for improved instruction in the foreign language. It is proving to be especially helpful when the teacher is not fully competent in the oral language, a situation that is unfortunately characteristic of the majority of modern foreign language teachers in secondary schools. The aural-oral teaching of foreign languages is made possible and effective by the use of the electronic laboratory. Assuming the ready availability of an abundance of tapes that introduce the learner to the foreign tongue through stories and sayings well known to him in his native language, efficiency and effectiveness of instruction should be vastly improved. Unfortunately, tape libraries in many schools are limited to little beyond materials that match the textbook. This means that the advantage of the electronic laboratory is limited to providing native pronunciation. This situation calls for major improvement. Whenever moving pictures, or even illustrated book material that the student can hold in his hand, can be synchronized with the audited foreign sounds, the instruction can be made that much more effective. This means that the eye is enlisted to help the ear in the learning process.

If electromechanical developments and human imagination can provide means by which elementary pupils and their teacher can learn together oral techniques and the basic vocabulary of a foreign language, this might pave the way for bilingualism in more Americans. It might help to give the high school a chance to lead the pupil on to mastery.

The overhead projector is a device of multiple possibilities, although certain other changes in the school must come with it if it is to be truly effective. Commercially produced overlays are useful but have their limitations. The school that is to make the best possible use of such a device must have its own illustrator-artist, one who can take a teacher idea and order and turn it into an illustration of professional quality in a short time. Such a para-professional, as mentioned earlier, might also work at times with students, helping them to develop techniques for illustrating their ideas, thus adding an important dimension to the learning.

An overhead projector used by the teacher merely as a device to get his outline before the students as he proceeds with his lecture may do more harm than good. As is true of all other special devices, effective use is preceded by thought and planning, often by dry runs or rehearsals. For these the teacher must have time and often skilled help, the artist-illustrator aide being an important example.

The three-dimensional object is a seriously neglected tool of learning in most academic areas. Realia of a wide variety, the mock-up, the model, the artifact: all have excellent possibilities. The impact of the three-dimensional object upon learning is often startling. For example, one has no real conception of the size and span of the human liver, save through the study or practice of medicine, until he becomes acquainted with a human torso model whose parts may be unhooked and removed for study.

Few schools have made notable gains in this area in recent years. Often the new school buildings, stark and dull in exterior architecture, are merely institutional, barren, and antiseptic on the inside. Instead, every classroom and work-study laboratory should have a variety of objects that give evidence of both the subject and the absorption of the teachers and students who work there. Many of these may well be objects that students have made, to be replaced by other student-made objects when better ones are produced. This is a matter that has long deserved more thought and attention by both faculty and administrators than it commonly receives.

The 16-millimeter educational film, although now more than a long generation into maturity, is still less than adequately exploited by many high schools. The lack of a few budget dollars for film purchase and rental and the failure to develop an active faculty film committee are two of the reasons for this condition. A third important reason is the teacher's understandable distaste and inadequacy for the mechanical responsibility. Hence the importance of the electronics-gadgeteer aide. In schools that do have an audiovisual director, no small part of his time is invested in the work of such an aide, making that level of service expensive.

USE OF LOCAL RESOURCES AND PERSONS

Local resources and persons constitute a learning resource that too often remains unassessed and unemployed in the instructional processes. It is possible that as this is written, the exploitation of community resources for learning is decreasing rather than increasing in the nation's high schools. That this is a distressing probability is evidenced by the recent frequency of newspaper reports concerning defeated tax levies in many communities and consequent cutbacks in expenditures for such purposes as field trips in school buses.

Generally speaking, science teachers have made the most frequent use of local resources in instruction. Outdoor laboratories, particularly for the life sciences, have grown in number and variety, but quite slowly. Some biology departments have set up programs for exchange of specimens with schools in distant parts of the nation. A better lesson on the relationship between environment and species would be difficult to imagine.

Although both social studies and business teachers make occasional use of local resources in their instruction, the school usually makes an inadequate effort to acquaint its students with the world of work. Many examples of the world's work can be found near the schoolhouse door, but the instruction within the school goes on as if the building were surrounded on every hand by hazardous desert or enemy territory. The business class talks and reads of the work of an auditor, overlooking the fact that an auditor with a friendly attitude toward education is at work only two blocks down the street. Likewise, the social studies class often makes no contact with public officials.

It is unnecessary, often unwise, for students to descend in hordes upon those whose understandings they would exploit. A single student, or a small committee of students, having been thoroughly briefed on procedure and possibilities, might well interview the useful human resource and report back to the class and teacher. Usually, of course, the teacher will have been personally in contact with the person earlier. The teacher has also a responsibility to see that resources employed are fruitful and appropriate, as with other materials of learning.

English and mathematics teachers are among the more

reluctant users of resource persons and things. The community, however, is forever beset by communications problems in every phase of its economic and social life. As for mathematical phenomena, they are everywhere, both inside and outside the school. Few are the English teachers who have wisely and thoroughly exploited representatives of the law, the ministry, and journalism in motivating their students' respect for and deeper interest in preciseness and character of expression. Similarly, one county engineer in a quite populous county told a high school mathematics teacher that he was the first such teacher in twenty-five years to request copies of blueprints for highways and bridges, in order that he might acquaint members of his classes with mathematics at work in their environment.[2]

This is not a full treatise on the use of local resources in learning. It is hoped, however, that the illustrations given have been sufficient to convince the reader that the possibilities for making learning more real and lasting are intriguing and virtually limitless. Good teachers have always taught their students to open their eyes and ears and minds and to learn from the persons and things about them.

UNIFIED STUDIES

Real gains have been made with unified or closely allied studies in many high schools in recent years. The correlation and fusion of subject matter from different fields has been an often-proclaimed goal in education for many years. For more than forty years high schools have offered fused courses in the social studies, the most common example being the twelfth-grade course in problems of democracy. Such a course draws content from political science, economics, sociology, geography, and history. Similar courses in social science have been offered by many colleges, usually termed survey courses.

Academic purists often find fault with fusion courses, maintaining that the true essence of the discrete discipline is genuinely relished only when it is presented in undiluted form. Despite such

[2] Burton W. Gorman, "Every Day Must Be 'Career Day,'" *The High School Journal*, 43 (May 1958), pp. 97–100.

claims of neutralization, fusion courses and carefully interrelated or allied courses continue to grow. English composition and literature were in earlier days almost universally presented as separate courses. In the transition stage, each was given a full semester of attention, often by the same teacher. Today they are often unified and are regularly used to support one another.

Perhaps the most common and recent further extension of this idea is found in the unified American studies, usually found in the eleventh grade. This is achieved mechanically by the simple device of what is often called "back-to-back scheduling," that is, placing American history and American literature and composition on the schedule in successive periods, with the same students in both classes. In its more elaborate or refined form, a music and an art teacher are added to the teacher team, thus bringing the work of four teachers to bear on the student's more complete understanding of his American heritage. The thinking is that the student sees all aspects more clearly when he sees them in their interrelationship, when he has the opportunity to look through the eyes of four different disciplines but is at the same time helped to appreciate and understand the connections.

Unified studies seem destined to continue to expand and to serve the high school well for the following reasons. First, the idea leads teachers and pupils to view their subjects more broadly and more meaningfully. Second, it encourages a natural kind of interdisciplinary teacher teaming, thus promoting professional stimulation of teachers and cross-fertilization among different disciplines. Third, it can scarcely avoid the stimulation of wider reading by both teachers and students. Fourth, the longer time span makes possible appropriate field trips, the showing of longer films, and other flexibilities. Finally, each significant idea holds the possibility of support from the different disciplines, thus enhancing the quality of the student's learning and his chance of functional retention.

HUMANITIES COURSES

Humanities courses involve not only certain modifications of method, but they also tend to lead the high school student into curricular areas that have for many years had little attention in secondary schools. Along with the unified studies concept, this movement is aimed at tone rather than merely at speed or muscle. Both are wholesome rebellions against the fragmentation of learning. The noble aim of the humanities course is that of helping the pupil to see life whole and to see himself as a moving force in it. Properly developed and expanded and granted reasonably appropriate teacher staffing, no change of the last fifty years promises greater potential for making the American high school experience more worthwhile to the student.

In the first chapter of this work, attention was drawn to the offerings of New York academies in 1837. They included such subjects as logic, mythology, natural theology, moral and intellectual philosophy, biography, and Biblical, Grecian, and Roman antiquities. Collectively, the aim of such subjects was similar to that of the recent humanities courses. They helped the student to understand human life and its human purposes. Hence the humanities courses do not represent a really new concept, just a revived one in a new dress.

Value of Humanities Courses to All Students

Unfortunately the humanities course has been developed in a very small percentage of the high schools. Those into which it has come typically offer it to only limited numbers of their students. It would be a catastrophe to have this experience seen as only for the most able students or for some other highly select group. All students need to learn about life and its problems. Those whose plans do not include college are, in fact, in greatest need of such a high school experience.

The limited offering of the humanities course is understandable. It is not the kind of undertaking in which a teacher can be handed a textbook and commanded to get under way. The teacher must be a person whose own education was rich and broad and whose reading interests are expansive. He must be perfectly secure without either textbook or curriculum guide. His interests should have led him into philosophy and perhaps into the history of art, music, and drama. He should be widely read in history and in literature. He should be able to take a few dozen carefully selected paperbacks and design his own course, at the same time leading his students to explore a wide range of reading materials with him.

Since this type of teacher is less often found than needed in the high school, incentive differences could be held out to attract the desired teacher. As suggested in the discussion of teacher personnel, such incentives might take the form of added pay for educational qualifications, assurance of summer school employment, or fringe benefits such as expense-paid attendance at such centers as the Aspen Institute on the Humanities in Colorado.

TEAM TEACHING COMPONENTS

The term "team teaching components" is used because, as pointed out earlier, team teaching involves a bundle of ideas and devices. As usually interpreted by its most devoted proponents, it involves arrangements for large group instruction, small group discussion, and independent study, plus the cooperative effort of two or more teachers. As employed in some schools, the team sometimes includes a teacher aide or a student teacher, or both. Usually the team is made up of teachers who work within a single teaching field and at the same level.

A very significant effect of team teaching is that interest in it has tended to stimulate considerable related experimentation and inquiry. The large lecture sessions, for example, have frequently been responsible for useful discoveries about the instructional potential of the overhead projector. Any plan that requires teachers to work together on aims, content, and instructional method normally leads to the generation of new excitement for all. Similarly, team teaching has tended to promote movement toward more flexible scheduling, toward the employment of a wider variety of instructional materials, such as paperbacks, and toward a further employment of the ungraded or nongraded organization.

Stimulation of Flexible Approaches

It is entirely possible that team teaching, in its present form, does not represent a relatively permanent school reform. The questions that its proponents have raised, however, are momentous and far-reaching. Its greatest service is that it has raised again the old question, Under what conditions does optimum learning occur? In part, the proponents have answered that learning opportunity is by no means limited to the time that a student spends sitting in the presence of a teacher with twenty-nine other students. Dr. Lloyd Trump and his persistent disciples have forcefully reminded secondary school leadership that the institution has long been victimized by a rigidity of organization, by the employment of too few routes to study and learning, by the inefficiency that always results from the lack of variety in both method and material. For cracking the long-resistant shell of the unmixed approach to learning, the high schools will long be in Dr. Trump's debt.[3]

Emphasis on Independent Study

The most promising element of the team teaching mix is the emphasis it gives to independent study. To date, however, there appears to have been insufficient emphasis upon the complementary element so necessary to make individual study effective—the tutorial assistance of a teacher. Independent study, it must be added, may receive emphasis in any school, whether team teaching exists there or not. If fruitful, it must be supported by a scheduling that provides student time for such study and teacher time for individual consultation.

Regarding small group discussion, certain questions must be asked. How many teachers can be brought to a level of effectiveness in stimulating and guiding such discussion as will make the results truly rewarding? Can discussion provoked to order two days a week be made real and consistently educational? Why not create schedules and conditions that encourage discussions to evolve, with teachers and paraprofessionals participating as they happen along or as they are invited? Does the period immediately after lunch have possibilities, the eating accommodations being made compatible with conversation, as the discussion part of the

---

[3] J. Lloyd Trump and Delmas F. Miller, *Secondary School Curriculum Improvement* (Boston: Allyn and Bacon, 1968), Part IV.

day? This practice has a long and worldwide tradition in the adult realm to commend it. Is it necessary that the eight or ten participants represent the same academic class? Might they not have more to offer each other if ideas bearing upon the topic came from a variety of classes and sources? Might not the practice also help to create that community of spirit so necessary to a lively and enlivening school? We are frequently forced into narrow and rigid practices because we think more about grading or marking students than we do about educating them. Consequently, we find it difficult to promote anything not directly related to marks and credits.

The large lecture or demonstration section must not be too large, and the lecture sessions should not become too large a portion of the course, perhaps not more than 20 percent. Furthermore, if one is to lecture to high school students, the lecture should be well prepared and skillfully delivered. Only the teacher who has attained expertness in the lecture, or one who is willing to work strenuously to develop it, should be given such an assignment. The public address equipment should be available, with the lavalier pickup, wherever acoustics are less than highly favorable. The lecturer's teaching load should be adjusted to allow for preparation time, and he should have competent help in preparing effective visual aids.

Present Limitations and Cautions

Team teaching, as now ordinarily managed, is a bit mechanical in nature. It tends to substitute for one too rigid pattern another that is also too rigid, although possibly less monotonous. If the pattern can be somewhat relaxed, especially in the management of the discussion sessions, and if the tutorial assistance to sustain the independent study can be made available, team teaching has a future in the fields of instruction that lend themselves to its techniques. Another essential ingredient, of course, is a team of teachers who are interested or can be led to work together congenially, under the management of one of them. The successful team in any enterprise usually has a manager.

INDIVIDUALIZED AND VARIED SCHEDULING

There are numerous ways of varying the schedule of classes and many ways of individualizing a single student's schedule. This is the reason for avoiding the frequently used term "flexible scheduling," which to many minds calls up the idea of the modular schedule. The modular schedule is built up of time modules of ten, twelve, or twenty minutes, or some other predetermined unit of time, making it possible to schedule a class of any duration that is a multiple of the modular unit. This is a relatively modern scheduling invention, but only in the extent to which the idea is employed and the terminology applied. The principle itself is almost as old as the school schedule.

Flexibility in the Past

Flexibility in the construction and in the management of the class schedule is not new. The secondary school schedule has always been characterized by certain kinds of flexibility. The academies, for example, and the high schools prior to about 1910 offered many subjects on two-, three-, or four-day-a-week schedules. In this respect the schools of the past fifty years have been much more rigid than the earlier schools. The practice survives in many schools in the scheduling of physical education, music activities such as band, orchestra, and choral groups, and sometimes in other areas. This is one kind of flexibility of schedule. As a high school principal, the writer employed this type of flexibility almost thirty years ago by offering the second semester seniors in a small high school their choice or choices among four different English courses, each taught either two or three days a week. Each student elected to take, as he chose, only one of the four, any two, any three, or all four—quite a degree of flexibility.

With the coming of laboratory science, home economics, agriculture, and shop courses came the necessity for another kind of flexibility of schedule, the addition of the occasional laboratory period. Incidentally, this involved the principle of the module, although the term was not used at that time. If the single period of that day be thought of as one module, the laboratory was given two modules, or twice as much. When the cafeteria became attached to the school, some principals with a greater flair for efficiency than for education conceived the idea of feeding two groups of students in a single class period. Thus students gulped their food in a half-period or a half-module, another type of flexibility.

When the clock makers of New England began to help principals manage their schools, they saw sales possibilities in flexibility. They provided clock-bell systems that would ring four or more different daily programs or schedules just by flicking off one switch and throwing another one. The most frequently employed variation in many schools was the "assembly schedule," which meant that the assembly program replaced no class; rather it stole its time, a little from each class. The practice undoubtedly still prevails in many schools. With imagination it was possible for a school to operate for at least four successive days on four different class schedules.

There is much basis for the argument that not all classes require or find profitable an equal length of time. One of the underlying ideas of this work is that very few classes should hold formal meetings five days a week. Furthermore, individual pupil schedules—that is, the attendance required of the pupil in classes for which he is registered—must often be modified in the interest of his optimum learning, perhaps only within a single course or perhaps within his entire school program. As mentioned elsewhere, in every school that is organized to serve the student's education rather than the school's organization, there will be times that the student will be excused for several successive days from attendance in a given class, or in all classes, to pursue an interest that is at white heat. Why should it not be so? This may easily be the most important thing that has happened to him, educationally, all year. It is the kind of situation toward which we have worked and for which we have hoped, but we are often unprepared and unwilling to be yielding enough to capitalize upon it when it arrives.

Serving the Individual Student

Flexible scheduling, both for the school and for the individual student, the superior principal and his faculty will always want and will strive to install. It will be installed, however, and administered with the student's total education and total development as a person in mind. It will be undertaken and managed with clearly conceived and generally agreed-upon educational aims in mind. It will not fall into any given popular pattern simply because that is what the ingroup is doing. Above all, it will seek to serve students individually and personally. It will involve large doses of the tailor-made concept. It will seek to rescue the individual from the mass rather than getting him lost in the mass.

THE PAPERBACK REVOLUTION

One of the most promising of modern technology's gifts to education is the relatively inexpensive paperback book. This is so because one of the surest routes to an education of higher quality at all levels is the one that widens the range of materials employed. It is an essential handmaiden of that other essential of quality education, variation in method.

Alexander Butman calls the paperback "a new educational dimension" and says it has undergone constant refinement since its first introduction to the American book-buying public in 1939.[4] The paperback facilitates variation and individualization in assignment and is an encouragement to independent study because it is easily transportable and is less formidable in appearance. Lou La Brant reports that she experimented with leaving a paperback on her desk in such a way that her student conferees could not fail to see it. Thus she had *Return of the Native* borrowed, read, and returned eleven times in a single semester, while the hardbound library copy had not left the shelf.[5]

The smallest and poorest of high schools no longer has any excuse for not bringing before its students a wide variety of reading materials. There is no longer an excuse for sole reliance upon the four-pound history text or upon the three-and-a-half-pound anthology of literature, nor does science or mathematics instruction need to depend upon a single source. The school that initially

---

[4] Alexander Butman *et al.*, *Paperbacks in the Schools* (New York: Bantam, 1963), p. 2.

[5] *Ibid.*, p. 20.

invests $200 per teacher in the field of English, social studies, and science for well-chosen paperbacks and that will sustain this investment by spending an additional $100 per teacher in each of these fields annually will soon have a wealth of useful supplementary material. A better investment in improved teaching and learning would be difficult to imagine.

Stimulation Through New Materials

Were there a way to verify it, the first few weeks of the fall semester would probably be found to be the most productive part of the school year in terms of new pupil learning. If this is correct, one of the main reasons for it would be the fact that many new materials are placed in the hands of the student at that time. If new materials have this stimulating effect—and many believe that they do—then schools must be organized and managed to ensure that new materials are placed in the learner's hands much more frequently than once a year. Among other possible answers to this need at the secondary level, paperback books appear to be among the readiest and most economical. They are effective encouragers of reading by teachers as well as pupils, and because of their cheapness no librarian is required to look after them. Many high schools are now making extensive use of them, but many others are still bound to textbooks.

Paperback Usable by Any Teacher in Any School

An enormous advantage of the paperback library is that its effective employment depends neither upon any accompanying reform nor upon any degree of faculty-wide agreement. One teacher in any school, whether small or large and however organized, can start the paperback revolution in that school.

Books appear to be destined to continue as a central source of learning for some years to come. The more varied the books, the more diverse the students who may be lured by them. The principal holdback appears to be the comparatively small number of teachers whose own reading ranges far and wide.

When it is fully appreciated that almost every student, no matter how apparently indifferent, has his sensitive points and can be reached, and when this realization is more regularly and more widely acted upon, the result will be vastly better education. The paperback offers one route to the discovery of those sensitive points and to the stimulation of genuine involvement where none previously existed.

OTHER INNOVATIVE IDEAS OF HIGH PROMISE

The next five innovative ideas appear now to have the greatest potential for the secondary school of tomorrow. These are the ungraded idea, the use of paraprofessionals, independent study, the restructuring of subject matter, and the reassessment of human potential. Some may not regard the last as an innovation at all, although it is certain to give the school a new appreciation of its lengthened reach, a new hope. Reasons for assigning a superior status to these five include the following. First, their reach is broader; they are capable of touching the whole of the curriculum, and in more different ways. Second, they seem to promise an almost endless variety of ongoing developments and are more likely to make a difference twenty, thirty, or fifty years from now. Third, they appear to be more firmly rooted in matters related to philosophy, more solidly and more variously related to the further civilizing of man and society, more closely allied with man's currently rising thoughts about himself and his problems.

EXTENSION OF THE UNGRADED IDEA

All grading or classification of pupils, at whatever level, is in reality a myth. Even in those limited aspects of human development that we have learned something about measuring, the variation from one human being to the next is almost beyond understanding and analysis. The measurement authorities tell us, for example, that the mental age of a representative room full of first-grade children ranges from just over four to just under nine. This means that more than twice as much mental development has taken place in the lives of some six-year-olds as in the lives of others.

Inadequacy of Grading

Dean Cook of the University of Minnesota has reminded us that the demotion of the slowest eighth grader to the fourth grade would still find him achieving beneath the median of his new classmates. He has similarly indicated that the acceleration of the brightest fourth-grade child to the eighth grade would find him achieving above the median of his new classmates.[6]

Again we call upon William S. Learned's Carnegie Foundation study of high school and college students in Pennsylvania, one of the most significant pieces of research in the history of American education and one that has received too little attention. With the help of a distinguished battery of psychologists, university experts in the several fields, and technical critics, the directors of this study assembled a battery of examinations covering the sciences, the humanities, and the arts. The initial version required twelve hours to administer; the later condensed version, eight. The tests were found to have quite high reliability coefficients and to measure effectively educational growth in college, since the tests were given in 1932 to forty-five groups of college seniors who had taken them as sophomores in 1930. Correlations with earned college grades and honors were also high.

The Pennsylvania inquiry represented more than a decade of effort. No resource was lacking, no care omitted that Carnegie Foundation money could attract. The battery of tests were taken by 5,747 representative sophomores in forty-nine collegiate institutions in 1930; by 3,720 of the same persons as seniors in forty-five of the same institutions in 1932; and by 1,503 representative high school seniors in 1933 and 1934.

To the astonishment of even those who were directing the study and to the unbelieving consternation of school people generally, the following findings stand out:

> 1. Of the college seniors examined, 28.4 percent did less well than the average sophomore.
> 2. Almost 10 percent of the college seniors did less well than the average high school senior.
> 3. Fully 22 percent of the high school seniors scored higher

[6] Walter W. Cook, "The Gifted and the Retarded in Historical Perspective," *Phi Delta Kappan,* 39 (March 1958), p. 251.

than the average college sophomore and exactly 10 percent of them higher than the average college senior.[7]

Findings like these should be sufficient to fill anyone with grave doubts about our capacity to classify with confidence either students or subject matter at grade levels or in any other manner. There is small reason to doubt that a similar study, repeated today, would bring forth similar findings.

Recent Development of Grading

Historically, the classification of pupils into grade levels is a relatively recent development. American schools were operated without it for a little over two centuries. During that time the pupil and his parent took the initiative in deciding when he was ready for a school presumed to stand at the next highest level. The headmaster of the Boston Latin School, or his examining committee, decided upon the fitness of a candidate for admission. Likewise, the college president or examining committee decided upon fitness for admission to college. There was no talk about grades completed, because the student was judged upon his performance.

The reports and impressions of American educators visiting Europe in the 1830s brought the notion of grade levels to American schools. Horace Mann of Massachusetts and Calvin Stowe of Ohio were among the European visitors of that era who were much impressed by the apparent quality of the Prussian schools, where systematic promotion through grade levels was the rule. Horace Mann transplanted the idea to Massachusetts; from there it spread throughout the budding nation. About a hundred years later, educators began to question this concept.

Ungraded School Activities

In some ways our schools have persisted through the years in the use of the ungraded or nongraded concept. Athletic team and squad membership from the beginning has usually been un-

[7] William S. Learned and Ben D. Wood, *The Student and His Knowledge* (New York: The Carnegie Foundation for the Advancement of Teaching, 1938), pp. 19–21.

graded. The orchestra, the band, and the choral group membership has usually been determined without reference to class or
grade level. If the student is enrolled in the school and if he
possesses the necessary abilities, he is eligible. The same has often
been true of the debating or dramatics club or class. This is the
true example of the ungraded idea. Variations of skill, interest,
and ability are conceded and utilized within the organization, but
no one is shut out merely because of his grade level. Furthermore, ordinarily no formal attempt is made to place a tag on the
level of his contribution to the organization.

Art classes, especially anything beyond the beginning class,
have often been ungraded; that is, the teacher accepts second-
year, third-year, and fourth-year students into the same class. A
similar practice has been applied to mechanical or engineering
drawing, to shop, and even to mathematics. In these situations it
is assumed that there is very little teaching of the group as a
group. Rather, students are put to work, each at his own presumed level, under the direction of a teacher. Is there any good
reason why the same cannot be done in teaching composition,
which is just as creative an enterprise as art? Can it be done in
literature, which is in any well-taught form as consciousness-
altering, as appreciative in nature as is industrial arts? The fact
that students in the same class may be writing or reading upon
different topics or levels enhances rather than limits their capacity
for sharing ideas that interest, inspire, or amaze. A Dartmouth
seminar for English teachers criticized "grouping" or "streaming"
as limiting "the linguistic environment in which boys and girls
learn English."[8] Thus we see that ungrading the school is the very
opposite of ability grouping or streaming.

Difficulty of Classifying

Who claims to know what constitutes a seventh- or a tenth-grade
composition? Who is capable of deciding which is a ninth-grade
poem or drama, which a twelfth-grade? Quite infantile composi-
tions are often written by graduate students while others reflecting

---

[8] *Education U.S.A.* (Washington, D.C.: National School Public Relations
Association, October 20, 1966), p. 46.

deep insight and maturity are at times produced by fifth-grade pupils. Some of the world's greatest literature has been written in quite simple language. Like a picture or a piece of music, literature is significant to a learner when it says something to him, when it moves his imagination.

Limits of Classification

Some currently touted plans riding under the nongraded or ungraded banner appear not to be examples of the ungraded idea at all. Rather, they are variations of ability grouping, enhanced by the opportunity for easy reassignment to a different and higher or lower group. One who creates three of five levels of work within a given grade level is not decreasing the graded character of the school. He is increasing it. The ungraded school and ability grouping really run in opposite directions. If one seeks to promote homogeneity of grouping, he may more closely approximate it by placing the "fives" of all class levels together, the "ones" of all classes together, and so on. Those who have spoken often and articulately about the merits of the nongraded school, whether they practice it or not, have rendered the high school a distinctive service. They have, often indirectly, led it closer to the teaching of individuals, and that is indeed a desirable goal.

The most plaguing problem that accompanies any and all attempts at classification of pupils is found in the variability of individual human nature. A student may be aptly classified today but still wrongly classified tomorrow. The individual's level of accomplishment, even within a single subject field, is not even. His level of performance, from day to day, is not even. One day he is up; the next, down. His application and his response vary with his energy output. Even a youth's reading level is not even. So much depends upon what the reading material is about and upon his experience with reality in that area. A teacher frequently has the experience of learning from a pupil, sometimes from one of modest scholastic endowments, that a given passage has meaning that he previously had not even imagined.

The ancient Greek Heraclitus observed that "one never steps

in the same river twice." To this we add that in fact, the stepper, as well as the river, is constantly changing.

The classification of human beings is at times expedient, but it is most unreliable.

PARAPROFESSIONALS, OR TEACHER AIDES

The use of paraprofessionals, or teacher aides, is treated in some detail in Chapter 8. It is mentioned here because it is regarded by many as an innovation.

The employment of paraprofessionals is regarded as holding a high potential for educational improvement for the following reasons. First, it is a means of increasing the effectiveness of the teacher by relieving him from routine, clerical, and monitorial duties and from providing technical or laboratory assistance and assisting with drill routines. Second, the provision of less highly trained assistants for the teacher enhances the dignity of the profession, which in turn enables it to attract more intelligent and more highly cultured persons into its ranks. Third, the teacher, being relieved of time-consuming routines, has more opportunity to individualize and personalize his attention to his client, the student.

The high school that earnestly desires to improve the quality of its educational practices will seek to enlist the services of paraprofessionals who possess expertise in clerical work, in monitoring, in illustrating, in managing electromechanical gadgets, and in caring for and helping students to employ intelligently a variety of learning materials. If, in addition, they can be perceptive in the area of a subject matter or in encouraging students to put forth their best efforts, so much the better.

INDEPENDENT STUDY AND DESIGN

Independent study is so vitally related to the central thesis of this book that anything short of the strongest possible position upon it here would be inconsistent. The plea is for more than independent or individual study. It is for individual responsibility. One is always the final architect of his own best learning.

Real learning is self-molding. Unless it is at least in part self-inspired, it cannot be real. Real learning makes one over; it changes the nature of his being. One cannot be made over against one's will. One can be led against his will to acquiesce, to assume an attitude of compliance or even of understanding, to pretend; but he cannot be led truly to learn until he desires to learn, until that desire becomes a part of his total nervous makeup. This is the reason for such stress of individual responsibility. In managing our schools, we must learn to capitalize upon—rather than fight or thwart—the essentially unique nature of the human clay with which we work.

Individual Variation

No schema of education that omits the exploitation and encouragement of individual idiosyncrasy can possibly be first-class. This exploitation is best achieved through individualized or independent study: by encouraging the student to pursue his own question, to follow in more detail an expressed or obvious interest or concern, to explore more fully his own curiosity, be it much or little. It calls for deep teacher perception and alertness and a willingness to stretch or alter what are ordinarily regarded as the outer boundaries of the subject matter being studied.

This conception of learning, it is readily granted, is least applicable to the areas of study in which the primary aims are the acquisition of specific and limited skills. If the objective of the course is learning to typewrite, no amount of research on the history of the typewriter will be significant. Such research may achieve a number of other useful educational purposes, but it will not turn out a student skilled in the use of the typewriter.

A course that is an introduction to the graphic arts might, on the other hand, permit any individual student the broadest possible experimentation with methods of reproduction. The possibilities are here limited only by the imaginations of both teacher and learner. Furthermore, the widely ranging experimenter might very well wind up with a broader, more permanent, and more useful understanding of the whole field of graphic arts than a classmate who completed with precision every exercise and assignment that lay within the course as standardly specified.

The Need for Self-Direction

Independent study skill, self-direction, the capacity to engineer one's own learning: these are qualifications that are more important to members of this generation than to those of any previous period in the history of man. Why? Because of the rapidity of change and the consequent necessity for reeducating oneself a number of times during the course of an active lifetime.

The capacity to direct one's own application and devotion to a task, to apply one's own ingenuity to the surmounting of problems encountered along the way is no less important to society than to the individual. A society whose individual citizens are in constant need of being told what to do next and how to do it is obviously an inefficient society. On the other hand, the society whose majority of citizens are self-motivating and self-directing is destined to a role of leadership and mounting influence.

Since the capacity to direct oneself is best developed through practice in directing oneself, the case for independent study and for individual student responsibility ought to be clear.

Ensuring the Effectiveness of Independent Study

Four additional points about independent study are in order. First, although independent study has often been associated with team teaching, it is in no way dependent upon it. Independent study, provided certain other conditions are met, may be launched in any school.

Second, student time and teacher time, in that order, must be set aside for the support of independent study. The student who spends 85 percent or more of his school day in formally organized classes, doing the things that teachers tell him and his classmates to do, is not likely to get far in independent study.

Similarly, the teaching staff that spends 85 percent or more of its school time in teaching formally organized classes and attending or policing formally organized study halls has little of either time or energy to devote to individual student conference, counsel, and encouragement. Student time and tutorial time are inviolable ingredients of independent study.

Third, a school that is unwilling to undertake reorganization something like that proposed in Chapters 5 and 6 can expect little progress with this innovation. As with other devices, new or old, its success depends upon the investment in it.

Finally, independent study and the development of individual responsibility must be thought of as something for all or almost all of the school's students. It is as much in need by all students as is the study of their native language. The students whose involvement will require the most teacher resourcefulness are, in fact, those to whom it can mean the very most.

RESTRUCTURING SUBJECT MATTER

Here again is an innovative idea with outer limits that are difficult to chart. What is included and what is omitted? Indeed, the idea is difficult to name, and many will be less than satisfied with the term selected here. Most analysts agree that the total package represents great potential for improved teaching and learning. Many are confident of an already more bountiful harvest.

The reader is placed on warning that there is here no attempt at an exhaustive treatment of the nature of structure as it applies to the different subject areas. Were we in the possession of expertise in any one of the areas, other experts in the field would nevertheless find grounds for disagreement. The treatment is deliberately incomplete, intended only to raise useful questions, to sharpen awareness of the extent of the possibilities, and to generate interest and renew hope in the underdeveloped potential that this educational revolution holds before us.

As one begins to examine this educational frontier, he can scarcely avoid wonder at the tardiness with which such thoughts have attracted attention and examination. The aim of the movement, briefly stated, seems to be that of providing the learner with a growing edge in the field. This means that he is helped to find a lever by which he is able to lift his own learning to greater heights. There is concern, too, with the natural corollary of permanence of learning.

History of Educational Ideas

If a basis for honest discussion is to be established, some history is necessary, a brief history of educational ideas. Social thought and social pressures are, of course, inseparable from the history of educational ideas, for one begets the other. Perhaps professionals in any field are able to concentrate upon only a limited number of problems in any given period. Perhaps the necessity for bringing the learner face to face with the responsibility for his own further education was far less pressing thirty, fifty, a hundred years ago—all eras of less rapid change. Perhaps the need of a technological society for making universal education universally effective has brought about enlarged concern for the structure of what is taught. All three of these are undoubtedly reasons for delayed attention to structure, despite the centuries-old pleas of educational thinkers for an education that might give greater attention to learning that would make a more permanent difference in the learner, for a learning that would do more than match formula to problem.

The pressures of nineteenth-century educational reform were largely social and political in nature. That era is sometimes characterized as the century that discovered the common man and his importance. It was the century of Charles Dickens and Nathaniel Hawthorne, of the founding of the YMCA, the YWCA, the Salvation Army, the settlement house, and the American Federation of Labor. It was a century that enhanced man's humanity to man, the century in which teachers learned to regard children as human beings. It came to an end with psychologists like G. Stanley Hall and William James, and with measurement-minded people like Joseph Mayer Rice on the educational horizon.

Throughout the first half of the twentieth century, interest in the individual pupil and in individual differences dominated

the mainstream of American educational thought. Early in the
century the thinking of Freud and the anti-repressionists played
their parts. Progressivism began to speak of the "child-centered"
school and of the "whole child" philosophy. Marietta Johnson
organized her school at Fairhope, Alabama, in 1907, with an
avowed determination to minister to the physical and emotional
as well as to the mental child. Frank Parsons initiated the guidance movement in Boston's schools in 1908. World War I brought
mass-administered intelligence tests. The first issue of the periodical *Understanding the Child*, begun and published by mental
hygiene societies, was published in 1931; the last issue, in 1957.
The pupil-centered interests of the first half of the twentieth
century did not ignore subject matter but were rather persistent
about its attachment to the interest of the learner.

Shift of Interest From Learner to Subject

With the close of World War II, interest shifted from the learner
to the subject, to an analysis of what is taught. Howard Fehr of
Columbia University declared that a seventeenth-century mathematician, could he come to life and speak the language of the
area of his resurrection, would be able to walk into the nearest
high school or college classroom and teach the subject without
further preparation, so little had the character of the mathematics taught changed.

Mathematics

Change in school mathematics was well under way by the early
1950s. Stagnation had characterized many phases of this school
study for hundreds of years. Consequently, it is not at all surprising that the revolution in subject matter struck first and hardest
here. It appears to be the only subject in which change has
penetrated the entire educational establishment. From kindergarten to the university, teachers speak of the new math, some
forms of which stress the discovery method and learning how to
learn in the field. The movement promises much, especially if it
can avoid getting lost in its own vocabulary and if it refuses to suc-
cumb to the constant temptation to substitute new formalities

for the old, simply for their own sakes. The grandest of educational designs can be killed by overformalization, from which some phases of the new mathematics may already be suffering.

The Sciences

Great attention to the sciences followed Sputnik, although the spread of the new mathematics was very much accelerated by the same stimulus. The scientists, in their new look at the structure of their subject matter, seemed to stress the need for the learner, no matter how young, to look at the subject area in the same way that a veteran researcher in the field views it. The boy of fourteen who studies the grasshopper and then the frog must learn the research biologist's methods of inquiry. He must acquire the same attitudes toward scientific analysis, the same habits of inducing truth from repeated observations of somewhat similar but different phenomena. The emphasis is upon the discipline as a method of inquiry. The view is that unless taught in this vein, the discipline is really not being taught at all.

One of the dangers of the naturally contagious interest in new method or new interpretation in any field is the tendency toward an overdependence upon method per se. By itself, a method will do nothing of consequence for any school or group of scholars. The tendency to rely too heavily upon the mechanics of change to achieve improvement has been too often in evidence in recent years.

A prime example of this tendency is found in the recent NASSP-sponsored Conant study of 2,000 comprehensive high schools of medium size. The heads of these schools were asked if they taught the "new physics," the "new chemistry," and the "new biology."[9] Particularly when standing alone, this question is not the important one, if the aim is to get an index to quality schools and quality instruction. It places too much emphasis upon the outline and textual materials used. A far more important question might be: Has the physics teacher had thirty-five hours or more of college physics? A second more important ques-

[9] James B. Conant, *The Comprehensive High School: A Second Report* (New York: McGraw-Hill, 1967), pp. 55–57.

tion might be: What does your chemistry teacher know about the new chemistry? or What effort has he made recently to bring his chemistry up to date?

The assumption here is that the teacher who knows his teaching field and the recent developments in it, assuming the other requisites of an effective teacher, can teach a good course with any outline or with none. He is capable of constructing his own. A further assumption: If he does not know his subject and recent developments in it, he is ill fitted to present an effective course, regardless of the outline or textual materials from which he teaches. Perhaps such teacher preparation was assumed by the Conant study committee, although investigations in the field of teacher personnel have demonstrated repeatedly that the preparation cannot be assumed, especially in subjects such as chemistry and physics.

Foreign Languages

In foreign languages the shift in emphasis appears to be toward simulation of the context in which the native learns his own language. The stress upon the oral-aural approach is a natural consequence of this thinking. In practice, however, many schools that have the electronic equipment are still teaching textbook French and textbook Spanish. The tapes owned and used are too often and too generally limited to text-related content. These schools overlook the fact that the typical child is master of a 2,000- to 3,000-word oral vocabulary in his native language before the first printed word is placed before him. If simulation of the learner's method of mastering his native language is to be a guiding principle in study of the foreign tongue, this realization cannot be ignored. Much oral skill will precede the introduction of the printed form. A revolutionary management of structure in the foreign languages probably awaits the revolutionary education of foreign language teachers.

English Grammar

Linguistic scientists have tried for many years to make a real difference in the teaching of English. Their success has never reached the proportions of a revolution in the secondary school or perhaps at any other level. Despite the lack of general accept-ance, they have reduced the English teacher's preoccupation with ritual through their assaults on the Latinization of traditional English grammar, on the inconsistency and incompleteness of definitions of terms, on the emphasis upon writing rather than speaking, and on rigid conceptions of correctness. Their contri-bution has been significant.

More recently the transformational grammarians have been rising in influence. The transformationalist places his emphasis upon the relationship of words within the sentence—upon the syntax. He sees the speaker or the writer as involved in a creative act, the act of putting words together in a unique form, but in such a way that the established principles of the system are observed. The transformationalist sees the basic problem of com-munication as that of devising as one proceeds a word relation-ship that will make meaning clear. Furthermore, he believes that the successful management of this task requires an understanding of the language's basic mechanics of operation.[10] At this point he appears to get closer to the traditional grammarian than does the structural linguist at any time.

One further implication of the transformationalist view seems pertinent here. Since he sees the student as a manufacturer of sentences that express the student's thoughts, the exercises in the transformationalist's textbook are designed to give the student practice in manufacturing clauses and sentences. He does not spend time and space in having the student correct the ineffective sentences of others, a better training for editors than for commu-nicators. Thus he departs from the traditional grammarian more notably in method or indoctrination process than in content.

Composition

In the teaching of composition, the emphasis is shifting from an almost exclusive cultivation of correctness of form and style to a stress of writing as a generator of thought and as a stimulant to logical organization and the understanding of relationships. Research has shown the traditional theme-correcting routine to

---

[10] See Paul Roberts, *English Syntax* (New York: Harcourt, Brace & Com-pany, 1964), pp. 8–16.

have little effect upon the quality of writing. Even the weekly theme, so much heralded in recent years, seems to be relatively ineffective in producing improved writing ability.[11]

Possibly effective writing may be undertaken only in connection with something about which the student feels an honest need to express himself, as was suggested in the type of student project described in Chapter 6. Perhaps it cannot be well done under stimuli and conditions that are wholly artificial. The task is a very difficult one. None that the high school undertakes is more elusive or more exacting. No department in the school calls for more imagination and experiment in leadership than does English. No teacher stands in more need of every encouragement, assistance, and support, financial and otherwise, than does the English teacher. His skills, the skills of communication, constitute the vehicle that carries much of the remainder of the curriculum. Such skills are no less important in the problems that plague society today.

Literature

The functions of literature, having long been significant, do not seem to have changed much, although the words used to describe them have. Literature is seen as an aesthetic experience, as a means of extending the reader's feeling to other times and places, as a way of recapturing life in another age or environment. Hence the reader has a tool for better understanding himself and his contemporaries. History recites only what happened. Literature adds the feelings of those who made it happen. It deepens insight into human experience. Its power to carry the reader across the world or back through history and to enable him to feel as he might have felt had he been there is one of the greatest manifestations of his humanity. "Through reading," says Professor Geraldine Murphy, "modern man can realize how a Renaissance subject felt about a king"—the adult can see "through the eyes of a child, the normal man can experience the world of an idiot."

---

[11] William H. Evans and Jerry L. Walker, *New Trends in the Teaching of English in Secondary Schools* (Chicago: Rand McNally, 1966), pp. 51–56.

Murphy also sees a moral function in literature as it provides a more genuine understanding, a "moral imagination" that "moderates moral intolerance."[12]

Perhaps the most promising change in the teaching of literature is related to the coming of the paperback, which enables the teacher easily to make individual adaptations, to introduce wider variety. Differences in individual pupil reading not only enrich the individual; they also give him more to contribute to his fellow students. Thus variety is added to an otherwise too confined curriculum, and the student gets additional experience and skill in directing his own learning.

Short Term Elective Courses

The English teacher's work covers so wide a range of objectives that the problem of inclusiveness is perhaps more perplexing in this field than in any other. The problem is no doubt partially responsible for the failure of English thus far to produce a dominant trend in innovation. One recent innovation that sweeps across the whole of high school English must have attention, however, in this section of the chapter. This is the trend toward making all or nearly all English courses elective and from nine weeks to one semester in length. In many places, too, such courses are ungraded; that is, each course may be elected by any student in the high school, regardless of his class level. Some high schools that have adopted this plan offer more than forty different courses, with typically only one or two required of all students.

Some curriculum specialists regard this advance upon curricular reform as reactionary. Indeed, it is reminiscent of the curriculum construction techniques of the high school of seventy-five years ago. Nevertheless, certain advantages must be recorded in its favor. First, it provides a flexibility for both students and teachers by offering the opportunity to teach and to study in an area that is consonant with personal interest. Second, the student, having chosen his course, is in no position to offer lack of interest as an excuse for indifference. Third, the teacher is in a position

---

[12] Geraldine Murphy, *The Study of Literature in the High School* (Waltham, Massachusetts: Blaisdell, 1968), pp. 25, 28.

that demands successful competition for customers; thus the incentive to produce is enhanced.

Experiment with this plan should lead to higher teacher satisfaction and higher teacher interest. The more interested teacher generally results in a more interested student. The plan is worthy of trial wherever this difficult subject has lapsed into pedestrian practices. But as with other innovations, the teacher most in need of stimulation is likely to be most resistant to change.

Social Studies

The predominant element in the new social studies, whether it is called reflective thought, the method of inquiry, or whatever, is designed to help the student escape from his imprisonment to the habit of thinking with his red corpuscles. It espouses rational thought. It urges the student to look beyond the obvious meaning of what he reads, to explore a number of additional or other possible meanings. It teaches the student to read between the lines, to reflect upon what the writer did not say as well as upon what he did say. The burden of teaching shifts from getting students to give answers to getting students to discover and explore meanings in answers. The teacher helps students to form the habit of dealing reflectively with wrong answers as well as with right.

The classic example of the teaching of reflective thought provided by Hunt and Metcalf is that of the conquest of Darius' empire by Alexander the Great with an army of 35,000 men.[13] The teacher questions the plausibility of the statement. Is it possible that a nation of millions of people submitted to an invading army of 35,000 soldiers? How or why? As the student pursues such questions, he eventually begins to realize some of the important differences between life in the ancient Persian Empire and life in his own country and time. He develops an appreciation of how little the millions of illiterates of early times really cared about who governed them or why.

[13] Maurice P. Hunt and Lawrence E. Metcalf, *Teaching High School Social Studies: Problems in Reflective Thinking and Social Understanding,* 2nd ed. (New York: Harper & Row, 1968), p. 71.

In essence the burden of this method is to develop in students the habit of weighing, questioning, and thinking about everything they see, hear, or read. In social studies they must learn to think analytically, soundly, and functionally about the matters that affect all society and themselves as members of that society. The aim is a long-held one but far less than generally honored. It calls for a teacher whose own depth of understanding is great. It is quite fully and ably interpreted in Hullfish and Smith's *Reflective Thinking: The Method of Education.*[14]

Nature of the Problem of Structure

Among the theorists who have attacked the problem of structure in generally applicable terms, no one has done so more clearly than Jerome Bruner, although he appears to make at least one seriously erroneous assumption that shall be discussed later.

Bruner sees certain advantages in all teaching and learning that give proper attention to structure. Among these are the following: First, structure makes further learning in the area easier. Second, through structure the specifics of the present lesson are related to the appropriate larger principles or general ideas of the entire field. Third, structure enhances the learner's independence by enabling him to go farther and deeper on his own. Fourth, structure emphasizes relationships and applicability. Fifth, it stresses permanent learning, enabling the learner to recognize throughout his life many variations of the phenomena now being studied. Finally, through structure the student learns what is basic, what is fundamental, what is foundational to all thought in his field of study.[15]

The error into which Bruner falls, one that has trapped many others, is an apparent belief that it is possible for secondhand learning to be first-class. Like Conant, he places too much faith in curricula or in the one who constructs the curricula. He says, "The first and most obvious problem is how to construct curricula

14 H. Gordon Hullfish and Philip G. Smith, *Reflective Thinking: The Method of Education* (New York: Dodd, Mead, 1961).

15 Jerome Bruner, *The Process of Education* (Cambridge: Harvard University Press, 1960), Introduction and Chapter 2.

that can be taught by ordinary teachers to ordinary students and that at the same time reflect clearly the basic or underlying principles of various fields of inquiry."[16] This view fails to make proper allowance for the fact that no teacher can teach what he does not know and fully understand. The only results that an ordinary teacher can get are ordinary results, no matter whose curricula is put into his hands. The only cures for an ordinary teacher are to take steps to make him extraordinary, to get rid of him, or to learn to live with his ordinariness. When will we learn that the great curriculum maker is the teacher, that it must be so in all education expected to approach what is first-rate?

Haven't many of our great cities demonstrated adequately over the past four decades, their bureaucracy having become too rigid, the deadening effect as well as the futility of the uniform curricula? Most state departments have abandoned such efforts over the same four decades, having exchanged their inspection functions for those of leadership and consultant services. Educational reform in the direction of the superb is not a matter of writing curricula. Whitehead reminds us that "knowledge does not keep any better than fish," and "it must come to the students—just drawn out of the sea and with the freshness of its immediate importance."[17] Incidentally, Whitehead is a great advocate of attention to structure, too. For the careful reader, he expresses all the ideas, although his vocabulary differs from that of the current disciples.

REASSESSMENT OF HUMAN INTELLIGENCE

The widespread interest in the reassessment of human intelligence and potential, which is more than an innovation, holds great hope for society as well as for education. In Chapter 2 it was suggested that one way forward in education leads us to recognition of the idea that unteachables are but few in number. Twentieth-century problems have finally forced society to accept a first-century idea. It is now recognized that even an affluent society like ours

---

[16] *Ibid.,* p. 18.
[17] Alfred North Whitehead, *The Aims of Education* (New York: Mentor Books, 1949), p. 102.

cannot afford to carry a fourth or a third of its citizens through life as noncontributors.

Scholars of each decade since the introduction of intelligence tests have doubted the capacity of these tests to measure human potential either accurately or fully. In the past two decades the doubters have greatly increased in number and in variety of background. The public schools of New York City have discontinued the use of such tests. In Britain, particularly among students of education and learning, there are mounting pressures for the abandonment of the "eleven-plus" examination, which has long determined admission to the academic secondary school. Conscientious directors of admissions in colleges and universities across the United States are ever more doubtful about their selection instruments, even when applied to students at the relatively mature age of eighteen years. These are simply some evidences of growing doubts about our ability to categorize human potential accurately at all.

In the past two decades the interest in taking another look at the social and intellectual potential of pupils has taken two forms. First is the examination of creativity in young people by researchers at the Universities of Chicago and Minnesota. Second is the growing interest in helping the culturally disadvantaged child, whether he lives in the city slum or in a pine thicket, to move into the mainstream of human society. These are very different aspects of a single but powerful educational idea, the reassessment of human potential.

Awareness of the criticisms hurled at the Getzels and Jackson and at the Paul Torrance studies on creativity prompts the observation that the quality of the studies, whatever it may have been, is not of concern here. What is relevant is the fact that there is a growing tendency to view more broadly human capacity to serve mankind, to view intelligence and potential in terms of an increased range of factors. The above mentioned are not the only studies on the creative interests and talents of young people. They represent pioneers in the area. Other studies will be made of social sensitivity or feeling for others and for still other neglected aspects of social intelligence or capacity. Just to call attention in tangible ways to areas of neglect is a signal service to education.

Efforts to make education practically as well as theoretically universal in a number of the nation's great cities have in recent years led to a startling reassessment of the intelligence of large portions of the population. What often has been written off as low intelligence has been revealed to be low incentive, low self-esteem, the result of limited cultural exposure, frequently the consequence of the individual's lack of vision of what he might do or become.

The net results of such experiment and investigation are leading to an ever more commonly held belief that promising intelligence is more widely scattered among the human species than many have previously supposed. (See the discussion of McGregor's *The Human Side of Enterprise* in Chapter 12.) Indeed, such findings raise serious doubt as to whether the distribution of native human intelligence follows the Gaussian curve at all. Perhaps only the opportunity for the development of human intelligence tends to follow the normal distribution curve.

Apparently the chief result of recent interest in the education of the culturally disadvantaged is that it has given both education and society new hope. Increasing numbers of people, educators and others, are coming to feel that intelligence and human potential are where one finds them and develops them. In the past educators have not been inclined to look very hard in some places, regarding the search as futile. Now there is new hope for the reality of universal education. Now it is becoming clear that neither the poor nor the ignorant must be always with us. More than ever, education threatens to become first of all a talent search, a search for talent in every individual, and then a developer of that talent.

Two scholars from the University of Hawaii more than lend their support to this thesis. They say, ". . . it is intelligence as output that should be the central concern of the educator." Among their other arguments for a revised thinking about the school's responsibilities are the following: First, since much American immigration came from Europe's lower classes, the hope for our nation offered by the Darwinian principle is not high. Second, definitive evidence on human potentialities is lacking. Third, people do their best when they are assumed to be capable. Fourth, there is more hope in an education in which the policies are based on optimistic assumptions about human capacity. Fifth, it is appropriate for American institutions to act in such ways as to create ability, increase intelligence, and develop interest. Finally, failure to establish real conditions of equal opportunity leaves the potential alternative of change through further violence and revolution.[18] These writers make quite clear the implications of their thinking for such devices as presently employed intelligence tests and ability grouping. Some scholars do not like it, but their thinking gives further evidence of how far the revolution in the reassessment of intelligence has advanced. Theirs, like ours, is a doctrine of hope.

SUMMARY

Innovative ideas affecting the high school are indeed widespread as the last third of the twentieth century begins. The pages of this chapter, hopefully, have opened up or reaffirmed for the reader the almost limitless potentials of the innovations discussed here. These ideas, intelligently and persistently acted upon, have the power to move education farther ahead than it has moved in the 400 years since Gutenberg. Such progress will occur, however, only if certain fundamental views of the whole school and the whole process of education are altered. Otherwise the school will be the same old show, with merely minor alterations in the mechanics of its staging.

Fundamental to a great harvest from innovation in the high school are deeper faith in the student and his interest in learning, more faith in the teacher as the curriculum maker, greater faith in the principal as the educational leader, more faith in variety of method and materials, less faith in the textbook and in outlines of whatever origin, less faith in precision and neatness of organization or in any mechanics, and finally, a willingness to encourage and to work with the individual student as he plays the lead role in the design of his own education. Any innovation, too, must keep its purposes clear and dominant, and its machinery subordinate to those purposes.

---

[18] William H. Boyer and Paul Walsh, "Are Children Born Unequal?" *Saturday Review,* October 19, 1968, p. 78.

11

Social Responsibility, a Major Aim

. . . we mutually pledge to each other our lives, our fortunes and our sacred honor.

Declaration of Independence

Rare is the school whose educational philosophy does not list near the top of its aims "preparation for responsible citizenship in a free society." Its wording varies, but it is always there. Its emphasis has been underscored since 1918, although the Reorganization Commission by no means invented it. To omit some such statement would be a breach of faith, bordering perhaps upon national disloyalty. The past dozen years may have given citizenship of certain kinds less emphasis, although even the most rightist critics do not advocate its elimination from school purpose. The school has long been recognized as the home's chief partner in transforming the neutral or selfish and antisocial child, depending upon one's philosophical viewpoint, into a positive, concerned, and reasonably altruistic adult citizen. To what extent is the school program directed at the realization of the aim?

Milton Eisenhower, president emeritus of Johns Hopkins University, recently observed that "we need a new breed of Americans who will devote as much time and energy to being wise democratic citizens as they do to being good physicians, engineers, or business men."[1] Like an increasing number of other leaders and thinkers, Mr. Eisenhower is recognizing that many of the gravest problems of today's society lie in the affective domain rather than in the cognitive. This is not to downgrade the importance of educational improvement in the realm of the cognitive. The school must move in that area, too. However, the behavioral or affective domain is equally in need of attention, because it is here that today's society hurts the worst.

Even an educational thinker such as Robert Maynard Hutchins, surely a conservative in curricular content, proclaims the business of education to be the development of wisdom and goodness,[2] and he berates the school for failure to develop social conscience. His position bears clearly upon both the psychological and social makeup of the individual. One who fails to turn his learning toward the long-range best interests of society, as well as of himself, can scarcely be cast as either wise or good. Personal behavior is involved. Social concern is involved. The things of the spirit, in the broadest and best sense, are involved.

How is it done? Patterns of behavior involve the formation of habit. One is habituated to a given mode of behaving by relentless practice in lifelike, preferably in real-life, situations. This means that citizenship cannot be taught from a book. It means that nowhere else is the laboratory method more essential. Nowhere else is learning to do by doing more important.

The teaching of citizenship or social responsibility requires the addition of an eighth element to Bloom's taxonomy of educational aims.[3] It lies far beyond translation, analysis, synthesis, or evaluation. That element might be called "involvement," with interpretive emphasis placed upon the useful and serviceable involvement of the student in problems within the school and in the society outside the school. To the degree that this element is neglected, to that degree shall the school continue to fall short

---

[1] Milton S. Eisenhower, "The Modern Imperative," commencement address, Kent State University, June 8, 1968.

[2] Robert M. Hutchins, *Education for Freedom* (Baton Rouge: Louisiana State University Press, 1943), p. 23. Hutchins' later books bear testimony to an unwavering view on this point.

[3] B. S. Bloom *et al. Taxonomy of Educational Objectives* (New York: Longmans, Green, 1956).

of its citizenship goal. This is an area where it is not enough to know; it is not enough to understand; it is not enough to appreciate; it is not enough to sympathize. It is necessary *to do*. Fairness to Mr. Bloom demands that his intentional limitation to the cognitive be recognized. The position here is that this is not enough.

THE AIM LONG HONORED

An examination of the ideas of a long list of respected educational thinkers through the ages reveals intensive and extensive support for the idea of education not only for interest in but also for adaptation and service to the society that nurtures the individual. It would seem to be self-evident that no society will for very long support an educational program that does not give young people substantial aid in adjusting to the expectations of life in that society.

Plato indicated the overriding purpose of his educational design to be "the greatest possible happiness of the city as a whole."[4] He pleaded also for an education that would develop wisdom and virtue, or at least for one that would work to bring these qualities to the top.

The Roman thinker Quintilian, in his *Institutes of Oratory*, indicated that he thought copybook exercises should be heavily charged with moral truths or lessons, further noting that he was sure that the impressions thus gained played a part in the formation of the youth's character.

Michel de Montaigne, the great French essayist and philosopher, made his educational priorities clear by noting that "after having taught our pupil what will make him wise and good, you may then teach him the elements of logic, physics, geometry, and rhetoric."[5]

"Reading, and writing, and learning, I allow to be necessary," said the British philosopher John Locke, "but not yet the

[4] Robert Ulich, *Three Thousand Years of Educational Wisdom* (Cambridge: Harvard University Press, 1950), p. 40.

[5] *Ibid.*, p. 294.

chief business. I imagine you would think him a very foolish
fellow, that should not value a virtuous, or a wise man, infinitely
before a great scholar."[6] Continuing his counsel on the selection
of the schoolmaster, Locke said:

> Learning must be had, but in the second place as subservient
> only to greater qualities . . . place him [the pupil] in hands,
> where you may, as much as possible, secure his innocence,
> cherish and nurse up the good and gently correct and weed out
> any bad inclinations, and settle in him good habits.[7]

The great American universalist, Benjamin Franklin, in both
his famous *Autobiography* and in his *Proposals Relating to the
Education of Youth in Pennsylvania* stressed the tremendous
importance of the development of personal qualities. Indeed, it
is difficult to measure the influence of the Franklin proverbs upon
American character in either past or future generations. That
Franklin saw education as a cultural influence is manifest in his
often-quoted observation that

> it would be well if they could be taught everything that is useful,
> and everything that is ornamental: But art is long, and their time
> is short. It is therefore propos'd that they learn those things that
> are likely to be most useful and most ornamental.[8]

Franklin used the word ornamental as we today use the term
cultural.

After elaborating upon his views of the subject matter com-
partments to be placed in the curriculum of the academy and his
specific expectations of each, Franklin closed his 1749 prescription for the education of youth with the following two paragraphs:

> With the whole should be constantly inculcated and cultivated,
> that *Benignity of Mind*, which shows itself in *searching for* and
> *seizing* every Opportunity *to serve* and *to oblige;* and is the

[6] *Ibid.*, from John Locke's *Some Thoughts on Education*, p. 373.
[7] *Ibid.*, p. 374.
[8] *Ibid.*, p. 444.

Foundation of what is called GOOD BREEDING; highly useful to the Possessor, and most agreeable to all.

The Idea of what is *true Merit* should also be often presented to Youth, explain'd and impress'd on their Minds, as consisting in an Inclination join'd with an *Ability* to serve Mankind, one's Country, Friends and Family; which *Ability* is (with the blessing of God) to be acquir'd or greatly encreas'd by *true Learning;* and should indeed be the great *Aim* and *End* of all Learning.[9]

Johann Heinrich Pestalozzi, whose interest in education grew out of his concern for a score of Swiss orphans of the Napoleonic wars, proclaimed his platform in *The Evening Hour of a Hermit.* He said "all human wisdom is founded on the strength of a good and truthful heart and all human happiness on simplicity and purity."[10] In *How Gertrude Teaches Her Children,* he has Gertrude in one of her more talkative moments advising a fellow teacher as follows:

You should do for your children what their parents fail to do for them. The reading, writing and arithmetic are not, after all, what they most need; it is all well and good for them to learn something, but the really important thing is for them to *be* something,—for them to become what they are meant to be, and in becoming which they so often have no guidance or help at home.[11]

The man who perhaps influenced thought and action in American education more than any other during the latter part of the nineteenth and the very early years of the twentieth century was the German, Johann Friedrich Herbart. He observed that

. . . those schools, whose main function is merely teaching and learning cannot be considered as serving education in the deepest sense of the word . . .

[9] *Ibid.,* p. 448.
[10] *Ibid.,* p. 483.
[11] *Ibid.,* p. 502.

It follows that education in order to have a permanent effect must try to use instruction not only for mere information but also for the formation of character.[12]

The first sentence quoted above should probably be read with an emphasis upon the *merely*, the second with an emphasis on the *mere*.

The wholeness of man, the complete and necessary unity of the human mind, motives, and spirit, the view that education in all its most noble fulfillments is essentially a function of the total human self: these are constantly recurring aspects of the educational philosophy of Friederich Wilhelm Froebel, the father of the kindergarten. They clearly and repeatedly imply that there is no real education apart from the development of character and total personality. It is the author's belief that they imply that no matter what is being taught, character is being developed, for better or for worse.

The great twentieth-century philosopher, Alfred North Whitehead, British-bred but mellowed at Harvard University where for many years he held a chair of philosophy, made indelibly clear his belief in an education that ministered to the whole man with a special emphasis upon character. "Moral education," said he, "is impossible apart from the habitual vision of greatness. If we are not great, it does not matter what we do or what is the issue."[13]

John Dewey, at whose work earlier educators often looked uncritically, and whose work has been in recent years condemned by those either ignorant of it or too anxious to be aboard popular bandwagons, warned against smug acceptance of the status quo. At the same time he fully acknowledged social efficiency, civic efficiency, and culture as legitimate and important aims of all education worthy of the name.[14]

Finally, President Nathan M. Pusey of Harvard University supported the intent of this chapter when he said, "... it is not

[12] *Ibid.*, p. 510.

[13] Alfred North Whitehead, *The Aims of Education* (New York: Mentor Books, 1949), p. 77.

[14] John Dewey, *Democracy and Education* (New York: Macmillan, 1916). See Chapter 9, "Natural Development and Social Efficiency as Aims."

sufficient for modern man to know, but he must also be and do."[15] At numerous other points he stresses his concern for the hearts as well as the heads of students.

A basic assumption listed in Chapter 2 stated that our secondary schools have achieved more in the bundle of aims that include skills, health, and vocational preparation than they have in the citizenship–character–personal development cluster. Our greater effectiveness with technical than with social man was noted. It will be recalled, also, that economist Barbara Ward, Herbert Spencer, and John Ruskin were called upon to support the stated position. Although numerous others could be listed and quoted, these, along with the other leaders cited here, surely provide adequate support from notable and respected thinkers who represent the best of Western traditions and thought.

STATED AIMS OF SECONDARY SCHOOLS

American secondary education was slow to state its avowed aims. No careful effort or clear statement was forthcoming prior to the work of the Reorganization Commission in 1916–1918, as was indicated in Chapter 2. The work of this commission has come to be popularly known as the Seven Cardinal Principles of American education and has found its way into school books on citizenship and sociology and wherever American education is discussed. "Aims" is a more accurate term than "principles," for the phrases used are in terms of aims. Although these aims have been juggled and restated from time to time and were expanded to ten by the Educational Policies Commission in 1939, who entitled them the "Ten Imperative Needs of Youth," such refinements appear to have brought little improvement over the 1918 pronouncement. It is worth noting, too, that no responsible national educational body appears to be on record as having renounced the Seven Cardinal Principles.

There is here no implication that each of these seven principles or aims is equally important. Any such weighting is a

[15] Nathan M. Pusey, *The Age of the Scholar: Observations on Education in a Troubled Decade* (Cambridge: Belknap Press, Harvard, 1964), p. 181.

matter of practical impossibility. It is interesting to note, however, that four of the seven, which were called earlier the modern
quadrivium, deal with the development of citizenship and character values. These are briefly phrased as follows: (1) citizenship,
(2) ethical character, (3) worthy homemembership, and (4) worthy
use of leisure. The remaining three, (5) health, (6) vocational
preparation and guidance, and (7) command of fundamental
processes, are not directly pointed at citizenship or character.
Broadly conceived, even these make indirect contributions to
character and development of the whole person.

EXAMPLES OF TEACHING SOCIAL
RESPONSIBILITY

Despite a rather general neglect of the planned teaching of
responsibility for one's environment and for the welfare of one's
community and fellow citizens, there are here and there both
principals and teachers who give this aspect of education persistent thought and careful attention. In order to make the argument of this chapter tangible and useful, the paragraphs that
follow provide real examples of such thought and attention by
a principal and by teachers.

Student Sense of Ownership in the School

A. T. McDonnell had been principal of the Oakwood Elementary
School for twenty years. He was respected and loved by 525
pupils and their parents not so much for his erudition and scholarship as for his forward-looking educational ideas and for his
convictions about the kinds of experiences important to young
people. One Monday his superintendent paid Mr. McDonnell an
early morning visit in his small and unimpressive office, in a
building then over fifty years old and showing its age.

   In the course of this conference there came into the office a
fourth-grade girl, who merely exchanged greetings with her
principal and then went to a simple and somewhat ancient
adding machine. From a paper she held in her hand she rang up

some figures and produced a total. Going next to the telephone and without checking with anyone, she called the dairy and gave the school's milk order for that week. Milk orders at Oakwood were regarded as a fourth-grade job.

Although some elementary schools in 1970 are just getting around to the establishment of central libraries, McDonnell had one at Oakwood more than thirty years earlier. It had a librarian on duty every period of the day each day in the week. Library service was a sixth-grade job. Few sixth-graders finished at Oakwood without having the experience for a period a day for at least a few weeks. And so it went throughout the school and throughout the year.

After the fourth-grade girl mentioned above had completed her work and left the office, the superintendent turned to the principal and said, "Mac, you do the best job of anyone that I ever saw of giving the students in your school a sense of ownership in it. How do you do it?" The principal, a modest man, was somewhat embarrassed by this high compliment, and after some delay pulled himself together and replied, "Well I guess you have to believe that it's important, and I happen to believe that such experiences are important to young people."

Thus Principal McDonnell announced in his way what the Kellogg Foundation studies in school administration revealed a few years later after careful and extended investigation: the convictions an administrator holds, those things he feels to be worthy of repeated and varied emphasis, do make the difference.

Self-Rule by Pupils

Miss Leona Wilson, a young sixth-grade teacher, had 46 pupils in her rather small postwar classroom. Despite the oversize of the class and the undersize of the room, there were in evidence six pupil projects in science. One was an astronomical mock-up with a pasteboard Mars suspended by a thread. Another involved a battery-fed light bulb that the pupils had constructed.

Miss Wilson's visitor, honestly puzzled, inquired, "How in the world do you manage such delicate projects under such conditions?" "Well," said the teacher, "we hadn't gone very far until the pupils themselves realized that something must be done about this. They realized the need for some rules or regulations. With my encouragement, they set up their own. They decided that no one should so much as touch any project unless a pupil who was on that particular committee was present to demonstrate it. Children are often more demanding of themselves," she observed, "than are adults. Further, they made the penalty high: a week's exclusion from all such activity life of the class." At this point her visitor, an experienced educational observer, said: "Miss Wilson, you are not only doing a good job of teaching science. This is a superb example of the kind of citizenship teaching our young people most need."

Students Involved in Building Learning Quarters

Young Mr. McAuliffe had just been employed as the vocational agriculture teacher in a fairly large high school where the subject for some time had lagged a bit. It was his second teaching assignment. He went to his superintendent, saying, "I just wish we could have a farm shop. It could be made to mean so much." "There's the carriage house, behind the Shively residence, which was a gift to the school system some years ago," said the superintendent. "Why don't you take that and see what you and the boys can do toward turning it into a farm shop? Wouldn't it be somewhat like the type of building that might become the shop on a fairly large farm?"

The teacher and his agriculture students rehabilitated the building, a farm shop project in itself. They overcame, to a degree, insulation problems, heating problems, bench and tool problems, and a host of others, with a minimum outlay of school dollars. Two years later the school board decided to encourage Mr. McAuliffe further. They provided a quonset-type steel building that permitted tractor overhaul and such activity. It is safe to assert, however, that no later group of boys in farm shop at this school ever had a richer experience than those who developed their own facility. The development of resourcefulness and self-reliance is a priceless educational outcome. It is basic to solid citizenship.

These are examples of the school serving as a genuine laboratory in citizenship development. The list could be extended. Readers of experience are able to add their own examples. Later in this chapter other examples are used for clarification.

The more skeptical reader may be inclined at this point to observe that the examples given represent only very rare persons, that schools generally cannot hope to move in such directions. This position is only partially true. The persons involved were in most cases not particularly rare in talents or education. In their scale of values, in their belief in the importance of developing personal and social responsibility in young people, they were indeed rare. They believed in the rewards that accrue to the young who are privileged to share directly in the burdens of the social group's forward motion, whatever its nature.

This raises a very important question. Are we ready to accept citizenship development as a high-priority school aim? If we are, then we must learn to behave very differently from the way we generally do now.

WHO IS TO DEVELOP SOCIAL RESPONSIBILITY?

It is a common paradox that the school task that is broadest and most significant in its reach is quite often one that is also neglected. What is everybody's job frequently becomes nobody's job. Yet there is no escape from the view that the teaching of citizenship is a job of the total school. It cannot be seen as the sole responsibility of the social studies department, for neither the understanding nor the appreciation the department can teach is the same as actually doing. Yet social studies teachers should be more deeply involved than they normally are. They should see themselves as conceivers and promoters much more frequently than is the case, and the formal classroom effort in the field should be linked to the doing in other fields more frequently than common practice reflects.

If citizenship education is any one person's job more than that of any other, it is the leader's job. The principal of the school, if imaginative, if alert, if convinced and constantly thinking of the necessity, is in the best position to see the greatest

number of possibilities. His vantage point offers the best overall
view of the school in terms of its total responsibility, in its relationships to the community, and in its shortcomings in servicing
its student clientele. If he is too easily satisfied, if he is smug and
complacent, the chances are good that the school will achieve
little in this area.

ASSUMPTIONS OF WHAT IS GOOD

Here it seems appropriate to state some further assumptions. It
is assumed that honesty, truthfulness, and fair dealing are essential in our kind of society. It is assumed that such behavior is a
matter of practical necessity, that our kind of civilization cannot
be sustained on any other basis. This truth was made vivid more
than thirty years ago by an editorial and a cartoon in *Scholastic
Magazine*.[16] The magazine had sought the best answer to a young
man who had written for a popular journal of the time a story
entitled "Honesty Does Not Pay." The school magazine, which
received many replies, pointed out that no one stressed the idea
that any advantage accruing to dishonesty is dependent upon
most others in the society being thoroughly honest. It further
noted that "Dishonesty feeds on trustfulness." The accompanying
cartoon, portraying a world-wide society of dishonest people,
showed questionable characters formed in a circle as if to play
"ring around the rosy" or "drop the handkerchief." In this case,
however, each player was lifting the wallet from the hip pocket
of the man just ahead of him. The implication was indelibly clear.
A dishonest society simply cannot survive. Quite apart from any
religious basis or Judaic-Christian ethic, honesty, truthfulness,
and completely fair dealing with our fellow man is a matter of
utter necessity. Its necessity and its practicality must be taught in
social studies, in literature, in assemblies, and throughout the
school's program.

[16] Editorial, "Honesty in a Dishonest World," *Scholastic Magazine*, 24:8
(March 24, 1934), p. 1.

Lawlessness Rising in All Segments of Society

It is assumed that the United States, along with some other parts of the world, is experiencing and has been experiencing for twenty years a widespread deterioration of moral and ethical values. The figures are too well known to require lengthy elaboration: The 1967 crime rate was 71 percent over the 1960 rate and 15.3 percent over the 1966 rate, increases that assure doubling in six years unless checked. Furthermore, the increase affects all kinds of communities, all segments of society, and all regions.[17] And criminals are younger each year, although moral dereliction is not limited to the youth or the culturally deprived. Let it be noted that President Kennedy, in requesting Congress for legislation to plug federal income tax leaks in 1961, estimated that tax evasions on building and loan dividends alone were costing the federal government almost half a billion dollars a year. That building and loan deposits are most often held by older people is generally acknowledged.

Many believe that moral lapses are found only among the lowly or culturally deprived. This is contradicted by the example of thirty electric manufacturing company executives arraigned before and sentenced by Federal District Judge J. Cullen Ganey in Philadelphia in early 1961.[18] Some of these men were vice-presidents of their respective companies and were regarded as highly successful persons. To them, however, signing non-collusion affidavits meant nothing at all. They contrived to "take" their government for whatever they thought they could make look reasonable. Thus they conspired to defraud all taxpayers of the entire United States.

In his book *Education and the Common Good*, Philip Phenix bemoans the generally low level of concern for the common weal. His thesis is that the "democracy of desire," growing as it does out of our worship of materialistic achievement and material possessions, has crowded the "democracy of worth," which promises a much more glorious future, into a very poor second place. So much have we emphasized things rather than people that the

---

[17] J. Edgar Hoover, *Uniform Crime Reports—1967*, pp. 1, 62–67.

[18] "Price Fixing Brings Jail Terms," *Business Week*, February 11, 1961, pp. 34–35.

schools are often severely criticized for not treating pupils as things rather than as persons.[19]

Moral Tone in Other Nations

A third assumption worthy of note and capable of support is that some nations or societies seem to be more effective than our society in maintaining moral tone. This matter appears to deserve more extensive and more intensive attention at the hands of educational leaders and teachers than it usually receives.

A recent popular magazine article was devoted to an analysis of the reasons behind the strikingly low rate of juvenile delinquency in Switzerland. Three notable differences from conditions existing in the United States were given no small share of the credit. First, auto driver licenses are not granted until age eighteen, thus curtailing the range of juvenile social operation. Second, adult movies are not open to youth and children, and the penalty for ticket sale violation is high. Third, and perhaps more important than either of the others, is the pressure that the industrious Swiss parents put upon their children to think about and establish early their vocational goals. Although Switzerland has enjoyed what is probably the highest prosperity level in Europe during most of the twentieth century, vocational success and prosperity must still be carefully planned. Consequently, parents keep saying to their children, "You must make something of yourself! You simply have to develop a plan for your life." In the reinforcement of this pressure, the rigorously prepared Swiss teachers no doubt give parents regular and recurring support. It is most probable that many fewer Swiss than American youth arrive at age eighteen with no notion whatsoever as to how they wish to invest their lives. Certainly this is a matter to which American educators, despite burgeoning counseling programs in recent years, have given too little attention. Clearly defined and regularly nurtured vocational goals provide one of the very best educational incentives and tend to promote in youth the stability that is required in every society.

[19] Philip Phenix, *Education and the Common Good* (New York: Harper and Brothers, 1961).

It is difficult to make comparisons between the goals and achievements of one society and another. Many have attempted, nevertheless, to compare Russia's strength in science and engineering with that of the United States. Americans often have expressed the fear that their nation is being outrun by Russia in certain segments of the scientific and technological fronts. Few have worried that Russia may be building into her citizens, present and future, a greater personal integrity, a more keenly whetted devotion to the general welfare, and a more cultivated respect for one's obligations to his fellow citizens. In Russian schools, however, an organization called the Pioneers, its motto "Always ready," has promoted and nurtured as its central aims devotion to one's compatriots and to the general welfare. Service to the community and to old or neglected persons is added to indoctrination to establish the dual nature of its method. Membership in the society is unlimited, and in many schools the flame-colored silk tie, its insignia, appears to be worn by a large majority of the pupils.

Other and possibly better illustrations than these may come to the reader's mind. He will seldom be inclined to question the assumptions, however, and the implications for school emphasis in social studies, in literature, and in the all-around management of the school.

HISTORY FOR PERSPECTIVE AS WELL AS LOYALTY

The gravest weaknesses of society in the United States tend to spring directly from its most notable strengths. Self-esteem, both personally and nationally, is an admirable and necessary quality, and it has its advantages. Carried to extremes, it also holds certain disadvantages. In some ways "we the people" are still heady from becoming such a success in such a relatively short time. Many would-be friends abroad see cockiness as a national characteristic. Humility is too seldom a significant element in our national character. We are reluctant to reflect real concern for weakness until we come up against a national crisis that demands it. This applies with greater force to domestic than to international crises. For example, all the problems relating to race, to social and physical blight, to impure air and water, have been with us for a long time. It is general concern and the will to act that have been missing. Would it not seem to be in the best national interest to exercise greater foresight through the analysis of weakness and, hopefully, the application of remedial measures before we come face to face with the full impact of the problem? Is the creation of concern for the future along with pride in the past a proper function of education?

The best citizenship and patriotism do not rest upon the pretense that evils, shortages, or weaknesses do not exist in our society. The school that is to strengthen its instruction in this area must make sure that it employs a teacher who is a genuine student of his teaching field. It must assure itself that he knows the difference between the pseudo or superficial patriot and one whose loyalty is based upon thorough knowledge and full understanding. Finally, this teacher must always work under the full assurance that school board and administrator policies provide him complete protection against unwarranted attack from any quarter. Only then can the teacher function as a professional. Only then can he help the student gain that honest perspective which will serve both his and the national interest most fully.

Norman Cousins editorialized in the *Saturday Review* as follows:

> . . . to have reached a peak in some fields today does not necessarily mean that civilization is now at a pinnacle from which man can look back upon and down upon long ages of mass delusion. We live a life of compartmentalization; some sections are marked with glittering splendor; others are as dimly lit as they were thousands of years ago.[20]

He might well have added that some areas of life were much more brilliantly understood and appreciated and had contributed much more to the edification of humanity in eras gone by than is anywhere true today. Note, for example, the superb and lasting qualities of Grecian and Gothic architecture. This theme,

---

[20] Norman Cousins, "Out in the Open," *Saturday Review*, April 2, 1960, p. 24.

however, will receive further attention a little later. In the meantime, attention is turned to some possible remedies for weaknesses, oversights, and failures either stated or implied in the past few pages.

GREATER RESPECT FOR PAST AGES

World history must be presented with a more appropriate emphasis upon the noble and great achievements of men and ages that are past. This means, for example, that a more careful and complete introduction to the life and thought of ancient Greece at her best is needed. Such perspectives must not be submerged in the labyrinth of military and political affairs. Generally speaking, the story of man's past has not been told with the purpose of cultivating deep respect for the achievements of earlier man's mind, vision, and patience. This is no doubt at least partly responsible for an unbecoming and unhelpful cockiness that, too often displayed by American tourists abroad, goes far to undo the better image that American billions funneled through State Department foreign aid programs have sought to build.

High Respect for Thought in Ancient Greece

Consider ancient Greece—or more precisely, Athens—and the city-state of Attica. Where else in such a short span of time, and with fewer than half a million people, has so much been contributed to the life, thought, and art of the Western world? Where, in modern times, in the United States or elsewhere, have we had the throne of the mind occupied in three successive generations by a Socrates, a Plato, and an Aristotle? For that matter, how often have we had a Euclid or a Phidias? Perhaps little Attica produced so many great minds between 500 and 300 B.C. because the better educated men of that day actually believed that life offered no higher calling than contemplation, analysis, and thought upon life's nobler purposes. It is quite probable, too, that at no other time in man's history upon this planet has there been such reverence for life itself and its possibilities. If citizens are to have balance and a proper humility, they must be taught a profound respect for the life of thought produced by the Golden Age of ancient Greece. Similarly, students must be taught to seek out and to respect other pinnacles of both long ago and far away.

With all of its eventual weaknesses, Roman society, too, had strengths that command the respect of moderns. The Roman genius for organization, both political and military, its amazing aqueducts and pure water supplies, its superb highways, its round arches, its public buildings and its cathedrals: all these were amazing developments for their day and time.

Great Patience of Medieval Man

Then the Middle Ages, especially the later Middle Ages, brought the construction of cathedrals, which sometimes took a hundred and fifty years or more to build and demonstrated a patience unparalleled by modern man anywhere in the world. Incidentally, they brought also all the wonders of Gothic architecture and the still unrivaled art of stained and leaded glass windows. All of this was the work of a people who had no printing press for the cheap and ready dissemination of know-how.

With respect to man's patience, the great Canadian arctic explorer, Vilhjalmur Stefansson, says that modern man has not demonstrated the patience to domesticate a single animal. Among the good chances that have been missed are the buffalo, the musk-ox, and perhaps a number of fowl.

GREATER RESPECT FOR TODAY'S UNSOLVED PROBLEMS

Many men of the Middle Ages lived miserably and narrowly, and the general health level was frightfully low. Many, however, eventually dared to dream of a better life, dared to venture and to promote change in a society unfriendly to change and adventure. The world today is immensely richer for the thousands who courageously faced new ventures of every kind, for those who dared to turn their backs upon practices generally accepted and generally approved in their day. We must teach youth that our country was founded upon and gained its strengths from the ideas of heretics, from people who found it oppressive and uncomfortable where great conformity was required. A free man must never fail to respect honest dissent and to respect the progress that springs from it.

Today's youth must understand that the world suffers from an excess of conformity, from a refusal to face problems no less real and no less frightening than those of the Middle Ages. Is it not the job of the school to foster a social perspective that sees today's city slums as no less degrading, no less threatening, than Roman slavery or medieval serfdom? The means to eradicate this societal cancer have been available to us for at least two generations. What has been lacking is a gripping sense of the proportions of the problem and a general will to act. What has been lacking is a cultivated regard for the long-range consequences. What Americans have consistently refused to do in this regard has been to devote themselves unstintingly to the promotion of the general welfare, as the Constitution's Preamble commands them to do.

Stated American Principles Forsaken?

Americans have often turned their backs upon their own noblest principles. They have conveniently forgotten that the Declaration of Independence, in its climactic sentence, commits them as follows: ". . . we mutually pledge to each other our lives, our Fortunes, and our sacred Honor." Often Americans have been unwilling to pledge a sufficient portion of their abundant fortunes, in either taxes or personal effort, to the social and educational rehabilitation of the slum, an increasing portion of the nation's great cities. The result has been a sharply rising delinquency, a sharply rising illegitimacy—in short, an ever larger number for whom life is utterly aimless and devoid of meaning. We have at long last awakened to the sad fact that the costs of the problem cannot be dodged, that previous neglect must now be paid in higher taxes and higher insurance, by providing sustenance for millions who have not been helped to develop the desire and the skill to sustain themselves.

It is the business of an effective education to teach young people that while experience is in truth the best teacher, it is also a dear teacher, and very often it is a destructive and a degrading one. The educated learner learns in less costly ways.

An education that fails to make the student keenly aware of the failures and unmet problems of society today is unjust and unfair not only to the society but also to the individual who will have to live with those failures and those unmet problems.

Unmet Problems Follow Gains

While our high schools teach in both world and American history of the wondrous changes wrought in ways of doing work, in lifting the burdens of drudgery from the backs of man—and it is important to teach this, and to teach it well—they must not fail to teach the unsolved problems that these changes have left in their wake. While the schools teach of the wonders of mechanical cotton pickers, they must not fail to teach of the plight of the Southern Negro who has been thereby driven out of the rural environment where his services had been wanted and into the least desirable and least encouraging section of a Northern or Western city where he has no marketable skill and where he seems unwanted. Here he bounces intermittently from one odd job or short-term employment situation to another, spending much time on relief roles and in utter boredom. The youth of America must know and understand that American machinery and industrial advance have not been unmixed blessings, that Americans have often been guilty of trying to extract the sweet without facing the bitter, thereby attempting to repeal an immutable law.

Even for the somewhat more typical and somewhat better educated worker, the transition from the seventy-two-hour work week to the forty-hour week has brought unsolved social problems. For many there seems to be only the choice between the inane pastimes of the mass media and a second job (moonlighting). The void of idle hours must be filled, constructively or otherwise. Social scientists of every stripe have been for some time calling attention to the failure to cultivate widespread interest in creative and rewarding ways of self-fulfillment. One evidence of the fact that this need is real and not merely the figment of philosophical imagination is seen in the recent waves of interest in commercially marketed do-it-yourself kits.

Self-Fulfillment as a Need

While schools, through the teaching of health and diet, have given attention to teaching their pupils how to live longer, they must give much more imaginative attention to teaching them how to live more purposefully and more rewardingly. The golden-age years, the years of retirement, are economically and physically comfortable years for an increasing number. They are years of mental and emotional boredom for far too many. Shuffleboard and bridge have their limits as major excuses for existence. Even foreign travel, for those whose means permit it, can soon be wrung dry unless it is firmly tied to ongoing and carefully cultivated interests of breadth or depth. A monthly or even weekly vaudeville or variety show was rewarding and harmlessly aided the regeneration of the spirit of many individuals a generation or so ago. Six to a dozen variety shows a week, however, presented by television, with or without technicolor, dull the appetite and tempt the viewer to go into the letters-to-the-editor business.

Activities for senior citizens, like activities for youth, must be constructively rewarding. They must lead to a feeling that what has been done matters, and preferably that it matters to someone besides themselves. Most retired persons, both male and female, are not only physically capable but would be far better off, both physically and mentally, if they engaged regularly in socially useful work from two to four hours a day, five days a week. In abundance such work cries out for attention, while the feeling of uselessness destroys many retired persons. Such uselessness is hardest to endure for those who in earlier years have been most useful. Our society has found very few shining ways to meet the problems of retirement. Only the problems of sustenance have been solved. Education for living is involved. School experiences that involve service to others, spelled out below, must be sponsored. Young people must learn, while they are young, of the great satisfactions, of the self-fulfillment that can come from involvement in real service to the community and to those persons who most need help.

The distressing distance between youth and age might well be bridged by imaginative projects in public work that now never gets done, but on which the forces of both might be joined with good, stimulating, and wholesome effects upon both. Youth might well furnish the greater part of the muscle and the leg work while age contributes more heavily to technique, judgment, and strategy. The social and emotional effect upon both is sure to be invigorating and rewarding.

HUMANITARIAN AND AMERICAN IDEALS

Man's centuries-long struggle for freedom, dignity, and self-realization must receive recurring emphasis in all possible phases of the school's total curriculum. Original documents, in translation where necessary, must be introduced more frequently and given careful, analytical attention. Contracts of human bondage, titles or bills of sale for human property, along with better known documents that concern the human rights of greater numbers will help to make meanings more vivid. Our schools are too frequently guilty of trying to get first-class results from the use of secondhand merchandise, overlooking the fact that a secondhand idea is no more appealing than a secondhand garment.

Whether the source is the death-chamber words of Socrates to Crito upon immortality or whether it is the Charter of the United Nations, in the hands of an imaginative teacher the original source is worth a dozen discussions about the source. The student must read the words of Magna Carta. Many of them are as clear to us today as when King John affixed his signature to them in 1215: "To no one will we sell, to no one will we deny, or delay, right or justice." The student must realize clearly that the principle of no taxation without representation, a phrase that was thrown back at England's King George by the American colonies some five and one-half centuries later, was established by this charter, that it was reaffirmed by numerous later kings, and that it was later written into the national Constitution and laws of every American state.

These needs and illustrations make abundantly clear why not just any teacher can be assigned an extra class in history or literature, a practice too often forced by expediencies of the past. They also underscore the need for the leader of the school to be a man whose interests reach beyond the provincial, whose reading and outlook are broad. He sees himself as the head of an organization that is expected to prepare young people for that mutual respect among world citizens which is the only sound basis for a universally prosperous and peaceful twenty-first century.

SOCIAL CONSCIENCE

By what means may a social conscience and social responsibility be developed? By the laboratory method, by the active and varied involvement of the learner, by practice in doing. Lip service cannot be depended upon to assure results. No amount of lecturing, reading, discussion, viewing motion pictures, or armchair analyses can be expected to develop such capacities.

Despite the detail with which the necessity for altered views and emphases in history and literature have been discussed in the past few pages, the main job of citizenship development lies in the activity in which the student engages. By way of summation for this chapter, these activities are broken into three categories with explanation and illustrations or means of implementing given for each.

School and Public Service Projects

Public service is here seen as either service to the school or service to the community, usually the local community, although there is no intent to exclude the county, the state, or even the nation. High school students might very well assist, for example, with improvements at a state park or shrine.

In and around any school there are countless opportunities for betterment through the expenditure of varying degrees of skill and human energy. Among the most valuable lessons any young human being can learn are those that come from constructive cooperation with others in the achievement of a mutually satisfying and visible goal which stands as an enduring testimony to the sweat and planning of all. Students, by investing their creative power and energy under the counsel and help of a wise teacher, are capable of making any schoolroom in America a more interesting place to be, a more functional place, and above all, a more educational environment.

The Group Project as a Class Activity

A suburban school the writer visited had doubled its size by a new addition some four or five years before. Beautiful and appropriate shrubs had been added to enhance the grounds, but those shrubs had been attended only by obvious and complete neglect from the day of their planting. They appeared to be fighting a losing battle with weeds and insects. Although within that school were held classes in biology, classes whose presumed function is an understanding of plant, animal (including insects), and human life, the laboratory outside the door was completely ignored. A home management class should find challenge in this situation, too. A high order of citizenship instruction, a sense of the management of and responsibility for common property, would result from intelligently managed student involvement in the rehabilitation of the school's landscaping. The strength and power of youth is not augmented by giving them everything and asking of them nothing. Furthermore, they do not appreciate it. Rather, they answer with boredom, and sometimes rebellion.

Effort in a Common Cause

In most communities are found public parks, gardens, old cemeteries, recreation centers, and other institutions that are objects of neglect. Most of these are capable of responding to the concern and attention of high school students. To them the rewards of involvement would run the range of educational aims.

The small city in which this writing is being done has a potentially beautiful, small, and historic river. In the words of a British visitor, however, the city "really doesn't make much of its river." Four successive mayors have talked about beautifying the river valley, but the project has advanced little beyond the contemplation (from the bridge) of what might be done. What might happen to this river valley if the interest and energy of a few hundred high school students were wedded to the direction, help, and know-how of teachers and a few dozen Jaycees? The electrification of every civic-minded group in the city and gifts of shrubs from as much as hundreds of miles away would not be too much to expect.

Civic projects represent an imaginative opportunity for the expanding summer school. Many students, especially those too young or unable to find summer jobs, might wish to make their major civic contributions then. At the same time the summer school may need the potential enhancement it might get from such projects by its supporting public, its program often having been rather narrowly conceived, limited in aim, and meagerly supported.

Artificial incentives being rather highly regarded in our society, it is proposed that student effort in behalf of the general welfare be appropriately recognized. It is assumed that participation is to be for the most part voluntary, that much of it will represent after-school, Saturday, and vacation hours. The school might arrange to present to any student making a significant contribution in this area a certificate or citation of public service. It might be called a Service Citation, a Public Spirit Award, a Better Life Award, or a Better Zanesville Award. If one wished to be more classic, the General Welfare Award (Preamble to the Constitution) or the Sacred Honor Citation (Declaration of Independence) might appeal. A feeling of demand would be carried by the Public Duty Award.

Awards should not be given for superficial or casual effort. The Saturday morning paper drive as a money-raising enterprise, for however worthy a cause, would not qualify. If only those about to graduate are to qualify, the demands would be greater than if awards are to be made annually. In this case nothing less than the equivalent of 30 eight-hour days, or 240 hours, should qualify for the highest citation, and care should be exercised to make sure that all certificates represent genuine effort. A faculty-student committee could establish criteria and pass on all citations.

Cultivation of Service to Individuals or Groups

Elsewhere in this work the growing number of humanities courses is discussed and commended. These courses help the student answer significant questions such as, Who am I? What is life? What is its purpose? What makes one more or less human? This is important, but the school must not stop here.

The brotherhood of man is affirmed not only by all of the principal occidental religions and philosophies but by oriental religions and philosophies as well. It has been reaffirmed in the credo of the United Nations. If the school is to make any considerable contribution to the development of the individual's capacity to serve as his brother's keeper, it must lose no opportunity to let him feel the satisfaction that comes from the experience of socially, physically, or psychologically serving others. This applies with special force to those others who for one reason or another lack capacity to help themselves: the aged, the blind, the crippled, the poor, the bereaved, and the ignorant.

That man's selfishness is one of his worst enemies is a long-accepted axiom. Similarly, from Horace and Ovid to the present, it has been acknowledged that the more one has, the more he seems to want. It is not at all surprising then, that both careful observers and sociological researchers should find that twenty years of widening affluence have brought a deepening of selfishness. This means that selfishness is normally greatest in communities that are materially the richest. For the school to excuse its oversights in this matter, considered on its own merits alone, is bad enough. For it to behave so when service to this aim would also serve other important educational goals is doubly condemning.

The Laboratory Method in Social Concern

What can the school do to cultivate in young people a greater concern for others, particularly for those less fortunate? The task is complicated by the thoroughgoing institutionalization of charity in our society. Furthermore, the student's father usually feels that he has discharged his responsibility fully when he has written his check to the United Fund. This, however, does little to cultivate social conscience in the son or daughter, perhaps not very much in the father.

For a practical example, let us commence with a class in home management. Near the school or near a class member's home there lives, on social security or other limited income, an elderly and partially incapacitated widowed lady in an apartment or house whose interior is dark, dingy, soiled, and neglected. Could one conceive of a more ideal project in home arts than for the class to undertake the complete refurbishing of the interior of this home, with the full agreement and cooperation, of course, of the inhabitant? Members of one of the school's industrial arts classes might join in the repair of furniture or the refinishing of woodwork. The reupholstery of a chair might be undertaken by members of either class.

Many variations of such a suggestion will be sensed immediately by the imaginative teacher. Not only does learning thereby get off the discussion and onto the laboratory level; such education also becomes more humanizing and real. It is practical for the learner, since the young married couple may soon be faced with rehabilitation of just such a dwelling for themselves. It is realistic because it is closer to the economic possibilities of most young married couples than are the usual examples shown in *Better Homes and Gardens.* It helps to reunite the older and the younger generation, with the development of greater mutual respect and appreciation as an expected outcome. It provides understandings important to the class in government, history, or problems of democracy. Finally, it is excellent public relations for the school, for the persons helped and all their friends are to support the tax levy. Furthermore, it creates high respect for the school from all the community's socially conscious citizens who learn about it.

Apply this pattern to the biology class. A yard and garden could be rehabilitated, providing experience expected to enhance the appreciation of plants, the meeting of disease and insect problems, and the understanding of soil chemistry. The learner gains in many ways, above all in a sense of usefulness to others.

According to a recent newspaper account, a community of over a hundred thousand involved teenagers in Project Candlelight. They did spring housecleaning for a blind couple, cleaned the backyard for an incapacitated woman, and tore down a garage condemned by the Board of Health. For the summer of 1970 the project will involve over a hundred youth, and requests for service exceed the potential of workers and leadership. A 4-H club sponsor in a nearby city of 12,000 took note. He involved teen-age boys all summer in similar activity, under the banner of SCIP, the Student Community Improvement Program. These programs bear testimony to the practicality of what is suggested above.

Here and there secondary school groups take their dramatic and musical programs to nursing homes, hospitals, and to other persons whose mobility is more or less limited. While not as effective as the other activities described here, because the involvement is more superficial and the contacts less intimate, such plans are worthwhile and should be extended. They cultivate the spirit of altruism.

INVOLVEMENT OF STUDENTS IN DECISIONS AND SOLUTIONS

In his great book *Theory and Practice of the Social Studies,* Earl Johnson emphasizes the importance of getting the student to realize that he is a very real part of the government, that "We, the people" is not just a dream, that government is improperly referred to as "they."[21] Why is this so? Perhaps there is no better reason than that so many have been so little involved in directly wrestling with problems of general concern, in working out solutions for them, and in being asked or even permitted to assume responsibility for making the solution work.

Does the school have a noise problem? Does it have trouble in protecting the property of its students and teachers? Does it have a littering problem? Can the school honestly say that it is preparing young people for future citizenship if it fails to involve students generally and actively in solving such problems? It must

[21] Earl Johnson, *Theory and Practice of the Social Studies* (New York: Macmillan, 1956).

insist, of course, that they make their solutions work. Why should teachers expend great effort in protecting pupil property? They should support students in any sensible and just efforts to protect their own property, but they should not do the job for them. These same students will soon be faced with problems of security in the neighborhood where they live. Would it not be a great help to these people to give them some experience in dealing with security in the school?

Does the city have the problem of dirty streets, broken curbstones, or inadequate tax revenues? Enlist both the services and the thinking of seniors who are studying government or problems of democracy. Democracy and responsibility begin in the cradle. In the well-managed and responsible society, maturity is well along by the time the individual enters high school. The development of democracy and responsibility is best furthered by their constant exercise.

TEACHING SOCIAL BEHAVIOR

There are still those who, after reading this far, will say that the persuasions of this chapter lie largely outside the range of the school's responsibility. A number of self-appointed educational authorities have in the past twenty years written books or articles in which they affirmed such beliefs. Such people are unaware of social reality as it impinges upon the work of the school.

The school is a social institution. In it teachers and students work together to serve social aims. It teaches, whether it wills so or not, by the most minute phase of its organization, by all things that students and teachers do and by the ways in which they do them. It is constantly fostering cooperation or dissent, concern for others or selfishness, respect for property or carelessness and destruction, kindness or disregard, forthrightness or pretense, social values or personal values, honesty or deceit, the superficial or the genuine. The list could be extended endlessly. The school cannot avoid teaching in the affective domain. Behaviors and attitudes are being modified or reinforced. A neutral position, were it tenable, is impossible. From the New England Primer to the present, the American school has never claimed neutrality in such matters. The Northwest Ordinance (1787), for example, said: "Religion, morality, and knowledge, being necessary to good government and the happiness of mankind, schools, and the means of education shall be encouraged."

SUMMARY

The plea of this chapter has been that high school efforts to develop social responsibility need a higher priority, more carefully planned attention, and subjection to the laboratory method. Both the stated school aims and the broad traditions of our society demand such devotion. The New England Primer, the Declaration of Independence, the Northwest Ordinance, and the continuing pronouncements of Presidents and Congress bear testimony to an unflagging interest in the cultivation of social conscience. These same sources often reflect faith in the power of the schools to provide ongoing help with the task.

In some ways the theme of this chapter reflects the theme of the book. Education for responsibility is possible and necessary. More attention to the affective domain is demanded by the problems of our times. It cannot be done, however, without the laboratory method. In no other aspect of education is learning to do by doing more essential. In no other aspect is involvement in reality of greater consequence. The tide of rapidly rising crime, indifference to environmental problems, and aloofness from internal social division must be turned. Citizenship is the vocation of all, and all must be prepared for it.

Self-respect and respect for others can be taught, but it must not be relegated to the incidental or the accidental. Young people can learn to live together and work together, but the school must provide laboratory lessons in it. A community and a leadership that believes in such educational goals will take steps to help youth acquire a stake in the community. Satisfying rewards await the flexible leadership and imaginative teachers who will take the trouble to do so.

12

Frontiers of Educational Potential

A difference, to be a difference, must make a
difference.—*Variation of an old saying*

If today's high school would leap to higher levels of service, if it
would make its education more relevant to today's society and to
today's problems, it must select with care the philosophical bases
from which such searches for refurbished or new purposes are to
be launched. The intent of this chapter is to show that the basic
views of this volume already enjoy staunch support in a wide
variety of contexts, enterprises, and minds. It shows that certain
trends in the furtherance of human freedom and in an essential
broadening of the base of human responsibility are in evidence
on a broad front. It reflects in matters of human behavior and
human considerations the further Americanization of America
that is taking place. It provides a digest of the philosophical
position of this work, just as the last chapter provides an abridg-
ment of the design in action.

One determination appears at this time to be indelibly clear.
The base of educational efficiency cannot be effectively broad-
ened, a larger number of people cannot be more rewardingly
taught, until there is at least among educators a deeper and
wider faith in human potential. This is to underscore the psychological principle that one person is useful to another in terms of

his growth and development as a person to the degree that the first believes in the second and to the degree that he is able to get the one being led to believe in himself. If universal secondary education is to be successful, and for reasons demonstrated earlier it must become so, such fragments of the Platonic theory of stratification and of European patterns of selection as still remain must be discarded. In the eyes of some, this may appear to involve considerable and drastic reform. To them it may be reassuring to note that many industrial leaders and thinkers, a number of careful students of the behavioral sciences, and a significant proportion of educators are actively promoting such departures from currently more general practices. Some of these sources, their principal thoughts, and the implications for the high school are cited in the paragraphs that follow.

REASSESSMENT OF HUMAN POTENTIAL

Human potential is undergoing reassessment on a wide variety of society's frontiers. One evidence of this is found in the field of industrial and business management, theoretical as well as practical. In 1954, under the auspices of the Sloan Foundation, Alex Bavelas and Douglas McGregor were commissioned to seek for a more promising theory of management. McGregor's research led eventually to his writing a book entitled *The Human Side of Enterprise.* In this he set forth the traditional view of management, based on direction and control, and labeled it "Theory *X*." The essence of Theory *X* is that the average or representative man dislikes work, seeks to avoid it, must be coerced and threatened, actually prefers to be directed, avoids responsibility and the exercise of initiative, and is most interested in security.

Against Theory *X*, which McGregor rejects, he sets Theory *Y*, which he represents as the "Integration of Individual and Organization Goals." According to Theory *Y*, the investment of physical and mental energy in work is natural, men generally have great capacity for self-direction and self-control, and they tend under favorable conditions to seek responsibility. Of particular significance to education is the following Theory *Y* characteristic: "The capacity to exercise a relatively high degree of imagination, ingenuity, and creativity . . . is widely, not narrowly, distributed in the population."[1] Finally, this theory notes that modern life only partially utilizes the average man's intellectual potential. It appears that McGregor sees control and direction most effectively furthered in enterprise by objectives—objectives generally understood, appreciated, and supported by the rank and file of participants in the enterprise. The basic ingredient of McGregor's favored Theory Y is faith in people.

It ought not to be difficult for principals and teachers to accept Theory Y, since belief or faith in young people is one of the best reasons one might give for a life of commitment to their richer and fuller development. However, as in other affairs in which human considerations are uppermost, the reaction is more often illogical than otherwise. The traditional machinery of organization too often comes to be celebrated for its own sake—by principal, by teachers, and by students. This, then, becomes the altar upon which most teachers' faith in individual pupil intent, purpose, and application is sacrificed. It takes considerable courage to break oneself loose from the firm grip of Theory X, it must be admitted, especially when few or no others in the organization appear so inclined.

EXPECTATION

Expectation may be the most important word in education. The lack of expectation can contribute materially to a bank's failure, to the sharp decline of a baseball player's batting average, to any human being's inability to perform satisfactorily a job for which his maturity and reasonably normal development and experience might otherwise fit him. There is growing evidence, on the other hand, that in any human relationship where there is a "minister" of any kind and one to whom he ministers, the full and unequivocal confidence of the former in the latter is a substantial ingredient in the success of the ministration. This appears to hold true whether the relationship is that of physician-patient, supervisor-worker, or teacher-pupil.

[1] Douglas McGregor, *The Human Side of Enterprise* (New York: McGraw-Hill, 1960), pp. 45, 48, and Chapter 3.

This point is quite vividly demonstrated in a study by Rosenthal and Jacobson. It is perhaps fair to say that their study, like many others in recent years, found its long-range motivation in a widening and deepening interest in the more effective instruction of the disadvantaged child. The elementary school chosen for the study served a mainly lower-class community, about one-sixth of the enrollment being Mexican children. The school experienced an annual turnover of about 30 percent of the 650 pupils, and might be described as a school whose atmosphere reflected "a feeling of sociability rather than of earnest endeavor."[2] The three ability tracks established by the school were based chiefly upon reading performance. The teachers, in the main, were regarded as dedicated.

The researchers in this study hypothesized that children would become brighter when their teachers expected them to do so. All children who were expected to return to the school in the fall were given, in the spring of 1964, a test that purported to indicate which children might be expected to show or demonstrate sharp rises in their academic capacity relatively soon thereafter. In reality, the test was a somewhat nonverbal test of intelligence. Follow-up tests were given in January 1965, May 1965, and in May 1966. Experimenters selected randomly an approximate 20 percent of the tested children and informed their teachers that here were children who "were about to bloom."

The researchers' hypothesis was confirmed by the retests of the children in 1965 and 1966. Later tests showed marked I.Q. rises in a number of the experimental children, considerable improvement in that group as a whole, some improvement in the control groups, more improvements in younger than in older children. Significant, however, was the finding that it took the influence longer to catch hold with the older children, but with them it seemed to remain longer, to become more permanent.

As the Irish playwright whose words inspired the title given to the report of this investigation put it (speaker, Eliza):

> . . . the difference between a lady and a flower girl is not how she behaves, but how she's treated. I shall always be a flower

[2] Robert Rosenthal and Lenore Jacobson, *Pygmalion in the Classroom* (New York: Holt, Rinehart and Winston, 1968), p. 62.

girl to Professor Higgins, because he always treats me as a flower girl, and always will; but I know I can be a lady to you, because you always treat me as a lady, and always will.[3]

HUMAN FREEDOM ON THE MARCH

In a number of ways, from the first chapter forward, this book points toward a high school education that is characterized by greater self-determination, more planning of both the large blocks and the minute elements of his learning by the student himself, more responsibility both allowed and demanded as the student attempts to advance his own education. This is seen as not only desirable for this age of man's progress but also as being forced by the turn of events in the last half of the twentieth century. Like it or not, schools at the secondary and higher education levels are being moved in this direction. All citizens, or at least significant numbers of representatives of all citizens' groups are today insisting upon more freedom, which is to say more individual autonomy.

Since autonomy without responsibility is unthinkable, school leaders and teachers, who themselves are pushing for and gaining more autonomy, ignore the challenge at the peril of both the organization they represent and their own collective and individual self-respect. Previously ignored and passive elements in society are today marching, with occasional rough interruptions, toward a more active role in the business of society. These elements include students, whose roles in their own education have been passive too often. This trend must not be viewed by the school as an inroad upon its ordinarily peaceful ways. It must be seen as an invitation to improve the quality of education.

The recently steeper incline in the ascent of human freedom is effectively portrayed in a U.S. Supreme Court case of 1960, that of Sam Thompson v. City of Louisville (Ky.), the only case in which the Court reached a unanimous decision during that session. The case involved for the Supreme Court the most minor

---

[3] George Bernard Shaw, *Pygmalion* (New York: Modern Library, *Four Plays by Bernard Shaw*, 1953), p. 295.

matters heard by it in many years. The fines totaled $20, but the human principles were significant.

On the early evening of the alleged violations, the defendant, Sam Thompson, was approached by two policemen while he was shuffling his feet to the tune blared forth by the cafe's juke box. He had been there about half an hour, according to the manager, had purchased no food (which later proved to be erroneous), but had in no way been unduly noisy or offensive. Neither the manager nor the patrons had objected to anything he had done. When the police officer asked him his reason for being there, he said he was waiting for a bus. The officer informed him that he was under arrest and took him outside. There the petitioner protested his arrest and was "very argumentative," according to the officer, whereupon a disorderly conduct charge was placed against him. The Louisville Police Court sentenced him to pay a fine of $10 or serve the alternate jail service on each count.[4]

Mr. Thompson, a handyman, had friends who helped him secure an able lawyer, who said the case could be appealed if Sam was agreeable. He was. Kentucky law provided no appeal to a higher state court from police courts, which left the Supreme Court as the only possibility. The contention was that Thompson was about to be deprived of liberty and property without due process as provided under the Fourteenth Amendment to the Constitution.

The Supreme Court found no semblance of evidence that the petitioner was guilty of violating Louisville's ordinance on loitering. Neither could it find him guilty of disorderly conduct for arguing, especially so since Kentucky law waives the defendant's right to later complaint if he fails to object to the arresting officer.

This and related decisions carry broad and strong implications for the operation of all institutions that deal with people, including secondary and higher schools. What is the basis for denying a given student access to this or that particular class? How often are young people in school dealt with in summary and arbitrary fashion? The school is usually expected, if not required, to teach the basic American rights. To what extent is it obligated to conduct its program in a spirit that is genuinely consistent

---

[4] 362 U.S. 199, 4L ed. 2d 654, 80 S Ct. 624, pp. 654–59, (1960).

with those rights? In the future the school can expect to be asked with increasing frequency to justify its procedures within such a framework. The school that finds means of sharing policy decisions, especially all those that bear on personal dignity and one's way of viewing himself, with students, or at least with student representatives, is not only doing a better job of preparing students for life in an ever more democratic society. It is putting itself in a better position to go about its business of education more efficiently, in greater dignity and with more respect from all. It is much less likely to suffer chagrin, embarrassment, and interruption in its work.

GOAL DETERMINATION FOR THE SCHOOL

Throughout this work substantial attention has been given to the need for reexamining the goal orientation of the high school. It has been sometimes implied, at other times stated, that an enhanced personal efficiency, a successful meeting of narrowly conceived industrial, defense, and business demands, and preparation for a continued education in a quality institution of higher education are not enough.

The superior school must be characterized by a spiritual bond and fervor that is valued for its own sake. The institution must constantly seek to make itself one that fuels and regenerates every human spirit that it touches. There must be something of the Benedictine commitment that Whitehead espouses. The word "enjoy" has been looked upon as an evil one for a number of years, a word that one had best not link with education. Yet who could convincingly argue that a student gets less, not more, out of schoolwork that he enjoys? To be committed, to be fully identified with one's work, is to enjoy it. And who would argue that having enjoyed one's schoolwork, one is thereby not better fitted to enjoy his after-school work.

Then there is the business of being a free man, a role that must be sought by each individual if it is to be attained. Students of philosophy and society are quite generally agreed that while the incentive to seek freedom may be inherited, the condition itself must be won anew by each generation and each individual.

And historians generally agree that freedom is constantly subject to extension, both within the person and among persons.

Each generation comes up against new threats to its freedom. In our own time people of all ages find themselves caught up in the technological, scientific, and social machinery that they and their parents have helped to create. Many would like to resist and get loose from it but either feel unsure about how to go about it or do not dare. Those most visibly in rebellion are the defecting groups, such as the various activist and protest groups.

There is little question that many Americans like the rat race they are in. They enjoy lives filled with very active nothingness. There is also little question that many others do not like it but continue to pretend that they do. These latter are pushed on by real or imagined expectations of parents, children, and friends. The third group, still relatively small in number but large in noise, and growing more rapidly than most of the first two groups like to think, thoroughly disapprove and express that disapproval in unmistakable but sometimes ridiculous ways.

The point here is twofold. First, in its best character the school is a place where the student is invited to stop and look around. He is encouraged and shown how to analyze and criticize what he sees, to reject with reason, and to accept with consideration of all possible consequences. However, the school can be, and sometimes is, a part of the emptiness, expending many of its resources in the sustenance of it. Second, the school is presumed to be committed to the support and extension of the great human values that the nation, and most of the Western world, for that matter, have long prized and espoused. This being the case, the school can scarcely avoid the responsibility of helping young people to get practice in carrying freedom constructively and developmentally, that is, in such a way that it leads to a more complete and ennobling freedom.

There is considerable reason to believe that the human goals indicated above have suffered an eclipse during the past two decades. What all the forces have been that have driven us in this direction is here unimportant. It is important that the issue be recognized and that steps be taken to put the development of the free man back into the center of education.

Archibald MacLeish put his appraisal of the problem as

applied to the college as given below. The application to the high school is of equal force.

> The college no longer exists to produce men prepared for life in a society of men, but men prepared for employment in an industry or profession.

> There is no quarrel between the humanities and the sciences. There is only a need, common to them both, to put the idea of man back where it once stood, at the focus of our lives; to make the end of education the preparation of men to be men. . . .[5]

In the insightful article from which this quotation is taken, Mr. MacLeish pleads for an education that will help man take charge of his own life, including the means at his disposal. He appears to be raising the question, Are we to be the victims of our science and technology rather than their masters? The potential cost to human freedom requires no elaboration.

RENEWED EMPHASIS UPON HUMAN VALUES

Among the disciples of a reoriented education is the Budapest-born Michael Polanyi. The holder of doctoral degrees in medicine and in physical science, he made important contributions in the field of metallic crystals and in measuring the determinants of the speed of chemical reactions. Today at Oxford University, he has turned his thinking to social science and to philosophy. He is convinced that today science is often misapplied, that some of the current ideals of physicists are false, and that they thereby damage other sciences and the humanities. He abhors a common tendency to try to bring the intangible into the realm of the tangible and to deal with it as if it were something that it is not. He reminds us, for example, that the computer cannot deal with meaning, which is dependent upon expression, upon man's gift of speech, the measure of his enormous superiority over animals.

Polanyi sees today no shortage of moral feeling but rather a widespread desire for brotherhood and righteousness. "All modern nihilism is a moral protest; the nihilists protest in the name

[5] Archibald MacLeish, "The Great American Frustration," *Saturday Review,* July 13, 1968, p. 16.

of moral perfection against a hypocritical society," says this scientist-philosopher.[6]

Throughout Polanyi's article there is constant reference to Hans Christian Andersen's fairy tale, "The Emperor's New Clothes." It will be remembered that the emperor's new clothes, according to the tailors who swindled him, were reputed to be made from a cloth invisible to any person who was unfit for the office he held or who was unspeakably dull. Both other adults and the Emperor refused to acknowledge that they saw nothing, which was what the Emperor really wore. A small boy, in his childish honesty, finally observed that "the Emperor has no clothes." Polanyi views the streets of the modern mind as filled with emperors without clothes, reflecting a civilization that has tended to surrender its decision-making faculties wholly to the forces of economics and power.

Every teacher and every educational leader must feel deeply his responsibility to serve human goals that will stand the long-range test. He has an obligation to serve more than the "in" group or even "in" ideas. The educator cannot be satisfied with merely enlarging man. He must enhance and ennoble man. Obviously the teacher can meet the demands of such a role only to the extent that he has broad roots in an understanding of man's conquest of the baser self, in the elements of civilization itself.

Even though a teacher may have a good grasp of the best that man has thought, felt, and done, it is the writer's conviction that the teacher does not best communicate this to his student in a school atmosphere that is overly formal, impersonal, and highly mechanized. The capacity of both teachers and students to think is best sharpened where conditions at least a part of the time will commit those involved to no rigid outline, where any question may be asked, and where any possible answer may be examined with respect. The work-study laboratory is designed to meet this need better than the formally organized class.

The school must be very careful that in its zest for the traditional earmarks of a well-organized school, it does not become an institution that encourages pretense and hypocrisy. Polanyi's

---

[6] Mary Harrington Hall, "A Conversation with Polanyi," *Psychology Today* (May 1968), pp. 20–25, 66–67.

position suggests only one of the many ways in which it is in danger of succumbing to this temptation.

PERSONALITY AND THE IMPERSONAL ENVIRONMENT

A professor of psychiatry, S. L. Halleck, examined student unrest in a recent article. He reported that activist students, according to sociological studies, come mainly from quite stable homes, thus sharply discounting the theory that such students come from indifferent or neglectful homes. That the permissiveness theory or the psychologizing of the population plays some part he is willing to allow. He makes it clear, though, that no one hypothesis provides adequate explanation; any hypothesis tends rather to shed "only a small light upon a highly complex phenomenon".[7]

Dr. Halleck examines a number of potential explanations that fix responsibility in society or in conditions of society, influences more external to the student. Not all of these are pertinent to our purposes. He notes a nation becoming much more densely populated, a society characterized by crowds, traffic jams, and all the social by-products of mass production. Like many others, he sees individuals feeling faceless and insignificant, the victims of anonymity. This factor applies to the student of the large high school as much as to the university student.

This psychiatrist also raises the question of how long we should expect youth to play only a passive role, having no part in the power structure and wielding no influence in society's business. He clearly implies that he thinks youth need commitment beyond their own selfish interests, a voice in matters that affect them. If nothing more, he thinks "we must at least begin to take a look at the impact of technological progress upon man's personality."[8]

Halleck goes so far as to say that the areas of technological advancement that are inconsistent with man's becoming a better

---

[7] S. L. Halleck, "Hypotheses About Student Unrest," National Education Association, *Today's Education*, 57 (September 1968), pp. 22–26.

[8] *Ibid.*, p. 26.

man must be rejected. He also bemoans our failure to study the psychological future of man. Finally, the last two sentences of Halleck's article cogently undergird the principal theses of this book:

> I doubt that man can live without intimacy, without compassion, without ideology, without faith, without autonomy, without privacy, and without beauty, and still be man. We must reexamine our time-honored reverence for affluence, power, and bigness and face the possibility that affluence bores, that power corrupts, and that big institutions diminish the stature of man.[9]

THE LEARNING SOCIETY IS POSSIBLE

Many have addressed themselves to the impact of technology and change upon education. No one has done it more clearly than has Robert Maynard Hutchins in a 1968 book in which he contends that the learning society is now possible and highly desirable, even necessary. By "society" he means virtually all persons, all except the severely brain-damaged. Since he thinks it no longer possible to evade the problem of educating everybody, he urges that organized education turn its energies to learning how to teach those with whom its success in the past has been limited. He thinks the substitution of vocational education for such persons to be futile, both because a technological society changes rapidly and because vocational education fails to fit them for their new leisure and their new role as self-governing human beings.[10]

Hutchins, whose book commemorates the 200th anniversary of *Encyclopedia Britannica,* and who has had the benefit of the criticism of at least ten distinguished scholars who represent both the Occident and the Orient in preparing it, is the guiding force of the Center for the Study of Democratic Institutions. He firmly rejects the Jeffersonian view of universal education, asserting that the school, not unlike the factory, tries to turn out the product

[9] *Ibid.,* p. 26.
[10] Robert M. Hutchins, *The Learning Society* (New York: Praeger, 1968), pp. 11–32.

that the society wants. It is clear to all, of course, that the school cannot long continue to turn out, often prematurely, a great many that are, as Jefferson believed, "destined for labor." Internal combustion, steam, and electronic horses have all but replaced manual labor in our society.

Like other authorities cited earlier, Hutchins deals with the principle of expectation, and he invokes the self-fulfilling prophecy. He questions generally held estimates of pupil ability, hence all ability grouping and streaming. Among others, he cites the judgment of the eminent microbiologist, René Dubos, who thinks that the most important recent finding of genetics is that less than 20 percent of the genetic endowment becomes functional.[11] The implication is that education must turn its attention from the question of how much ability the pupil has to that of how much it can induce him to employ in the interest of his own development and his potential contribution to society.

It is evident that Mr. Hutchins fully supports the view that the extension of general education is the high school's first responsibility to all students. It seems equally clear that he would support the estimate and eventual destiny of ability grouping indicated in Chapter 9.

Incidentally, it seems appropriate at this point to note that many educational leaders still see vocational education as the answer for those whom present schools have not been able to serve rewardingly. The proponents are usually vague, however, about the precise patterns of vocational education they have in mind. A high school that comes to mind offers the apprenticeship in barbering, but with few public high schools in barber training, the trade seems to be supplied with about as many operators as appear to make a good living. The number of machinists that our society can absorb is limited, and the same is true for auto mechanics. What might the situation be if every community in the nation had a trade school for the training of both? It is unlikely that the need for dental technicians will ever greatly exceed the number of dentists, who represent a very small portion of the country's employed persons. This is not to speak against the vocational education that can and should improve craftsmanship

---

[11] *Ibid.*, pp. 12–13.

among the tradesmen of our society. It is simply to point out the limitations of that avenue as a means of making universal education universally effective.

There is more to life, too, than learning to make a living, destined as it appears to be to occupying an ever smaller portion of one's time. Robert Havighurst told the nation's secondary school principals in their 1968 national conference that the era of the determination of an ethic based upon work is nearing an end. Pointing out that the typical work week is destined soon to be reduced to about 22 hours, he indicates that in the future, man's ethic will be based upon the ways in which he invests his leisure time. The view that was ushered in with the Protestant Reformation is the pattern of the past, says Havighurst, and the school must prepare its students to use their leisure to enhance rather than erode their humanitarian qualities.[12]

The lesson in this is that we must never allow ourselves to forget that the worker with the humblest 40-hour-a-week job lives another 128 hours each week just like the rest of us. It is in this larger block of time that he has the most opportunity to enhance or degrade his own humanity and that of all others with whom he comes in contact. Increasingly often he will have the opportunity to make his most important contribution to society in his off-duty hours. To the extent that his education has helped him to get a proper start and a proper perspective, he will be able to avail himself of this opportunity.

ATTITUDES OF THE ESTABLISHMENT

The reader of practical orientation might at this point be inclined to make an observation, with some justification, somewhat as follows: "The philosophers and authorities cited above are no doubt wise and sincere men, but they have no direct or indirect responsibility for the operation of a high school. What does the establishment say about these ideas?"

Possible replies to such an observation and to such a question take two forms. One is stated; the other implied. At many earlier

12 Robert J. Havighurst, "High Schools for the Future," National Association of Secondary School Principals, Bulletin 328 (May 1968), pp. 117–125.

points in this work, and at least once earlier in the present chapter the official organ of the National Association of Secondary School Principals provided solid support. Only a few pages back an article from *Today's Education,* the official organ of the National Education Association, was cited and quoted. Presumably the official journals of such organizations publish only articles that their editors think useful to their clientele, the people who are in direct charge of the schools. Thus the implied support is considerable.

A sample of the direct support for some priority ideas of this treatise is found in a monograph entitled *A Climate for Individuality.*[13] This document is a joint project of four of the most powerful and respected arms of the National Education Association. These branches represent the school superintendents of America, the secondary school principals, the Association for Supervision and Curriculum Development and the Department of Rural Education. It was written with the advice and counsel of eighteen persons who represented these organizations and who are well known to the establishment. Publications that might be more representative of the educational establishment are rare. Because the subject is so pertinent to the burden of this volume and the wording so clairvoyant, this document is quoted at length, with permission.

The first chapter is entitled "Storm Signals," and it includes observations as follows:

> . . . we see signs—signs indicating that an essential part of our American heritage is being eroded away.
>
> The foundation of our nation is its supreme commitment to the individual human being.
>
> .   .   .
>
> Individuality tends to be submerged in gigantic organizations, in chain-belt production, in monolithic economic enterprise, and in the complex cultural interdependencies of our society.
>
> Caught in this cultural drift, the schools too are veering toward impersonal solutions to vital educational problems. Mass

---

[13] *A Climate for Individuality: Statement of the Joint Project on the Individual and the School,* (Washington: American Association of School Administrators, Association for Supervision and Curriculum Development, National Association of Secondary School Principals, National Education Association Department of Rural Education, 1965).

grouping, standard curriculums, texts, and examinations, and standardized institutions are squeezing individuals into a common mold. Standard school products are demanded by short-sighted and frightened adults and frequently are accepted by school boards and teachers. With an eye to masses rather than to individuals, the schools are departing from their unique historic character by manipulating pupils and teachers into organizational patterns and by leaning on administrative and mechanical devices that tend to destroy the very quality which has made them great.[14]

.   .   .

We must find a *modern* way of nurturing the special character and unique strengths of each individual in a world in which that individual will be highly involved in groups.[15]

It is apparent that the thinkers behind this document would approve some type of high school reorganization such as the house system proposed in this book, where representatives of the house participate in its government and its programs. The writers observe further that presently employed attempts at the individualization of instruction tend to limit such tailoring to variations in rate through standardized lessons, thus ignoring the more subtle elements of individual difference. The writers mention grouping as a remedy as follows: "Similarly, systems of grouping, though designed to put each pupil in the most suitable learning environment, contain no guarantee of treatment as an individual."[16]

Other statements of special relevance to present purposes include the following:

Schools can and should seek out additional ways of dealing with the individual, but the fullest flowering of individuality can never be achieved unless the group life also makes its great contribution. Only in the group setting can individuality be transmitted into cooperation and leadership.[17]

.   .   .

[14] *Ibid.*, p. 9.
[15] *Ibid.*, p. 10.
[16] *Ibid.*, p. 11.
[17] *Ibid.*, p. 29.

History will support the rough generalization that a rise in human freedom will generate a rise in human productivity, whether such productivity is measured in terms of ideas and the arts or in terms of economic goods and services. A look at the productivity of American immigrants before and after they came to these freer shores makes the point.

For children, too, freedom is a tremendous stimulant.[18]

.   .   .

. . . our image is of another sort. It is an image of a child with a secure base to operate from as he forays out into the world that may be tough; a child with an accumulating reserve of experience that carries him courageously into new and risky ventures; a child with a concept of himself that nerves him to dare. It is anything but a soft and sentimental picture. For it assumes that life takes strength, and it is based on faith that a rugged inward strength can grow to a level of power most men never know they have.[19]

.   .   .

. . . any school devoted to the cause of nurturing individuality within its walls must also look out beyond those walls to active work in the community as a whole. Schoolmen need to see themselves as the community's outstanding cadre of professional agents for the full development of young people.[20]

Finally, in their last chapter, dealing with what the leaders can do, this careful and thoughtful publication admonishes the school administrator in this vein:

Conformity to existing conditions, uniformity of operations, rigidity, and undue regulations tend to suppress individuality. If the staff is restricted, children are stifled. Do the administrator and his staff challenge existing operations and programs? Do they keep restrictions to a minimum? Do they avoid regimentation and make exceptions?[21]

The representatives of the establishment who prepared this document could scarcely have been in greater agreement with the

[18] *Ibid.*, p. 31.
[19] *Ibid.*, pp. 39–40.
[20] *Ibid.*, p. 44.
[21] *Ibid.*, p. 55.

present writer had he been chairman of the group, with authority to select his own help, which was not at all the case.

SUMMARY

This chapter has shown that a variety of minds and organizations are deeply and persuasively committed to the major tenets of this work. Such sources of support are found both inside and outside the official education establishment. The major doctrine is one of greater hope for a wider segment of the human species than has ever before been induced to absorb extensive education. The utter necessity of making universal education universally effective has in this chapter been reaffirmed, with generous support from a number of sources. The broader and firmer reach for more freedom and responsibility by many has been reviewed, again with appropriate support from many segments of society. Even the establishment has proved that it recognizes the storm signals and the demand for change. All individuals must have individual attention, attention to their more subtle differences.

Of all the changes, of all the innovations that hold promise for a better education and a better high school in the future, none outranks the reappraisal of human potential that is now moving through the American mind. This movement, still beneath the surface in most areas of education and life, promises to replace despair with hope for humankind. It is a very difficult development for educators to face, for the school thereby robs itself of its best excuse for failure with many of its students. The dollar cost of the change is not to be its greatest; no development will cost the school more in the pains of a readjusted thinking. However, once these pains have been suffered through or overcome, no development promises greater educational gains over the next thirty to fifty years. The individual, with hope for himself, with hope in his teacher for him, moves once again to the center of the educational stage.

13

The High School of 1990

Some men see things as they are and say "Why?"
I dream things that never were and say "Why
not?"

Robert F. Kennedy's adaptation of
G. B. Shaw lines

In this chapter the reader is asked to move himself forward
twenty years. He is asked to look first at the educational thinking
and forces that are motivating the more alert secondary teachers
and leaders of 1990. Then he is asked to pay a personal visit to
one of the better staffed but not necessarily extravagantly supported high schools of that time. This chapter portrays some of
the learning activities he will see in progress. Even more importantly, it seeks to reveal the spirit or the atmosphere in which
those tasks are carried out, for it is here that the 1970 visitor to
the 1990 school will find the change most marked.

In 1990 the "people's college" will have attained the vener-
able age of 169 years, one and two-thirds centuries. The scope
and thrust of change in the high school between now and then is
destined to be the greatest the institution has experienced since
the last years of the nineteenth and the first years of the twentieth century. Educational historians and students of the high
school in 1990 will disagree as to when the current era of change
commenced. They will, however, agree that the change has been
momentous, that there has been no tendency toward plateau such

315

as that which characterized the period of the 1920s to the 1950s.

Some relatively certain alternatives will present themselves. The high school of 1990 will have either gained status or lost status. In the overall schema of the educational organization, it will be either a stronger or a weaker institution than now. It will be influencing the college more or less than today's high school. Its program will be helping more or less with the solution of society's gravest problems, both directly and indirectly. Its teachers and leaders will compare more favorably or less favorably in imagination, initiative, and resourcefulness, with college, elementary, and private school leaders and teachers. It will be trusted more and supported better, or it will be trusted less and supported less well. All those who believe in the ideals that the high school was designed to advance will want to play a part in achieving positive change. There will be no standing still.

Henry Ford I had a good car in the Model T. He clung stubbornly to it, however, for almost too long. Only the great resources of a Ford Motor Company permit such extravagance in any institution. A more current example is seen in the *Saturday Evening Post*, for many years the leading weekly publication in America. It waited too long to change and eventually changed too little. Only recently its refusal to recognize the need for basic change brought it to the announcement of its last edition after almost a century and a half of publication. The high school deserves a better fate.

THE THINKING AND THE AIMS

Many of the innovations so much in the literature of secondary education in 1970 will have been forgotten by 1990. Even the terminology employed in their discussion in 1970 will have been forgotten. That era is looked back upon as one whose interests centered upon mechanics rather than function. The leaders and teachers of 1990, however, acknowledge their debt to the innovation and experimentation that characterized the 1950s and 1960s. They know and appreciate the history of educational ideas more fully than the secondary teachers of any earlier American time. They hail their predecessors of those earlier days for their recognition of the need for change. They admire the courage with which many of their forerunners tested various footholds by which they might climb to higher fulfillment of the high school's purposes. Nevertheless, they understand that the experimental efforts of those post-World War II years were not always linked to clearly conceived and thoroughly American purposes. This error they are trying to correct in 1990. The progress of systems analysis and a deeper interest in measuring results in terms of stated purposes has helped them.

Personal and Social Responsibility

The changes that have come by 1990 center upon the filling of earlier educational voids. These changes sought correction of education's previous failures to serve functionally the noblest and best of the American ideals and traditions. (The reader may at this point wish to turn back and again briefly scan the basic assumptions set forth in the second chapter.) Major attention has been given to the development of personal and social responsibility, a long-acknowledged aim of the school. Attempts to measure success in this area were slow in coming, but they have now arrived. Much more of the school's energy is now turned in this direction, and much less into the channels of detective work.

Certain social skills, especially those of learning to work with other people and to consider others' viewpoints, are given central and obvious attention in this school. Everything the school does is geared to develop a self-managed citizen, one responsible for himself and to himself. Its studies of its alumni give major attention to their demonstrated capacity and readiness for social responsibility. They attempt to measure the degree to which the graduate has assumed responsibility for his family, his club, his community—in short, for the general welfare.

The school's serious concern for progress in this area was long delayed in part because there was widespread apathy toward the promotion of the general welfare. A more crowded nation and the diminished opportunity of an undeveloped frontier led the man in Congress, and finally the man in the street, to think more about it. Such a nation discovered that the problems created by the neglect and abuse of both resources and people became intolerable. Likewise, an education that failed to create concern became intolerable.

The school now recognizes that continued success of the American experiment requires an ever wider dissemination of social conscience or social responsibility among the citizenry. The school helps its pupils realize that an environment is healthful and wholesome for none until it is so for all. It fully acknowledges that the ancient truth that man does not live for himself alone seems to be one of the most difficult to teach. Unlike the high schools of the 1950s, however, it is not about to give up on that realization. Both the school and society generally now realize that the future hinges upon our surmounting the barriers.

Faith in Pupil Desire and Capacity

The teachers and leaders of the high school of 1990 have an abundant faith in the capacity of the masses of pupils to learn. They are recognized and rewarded in terms of their adeptness at finding and developing incentive, talent, and ability in all their students. Department chairmanships and summer school teaching are assigned on the basis of such demonstrated interests and capacities. It is generally recognized that almost any learner has enough ability. The school knows that the failure is that of the environment to cultivate concern, that of the parent and the teacher to hold hope for the student, that of the student's lack of hope for himself. It is fully realized that one does not ordinarily reach for anything that he has no hope of grasping, and the school acts upon that realization. Consequently, the school no longer wastes precious time in giving, scoring, and recording what was only a few years earlier called I.Q. tests. It asks not how much ability the pupil has but how much of his ability can be developed and turned to the service of society? It is less concerned with classification of the pupil than any previous secondary school in the United States or Europe. Its main concern is with helping people find the way toward the top of their potential.

This high school of 1990 has long realized that it cannot write off 20, 30, or 40 percent of its potential clientele. It has

recognized that the answer to the education of the more difficult-
to-inspire students does not lie in shunting them off to some
other institution with some other kind of name over the door. It
is realized that the chief educational capital of the special institutions that have been set up to serve special groups, where they
are succeeding, lies almost wholly in the attitudes of their leadership and their teachers toward their clientele. It is agreed that
they are doing business on their faith in youth, a faith that has
elsewhere and too often been withheld from them. It is presumed
that the desire for success is an almost universal human trait, and
that presumption is acted upon. Even outside the school, in the
world of industry and commerce, nearly half the leaders are
consciously trying to harness Douglas McGregor's Theory Y,
whereas those doing so in 1970 had been not more than 10 to 15
percent. Faith in the masses of people generally makes it much
easier for the school to act on this theory. (See the discussion
of McGregor's theory in Chapter 12.)

It is widely noted in 1990 that the vocational schools established in the late 1960s and 1970s, with rare exceptions and by
whatever evolutionary processes, have become comprehensive
secondary schools. It is noted that many of the graduates of such
schools are going on to enter colleges and universities and that
they are doing well in their higher education. And, alas, it is
observed that a number of college and university admissions
offices are reporting that the graduates of such schools are often
better scholastic risks, in both technical and nontechnical curricula, than are the graduates of the traditional college preparatory high schools. It is understood, of course, that this is not
because of major differences in the curricula or quality of these
vocational schools. It is rather because of the experimental-
mindedness of such schools, which found as they were being
established that they were attracting more experimental-minded
leaders. It is because these schools have had faith in their
enrollees, because they have courageously shouldered the blame
for their own failures and have resourcefully sought remedies for
them. It is because they have made it their business to help their
students find themselves, to find motivation, to find reason for
being. It is in part because such graduates have attained a more
mature responsibility, because they have achieved a greater

mastery over themselves, a higher degree of self-discipline and
self-respect, a keener sense of direction than did the high school
graduates of the 1960s.

Again, the purpose served by deeper faith in the learner is to
give him deeper faith in himself. The best literature of the 1960s
that concerned itself with the socially disadvantaged, the culturally deprived, the slum child, frequently referred to his need
for a more promising self-image. Most teachers of 1990 realize
that this is the principal need of a vast majority of young people
everywhere. They know it to be a common need of the psychological or emotional deviate, regardless of intellectual potential.
They see it as a deep need of the parentally harassed youth,
whether that harassment springs from the parent's scholastic,
vocational, or social ambitions for the youth or whether it is an
outlet for the parent's own frustrations and inadequacies. They
think of it as a deep need of other young people, each of whom
in the last analysis they view as fitting only into a category of his
own. Consequently, they are channeling far more energy into
the building of each student's confidence and self-image.

Cultivation of Self-Direction

The third important aim of the high school of 1990 is closely
related to and lends support to the first two. Its practice as an
institution is pointed at the most pressing educational demand of
the twentieth century's highly technical and rapidly changing
society, the demand that the individual be turned out of school
with a highly developed capacity for self-instruction. Consequently, many of the school's most important assignments are
assignments that the student has given himself. Of course, he
makes frequent and extensive use of the teachers, librarians,
teacher aides, and other technicians employed by the school in
pursuing his goal. The school has finally taken seriously the
admonitions of such earlier thinkers as Jerome Bruner, Robert
Havighurst, and Ernest Melby. It confidently stresses teaching
the student how to learn by himself and for himself, knowing
that the rapidly changing world of his active days will demand
this as a priority skill.

This does not mean in any sense that the school has returned to aimless permissiveness, if indeed such a condition ever prevailed on any wide scale in American education. It does not mean activity for activity's sake. It does not mean the release of the teacher from responsibility for what goes on in the school. It does not mean a curriculum based upon the passing whim or fancy of the moment, be it either the student's or the teacher's transient delight. It does mean, on the contrary, the kind of teaching that promotes excitement in young minds, that opens up to young imaginations fruitful questions or issues they wish to pursue. It means that the teacher's responsibility is greater, not lesser. It means that no small part of the learner's time is engaged in pursuit of an issue, a question, a phenomenon, a hypothesis that is real to him and of concern to him. This is the kind of question that in earlier classrooms was too often swept under the scholastic rug.

The student can do some daydreaming in the high school of 1990. Not only is he allowed to dream; he is even encouraged to dream, and he is assisted in every possible way and by every possible resource that the school has or can find to translate that dream into a self-imposed assignment. He gets much help from one or more teachers in refining this assignment, although he is free to accept or reject such help or suggestions without penalty. Such freedom encourages his continued seeking out and weighing of the value of such help. Thus a great deal of the initiative for learning is restored to the hands and mind of the learner, where it functions most fully and most genuinely. The school system, from kindergarten forward, guards against taking from the learner his opportunity to develop strength in the decision-making process. His teachers know that he must try a wrong method if he believes in it. They act on the principle that to revel in the rewards and suffer in the consequences of one's own decisions is to develop maturity and skill in making wise choices.

Independent study is much more broadly conceived and applied in far more subtle forms than anything that was done in the 1960s. The term, in fact, is not even used, because it came to be thought of as merely individual pacing through materials that were anything but highly individualized. The independence of the individual student of 1990 expresses itself in two ways. First, it starts with his own conception or question. Second, he is more frequently given the opportunity to experience the consequences of his own decision.

Leaders and teachers of 1990 have identified a grave inconsistency of earlier days, and they have corrected it. They no longer talk of independent study with the mind's left hand while preparing with the right a schedule and an organization that discourages individual or independent thought and action in both teachers and students. The teacher's schedule is arranged upon the assumption that he will spend a number of hours each week conferring with individual students about individual problems and projects, many of which have been individually inspired. The mechanics of organization are less rigid than in earlier days. The student, for example, can slip into the library without finding it necessary to get a ticket signed by a teacher or other authority. When the library finds itself overrun with customers, it reacts in the same way that a merchandising organization does when it experiences such a happy situation. It enlarges its facility or decentralizes by establishing branch stores. In some respects each work-study laboratory becomes a branch for the library's products.

Warm, Personal, Unified Organization

The high school of 1990 has for some time operated on the assumption that the way the student feels about his school and the nature of his relationship to it has a powerful influence upon the quality of the learning and development that he as a person can draw from it. This has come about not solely through a shift in educational emphases. It has come in part because of changes in society and in conditions around the world. Thinking in 1990 is conditioned by three very important developments. The first is that the United States and other world powers have been involved in no major conflict for more than forty years. The second is that birth control, having been generally accepted for thirty years in the Western world, is now the rule in almost all parts of the world. Both of these phenomena have tended to give each human life more respect. Humanity is regarded as far less cheap than was the case through the first three-fifths of the twentieth century. A third force of great impact is that there has been a change in the way law is viewed. Not too many years earlier men were fond of saying, "Ours is a government of laws!" Thinkers in 1990 are emphasizing the spirit and unity of the people, their respect for one another. They know that no law is any better than the degree to which the people generally wanted it, accept it, and are willing to observe it and to insist upon its observance by others. Distressing experiences for thirty years have underscored this point.

The kinds of changed thinking that have overtaken the society of 1990 are modifying school thinking in significant ways. There is a primary emphasis upon the quality of life in the school for teachers as well as students. It is now understood that those trying and persistent teacher personnel problems of the 1960s and 1970s were based less upon economic issues than was commonly supposed. Rather, a major cause was found in the frustrations that came from the type of organization and conditions under which the school program was being carried out.

The opinions of 1990 teachers upon educational issues are highly respected because they are more sophisticated opinions. They are based upon a broader and more thorough knowledge of the processes of learning and the development of young people. In turn, the respect of teachers for their pupils and pupil opinion has been significantly enhanced. A conscious effort is made to apply in the school that great American principle that any and all are presumed innocent until proven guilty. Hence one is struck as he moves about the high school of 1990 by the evidence of mutual trust and mutual candor that marks teacher-student and student-student relationships. The school has moved far toward the elimination of the hypocrisy that prevailed in earlier days, that of teaching one thing and practicing quite another. Thus the quality of life in the school has moved to a higher level—not high enough, but it has moved.

The house plan employed in the 1990 high school, the house of about 200 students, provides the student with a circle of friends and colleagues with whom he can more warmly and fully identify. The half-day-a-week activity that students of the house experience in common provides a community bond, a social cement that had been needed from the time that high schools first began to enroll more than three or four hundred students. The house serves as a sounding board and as a channel through which student frustrations and concerns make themselves felt by both teachers and administrators. It has become an instrument of improved communication with students. It helps the school to meet and solve problems before they become rebellions. It is a means by which the school teaches the application of reason, understanding, and compromise to problems rather than demonstration, defiance, and coercion. It is the tool used by the school to teach the application of intelligence to problems in human relations.

The restructure of the high school as a social institution has been under way for twenty years. Collegiate experimentation aimed at meeting the same problems has been useful to it also. We recall that the impact of this need struck first and hardest at the collegiate level, where student bodies became too large, as did lecture sections also. Sometimes professors became too busy with their research to talk to their students. These were phenomena of the 1960s. They began to take their toll in student impersonalization and rebellion.

Eventually the colleges and universities began to take notice of the toll that bigness without reorganization was exacting. They finally stopped building dormitories of ten to twenty-four stories. They began to break their colleges into smaller colleges. They organized smaller groups of students who lived in the same dormitory or dormitory section, who ate together, who had two or three specific courses or professors in common. They began to build identity with a unit, with a solid social community. They began to think about what young people pursuing their personal development can mean to one another. They sought to personalize, to introduce greater intimacy into education. They began to appreciate more fully the degree to which students learn from each other, the ways in which they support and give confidence to one another.

The colleges found that such reorganization salvaged many potential dropouts, improved the mental and social health of students generally, and rescued many from isolation and boredom. They found also that it opened avenues of communication between faculty and students. Colleges suffered earlier and more drastically the consequences of an impersonalized education. Thus they were in a position to offer leadership in overcoming it.

Not always has the influence of the college and the university upon the high school been a wholesome one. In this instance, however, the influence filtering down from the college has been helpful. Some high schools have helped by setting examples, too. For instance, the high school at Brookline, Massachusetts, had been divided into houses for several decades, although its units were quite large and their social identity was less than completely functional, at least as envisioned here. Other high schools made earlier efforts to break their school enrollments into units, but they were often as large as 600 students, and the social identification was very incomplete. These earlier efforts generally failed to provide activities in common, the social cement needed to hold them together.

The greater informality of the organization of the high school of 1990 makes for greater unity in other ways. The teacher is in individual contact with the learner much more frequently. As a result he has a more intimate and personal knowledge of what the student is doing, not only in his own class but in the courses of other teachers with whom he is enrolled. This teacher knowledge of learner interest and activity facilitates the introduction of many more student projects that cross subject-matter boundaries.

The fragmentation of earlier secondary schoolings has not been overcome entirely. It has been recognized, and steps have been taken toward overcoming it. A crude but telling cartoon of some years earlier comes to mind. It pictured the bedraggled and frustrated student laboriously dragging along his weary way through the high school a huge gunnysack in which he was seeking to stow safely the sixteen units required for his graduation. There was obviously little or no plan for orienting this student to ways in which the loading of the sack could be made personally relevant to him and his goal. There was even less attention to the interrelationship of this collection of sixteen or seventeen units. Each unit was seen as a discrete entity, complete unto itself and somewhat insulated from all the others. Finally, there was no apparent effort to pull the top of the sack together and tie it, once it was filled.

For many years such omissions characterized most high schools. Personal relevancy, interrelationships, and unifying or capstone experiences had been rare but pleasant exceptions, not the rule. The high school of 1990 has achieved much of this for most of its students. No two of its current seniors will graduate having followed precisely the same curriculum. There is constant effort at individual tailoring that is tied to individual goals.

Student Orientation to the Task

A student cannot intelligently share in defining his school task unless he understands what that task is about. What is its purpose? Why does society support schools? What does it expect to receive in return? What does the school expect to do for the individual? How does it propose to make him more useful to society? What is the philosophy, the hope of this particular school? Why does it share critical decisions with the student? Why not simply tell him what to do?

The high school of 1990 gives more attention than any previous high school to such questions. It does not consider them beyond its resources and beyond its students' comprehension. One might even say that there is a degree of indoctrination. That kind of indoctrination, however, is no longer feared. It is realized that wherever people work together toward common goals, there must be some elements of indoctrination. The responsibility for the quality and the pertinence of this indoctrination, however, is keenly felt.

Secondary school thinkers of 1990 are shocked by the knowledge that it took school people so long to realize that they were teaching about all aspects of life except their own institution. However, they understand that the purpose of education is a subtle thing, that people found it difficult for centuries to grasp its essence.

Careful and calculated attention is given to the school's function, to its aspirations for the student. He dwells upon such matters in his first days in the school. He is encouraged to ask questions that are difficult to answer. Such orientation to his task is salted into the required English, the required social study, and into the student's special interest area such as music, art, or shop. It stresses ways in which the school can help him realize his worthwhile goals. Indeed, it helps him to find and clarify these goals. Above all, it seeks to clarify in his mind what is expected of him through responsibility for his own profit. His attention is redirected frequently to such questions throughout his association with the school.

The aims of the humanities courses, which developed in the high schools of the 1960s, have come to permeate the entire curriculum. These aims dominate the whole house activity and program. The oneness of education and life has finally come to be appreciated. The practice of the school reflects this faith. The learner, in examining any problem, issue, or literature, is urged to examine it in terms of what it means to him. Then the school's procedures are geared to encourage his testing those meanings against the views of his teachers and his fellow students.

How schooling is related to life is given careful attention in the student's orientation to the school from the first day. He is made aware of the means by which his school opportunity is provided. He is helped to understand why society is willing to invest in him, what it expects to harvest in return. Then these understandings are kept alive in a thousand ways as he advances through the work of the school. They help to give his school experience a wholeness that it did not formerly have. They are nourished frequently and richly through the activity and ideas that move the whole-house part of the program, the one-tenth of each week that is common to all house members. Each faculty-student committee, as it discusses future programs and evaluates past programs, frequently asks: "Is this life-giving? Is it life-revealing? It is life-fulfilling? Is it educative? What can we do to it to make it meet these criteria more fully?"

A DAY IN THE SCHOOL

Let us now make a personal visit to a 1990 high school. The high school at Deauville has been selected largely because Deauville is a city that is average in most respects. It is an industrial city of 30,000 people. It might be in the Midwest or upper South.

Average family income is about the same as for the nation as a whole. Cultural and recreational facilities and interests are neither superb nor poor. Community wealth and state wealth are average. The percentage of the school's graduates going on to college or university is each year either a little above or a little below the national average.

Even the age of the school building is about average for the nation's high schools. It was built in 1960, and the extent to which it fits the 1990 program is the result of adaptations. Physical things, however, get only incidental attention, only when they are functional in changed purposes and in changed attitudes. In addition, the principal, the teachers, and the students will not let us talk long about physical facilities or items of equipment. They are absorbed with exciting activities and projects. They want to tell us what they are planning to do next. We do discuss the environment at points where we find the students themselves involved in changing it.

The decorum of school visits has not changed. Consequently, our first point of call is the principal's office. The weather is fair. The day of the week is Tuesday. It is mid-April.

We are met at the visitors' parking area by a student host, a young man who is a senior. As we drive up we notice he is sitting on a nearby stone bench, reading a paperback book. This, he explains, is one of the many books published a number of years ago about United States involvement in Vietnam back in the 1950s and 1960s. Further questioning reveals that he has under way, as his individual project of the moment, an investigation of the "Vietnam Revolution." By degrees it becomes clear that the word revolution is here used to mean a revolution in American thought, a revolution that was initiated by dissidents who began questioning the morality of United States participation in Vietnam, but that spread rather rapidly to a number of other social, political, and philosophical issues.

Our escort, Hank, to us poised and sophisticated beyond his years, responds with obvious pride to the mention of his principal's name, in whose selection for the post student representatives played a part. Deauville High School, it is clear, has a highly respected leader, one who is also trusted and admired.

Hank introduces us to the principal's secretary, with a word about her ready kindness and helpfulness, and, getting the all-clear sign, ushers us into the inner office, where he introduces Joe Kaczor, the principal.

The Principal

Joe Kaczor appears to be about thirty-eight years old. He holds a doctor's degree, but he forbids both his colleagues and students to address him as "doctor" because he wants and needs no artificial props to support his status or respect. In fact, he is addressed by most faculty and students simply as "Joe," and he asks that we do likewise. He does not think that this, in and of itself, is tremendously important, but he thinks that it helps somewhat to create a sense of partnership in all, a condition that he seeks to sustain in numerous ways.

As we talk with Joe, we notice that he does not stress the things that the school has. Rather, he stresses what the school does. He stresses the human behavior in it. He stresses goals commonly sought. He spends no time explaining what he cannot do because of limitations the superintendent or the school board has placed upon him. He does not even make any excuses that he attributes to lack of funds. He knew how much money per pupil he would have at his disposal when he took the job, and he understood clearly what the financial limitations of the school for several years ahead were likely to be. He has been on this job for four years.

Incidentally, Joe's doctoral study did not deal with tax rates, school buildings, transportation costs, or even public relations. It was a problem that called upon him to combine philosophical and psychological analyses, and it attempted to get at some of the factors that move and motivate the sixteen-year-old adolescent.

The first serious question we ask Joe is, "What makes possible the kind of school you have here?" He answers that he was given, even assured, of the conditions that make it possible for a well-qualified and courageous leader to develop a superior school.

"What were those conditions?" we ask. "To start with," says Joe, "I was assured that I would be my own man, that practically any autonomy I requested I would get. This gives me a chance to be the servant of the 1,628 students we seek to help here, and the servant of the 82 teachers and 21 teacher aides we have here." Clearly this is a man who relishes responsibility. He accepted the job because it carried heavy responsibility.

Joe continues, "Our funds are assigned on the basis of the number of students in average daily attendance. With the counsel and approval of my administrative committee, composed of five elected faculty members and three students each from eleventh- and twelfth-grade houses, we have almost unlimited control of these funds. For example, this year we have one less faculty member but three more teacher aides than last year. That decision was made in this building. We have the option of spending our money where it will buy the most and best education for our students. The limits of our authority are set chiefly by state statute and by State Board regulation, very few by the local board. We forward to the board, of course, an annual report that gives a careful account of our stewardship." Joe is obviously proud of the achievements that have resulted from the exercise of his autonomy. He explains that he recommends the employment of the building's teachers, again with the counsel and approval of a building committee on faculty, a committee whose membership always overlaps the administrative council's membership.

High schools have moved toward more autonomy for their leaders, Joe explains, for about twenty years. He turns about and pulls from a nearby shelf a book written and published by a Midwestern education professor in 1970. He opens the book and calls attention to the following quotation from Ernest O. Melby, as he addressed a summer assemblage of educators at Southern Illinois University:

> Recently an unusually successful high school principal in a large city has resigned in discouragement because the centralized controls from the board of education offices leave him so little chance to act in a creative way. This brings us to *a prime weakness of our present administration,* namely, *its excessive centralization.* We have tended to copy industry rather than medicine in our concepts of organization. In medicine decision

making is close to the patient, in industry it is far removed from the assembly line. We are more like the assembly line than like the operating room in the hospital.[1]

Achievements of the School

The principal's reference to pride in the achievements of his school prompts us to observe, "Joe, you have obvious and no doubt justifiable pride in your school. Would you be good enough to tell us, a little more specifically, about some of the features or conditions in the school that make you so proud of it?"

"First," says the principal, "our students feel a real sense of ownership in this school. They regard it as theirs. They see its weaknesses and inadequacies as in part theirs to correct. They leap to its defense whenever it is attacked. They shame and socially ostracize the student who abuses its reputation or its property. This is fundamental to the kind of educational community for which we strive.

"Every student and every teacher here has his own chance, his own kind of chance," continues Joe. "This is a second school characteristic of which I am very proud. We cater to individual idiosyncrasy. A survey taken just two weeks ago showed that only 48 students out of a student body of 1,628 were not on that date officially engaged in projects unique to each of them. Some, of course, push their projects with less regularity and less devotion than others. This means that 1.5 percent of our students, an average of six from each of our eight houses, are not engaged in individualized learning. Furthermore, no meeting of a house faculty is held without reference to the individual names of uninvolved students. New names get on the active role daily. These are offset to some extent by students who finish the projects they have been absorbed in without having a new one to turn to at once. Such students represent a minority, though, and the problem of 100 percent participation is never laid to rest.

[1] Ernest O. Melby, "Needed: A New Concept of Educational Administration," *The Community School and its Administration,* Mott Program of the Flint Board of Education 3, no. 11 (July 1965), pp. 2–3 (italics added).

"Finally," says Joe, "we are proud of the quality of life in the school. This does not mean that we are not proud of the quality of learning or scholarship. The two aims work together and support one another. In fact, we think our learning is more genuine because it is nurtured in a social community of quality. It is much more often self-inspired. It more frequently springs from real rather than trumped-up propositions, less often from blanket teacher assignments.

"The quality of the school community," Joe continues, "must be credited chiefly to two sources, I think. First, to our house plan, where community interests and solidarity are cultivated. Approximately one-fourth of the house time is devoted to house and school problems, although the manner in which such time is deployed varies considerably from house to house. No minority group must demonstrate here in order to get itself heard. We want feelings and reactions heard, for we regard them as great educational capital.

"The other great molder of the school as social community," says the principal, "is the work-study lab, which gives the student regular opportunities of meeting and talking informally with teachers, teacher aides, and other students. Out of experiences in these laboratories, out of questions raised there, often comes the clue for the emphasis or stress in the formal class. Thus the influence of student interest and student problem upon curriculum is facilitated. Teachers are sensitized to it under conditions that enable them to understand it best. Then the teacher has time to evaluate what he has learned and to strike a plan by which his class may profit most fully. In this way, the insight he has gained in the work-study lab, through informal association with his students, is put to work to serve all students in his classes. I hope you will look for the germination of such classroom sessions as you visit our work-study labs."

The Principal's Most Difficult Barriers

"What do you find the most difficult obstacles to the development of a school like this to be?" we then ask the principal. His answers to this question will come as no surprise to any reader who has attempted leadership in nontraditional directions in any enterprise.

"Convincing the most doubting one-third of the teachers," answers Joe, "that we can find merit, interest, capacity, initiative in all students is the hardest job of all. Faith in student potential and seriousness of purpose is basic to our kind of school. Some teachers are still disposed to believe, with Jefferson, that a substantial number of human beings were 'born to serve,' not to think.

"Coupled closely with this failure of teachers' faith in their students is a lack of faith in themselves. Sometimes they do not think of themselves as being resourceful enough to help the student find and develop his own curriculum. They are as a consequence a bit uneasy and insecure when asked to move beyond teaching that is textbook-bound. Once they have overcome this fear, however, it is gratifying to see the professional growth and the satisfaction that overtakes them."

Joe now suggests that we have listened to him long enough, that we ought to look about the school and observe for ourselves, talking with students and teachers as we like.

Organization No Slave to Mechanics

As we go about the school, we are impressed with the degree to which it has freed itself from that unwavering servitude to mechanics that long characterized the high school. We discover, for example, that in all possible cases students report their own absence in advance. The absent student telephones the records office and asks that word of his absence be relayed to teachers and to any student committee in which his work will be missed that day. Thus he is learning the kind of responsibility he needs as an employee later. He is regarded as a responsible person, and he tries to live up to that trust. When he is ill or injured, a member of the family or a friend does this for him. He is made conscious of the fact that in this matter as in all others, he writes his own record.

There are no startling or grating bells or buzzers to mark the ends or beginnings of classes. Clocks are everywhere, but it took schools a long time to realize that they had taught teachers and students how to tell time. Besides, there is now a degree of flexibility in the schedule for most students much of the time. This would tend to make any bell system more confusing than helpful. This is one of many ways in which tranquility and composure have replaced flurry and frustration.

In no case is a student who is thirty seconds late to a class sent to anyone else to explain why he was late and to get a "pass." The occasionally tardy student slips in as quietly as possible and is politely unnoticed by all present, as is the practice in the adult society generally.

Students enter and leave the libraries and the work-study labs quietly and without formality or license of any kind. It is assumed that each knows where he is going, why, and how to manage himself after he gets there. And no one is called upon to report to anyone else in any form that nature summons him to the rest room, or on occasion outdoors, where he may catch a breath of fresh air. It is assumed that he is capable of recognizing the signals all by himself.

This freedom of student movement does not mean that an atmosphere of irresponsibility is tolerated. The entire school program is geared to the development of responsibility in the student. With rare exception the student holds himself responsible. When he does not, that failure becomes a matter for considerable and careful attention. The student is immediately taken to task, not for violating a rule, but for being irresponsible, for being untrue to himself and unfair to the ideal of the school. The weight of student opinion and student pressure is the great influence in setting him back on the track. He learns how uncomfortable one can become when he fails to meet the reasonable expectations of his fellows.

Control by the clock is less evident in many ways. For example, we talk with a senior girl, Ruth, about student appetite for what goes on in the school. We ask her to describe what happens when students first come to school in the morning. She explains that they arrive over a half-hour period, from 8:00 to 8:30. Ruth and most of her friends, whether they come in at 8:10 or 8:25, move at once or with a minimum of preliminary activity to the work-study lab, to the library, to a teacher conference (often prearranged), or to a committee meeting. (Many of the shorter meetings take place at this time.) Much constructive activity has taken place prior to the start of the day's first formal class. Committee meetings are often permitted to extend into first period work-study lab time, but not to borrow class time. Early morning informality is less prized than in the earlier high school, perhaps because there is more opportunity for informality and conversation throughout considerable portions of the day.

Formal classes are held in higher regard in this school, no doubt in part because there are fewer of them. Other reasons include the greater student participation, the constantly available opportunity of students to influence what goes on in the class, the greater use of students themselves and their interests as teaching and learning resources. The teacher is more of a coordinator, less a director or dictator. Communication is less and less a one-way affair. The teacher is often conceiver, at times designer, with the student serving as the modifier and executor. The student wants to be present in the class because he and his fellow students are the performers. He wants to see and hear his friends perform, and he wants them to see and hear him perform.

The Whole House in Action

We find the most distinguishing organizational marks of this 1990 high school to be its house plan and organization and its work-study labs. Between them they have replaced the study halls and 40 percent of the academic classes of earlier high schools. The whole house activity has also replaced on the average 10 percent of the class time formerly given to laboratory classes, such as shop and art, for its one free half day a week is inviolate. We move then to a closer look at the program of the house, there being eight of them in this school.

A local novelist and short-story writer who is also a part-time faculty member at a nearby college is about half way through with her presentation to the Burke House (named after a teacher who is this year retiring) as we take our seats in the small auditorium. The Burke House enrolls 196 tenth-graders. The novelist is discussing with them the problems of the writer. She explains how the writer must become at times a historian, at others a psychologist, always a master of rhetoric in order to portray his characters accurately. She tells some interesting stories about letters she has received from critical readers who found inconsistencies and inaccuracies in her writing. She explains how religious fanatics have accused her of misrepresenting a given religion, of being irreligious herself. Her contribution is felt in history, geography, and science, even though it was instigated by English teachers and students.

The novelist's lecture was preceded by a film that portrayed the nature and variety of fictional plots, an analysis of the devices of the writer. The lecture will be followed, after a brief recess, by discussion groups of ten to twelve students each, some of which will at any given time have a teacher with them and some of which will not. The novelist visits further for a few minutes with each of several of the groups. A further whole-group session of about twenty-five minutes is given to the lecturer's answers to some of the questions raised in the small group discussions. In the remaining weeks of this school year, the English classes of this house will give intensive attention to novels, using a wide variety of them, and including both early and late examples. The novel is emphasized as a means of revealing life, making it better understood; as a strengthening force in developing powers of communication; as a contribution to worthy leisure and to social understandings.

Earlier in the year the Burke House had centered a similar program upon the newspaper, with a journalist providing the pivotal lecture. That program, however, was followed the next week by field trips in smaller groups to newspaper offices and by visits to a newspaper's production plant. The newspaper was emphasized as an agency of communication and of social solidarity, as a developer of community pride, as a revealer of weaknesses, as an agent of the community's business life. The results, therefore, were capitalized upon in social studies and business education, as well as in English. Some students followed up by presenting to their house the results of investigations into such matters as the impact of cheap printing.

An eleventh-grade house of 185 students is preparing one of its four annual full-length plays for presentation at the house session next week. The cast includes only one student who has been in a full-length dramatic production before. The chief responsibility for coaching this play has been in the hands of a twelfth-grade girl who is an outstanding member of the school's Strut and Fret Club. However, she has had counsel from the club's faculty sponsor and irregular but more direct assistance from one of the house's social studies teachers who is something of a dramatics fan.

A third house, a twelfth-grade group of 243 students, is holding its semiannual field day this afternoon. All but four of the students will participate in at least one event. Students themselves, in most cases, carry the roles of starters, officials, judges, and safety directors. There are softball, marble, horseshoe and a variety of other tournaments. The program includes field events for both boys and girls, a softball throw for both boys and girls, and a pluto platter throw, among other unusual events. Sometimes there is a modified version of the joust, done from bicycles.

The twelfth-grade group, in case the weather is unsuitable for a field day, holds in readiness a substitute program on local government, one that features a film and a local judge, who agrees to be flexible with respect to date. Each house guards against being caught without a program.

A fourth house, another tenth-grade group, is featuring the role of animals in civilization in two successive house programs. The assembly part of this program, done both weeks with half the house members present, features films and students. It is tied firmly into the study of world history and biology, and the students featured in the assemblies have done extensive study and research on their topics. The half of the house not involved is visiting the nearby animal laboratory of a drug company and a nearby dairy farm. Next week the activities of the two groups will be reversed. This exercise promotes careful studies of such topics as vaccines, the spread and control of disease, conservation of wild life, vivisection, and animal protective leagues.

The range of whole house activities over a period of two or three years is amazing. Doctoral studies at state universities have contributed to the understanding of possibilities. We learn, by inquiry, that a kind of rule of thumb for assuring variety and student participation in whole-house activity is that approximately half of the programs shall feature students and student activity. Beyond that, an emphasis is placed upon bringing resources and persons into the school and upon taking students out to the local resources. This obviously contributes much to the maintenance of helpful community relations and support for the school, although the educational values of such programming are of first importance.

The Work-Study Lab at Work

As we visit the work-study labs, we discover that this is another instrument of school unity. We discover that few student projects are influenced by only one teacher. It is not uncommon for a student, in pursuit of his project, to be conferring with as many as half a dozen different teachers and possibly as many as four or five different persons in the community as well.

In the social studies lab, for example, we find George, whose current lab time is absorbed by a world history project he has entitled "Bridges Through the Ages." Many phases of history interest him little, but he is stimulated by problems of mechanics and design. Consequently, he is conferring regularly with a physics teacher and is now sure he wants to include the study of physics in his senior year. He has also conferred with two mathematics teachers and frequently has something of interest to report to his geometry class. His shop teacher is regularly helpful, also, and he has discussed elements of design with the art teacher and members of an advanced art class. He has also had conferences with an architect and with one of the community's civil engineers. The latter provided him with blueprints of two recently constructed bridges in the area. When his project is finally written up, his English teacher will read and criticize it before it goes into final form. He will also, he explains, spend several hours in each of four or five successive weeks in the applied arts laboratory, where he will receive aid and instruction in graphic illustration.

When this project is completed, the chances are good that George will be asked by the House Program Committee to make a twenty-minute presentation upon it in a whole-house session.

The day before this presentation, each student in the house will be provided with a duplicated digest (not more than five pages, including illustrations) of George's project. By then, of course, many students will have become interested in George's project and in him because of it. The digest will be prepared by a committee of four of his classmates in English. It will be reviewed and passed upon by the teacher, and it must be satisfactory to George. Thus students learn something of how the world of publishing works.

Interdisciplinary team teaching is characteristic of this school. George's project illustrates this clearly. Through its processes many persons have played a part in educating many others: students, teachers, and citizens. The learning society of a technological and intellectual age is at hand. Its processes, however, do not overlook the enhancement of humanity that comes from human cooperation and teamwork. The learning society, as reflected in Deauville High School, is one in which everyone learns from everyone else.

Graphic Arts Laboratory

The graphic arts laboratory of the school is not merely a service agency of the school. It is a teaching agency, one that is under the direction of a shop-drafting teacher who has also had special education in illustration. An art teacher assists, also, to make sure that the artist's imagination is a regular influence in the production that takes place there. It is attended all day long by a paraprofessional who helps students and teachers prepare a wide range of illustrative materials: graphs, charts, slides, models, and mock-ups of a professional quality. It is above all a learning laboratory, adding a dimension to learning that earlier schools did without.

Student and Teacher Teams

One group of students have collaborated on a most intriguing project that has given them real insight into changes in the way the world does its work. They have visited a sheep farm and have themselves shorn a sheep (animal husbandry, biology). They have combed and carded the wool, spun it into yarn, and woven it into cloth on one of the school's three looms (crafts). They have dyed the cloth with their own extractions from the sumac and from the hulls of black walnuts, thus bridging five thousand years of chemical evolution.[2] With this cloth they have then upholstered an old but sturdy and comfortable chair in the twelfth-grade English work-study laboratory. Thus the school's home economics, industrial arts, and science are merged in a firsthand learning experience.

Student Work in Evidence

Earmarks of former student projects are all about the school, which has become thereby a museum of history, science, craft, and art. There are murals portraying both local and worldwide history. We see works of relief, both base and high, even student-made relief maps of local terrain where student plans and work have brought improvement. The school has its sculptors in both stone and metal and its plaster casters. One student is now working on a bust of the former principal. When it is completed, a committee of seniors will decide on an appropriate mounting and its location in the building. A brass plate will credit it to its creator.

Few skills, either ancient or modern, are not somewhere in evidence in the school. Most are the work of students. The exceptions are the artifacts and works of craft and art that have been given or willed to the school by local citizens. These include fine wall hangings, such as tapestries and rugs, rare vases and urns, products of china and porcelain, and even a few pieces of fine antique furniture.

Taste is cultivated in this school. The former stark institutionalism is gone. Students learn from and are inspired by the things about them as well as by the people. It is now recognized that a completely predictable building and furnishings are as bad as a completely predictable teacher. This revolution in thinking started with the introduction of acoustical treatments and carpeting into schoolrooms approximately fifty and thirty years earlier,

---

[2] In other years students made their dyes from various barks, roots, vegetables, fruits, and weeds.

respectively. It took a long time, however, to move the extra step, from physical to aesthetic comfort. In the latter, European schools moved first.

Influence of the Work-Study Lab

Laboratory activity inspires classroom topics in this school. For example, we come into an English laboratory and find there that three students who are preparing a digest of a fellow student's project have fallen into an interesting argument. A question was raised by one of them concerning a proposed use of the word "go." Turning to an unabridged dictionary, they make the startling discovery that this simple word, in its various tenses and senses, has forty-five different meanings. When coupled with other simple words such as "about" and "through" it picks up forty-six additional definitions, thus making an astounding total of ninety-one meanings. The group takes this new discovery to their English teacher, who gives them the further job of leading a discussion on the subject, "Why the English language is so difficult and so rich." With their teacher's help they bring forward three other examples and these become the subject of discussion for an entire class period. The result: greater language power and deeper appreciation of language potential.

This example is merely one of hundreds of ways in which the different features of the school program cross-fertilize one another. Obviously, the work-study lab is an extension of the classes in that field. However, it is more than that; it is an interdisciplinary bridge. The same is true of the house. Both the house and the work-study lab are constantly influencing what goes on in the classes. Similarly, the house and the lab influence each other. Many a house program is born in the informal atmosphere of the lab, and many an inspiration for an individual or a group project is brought back from a house program or excursion.

WHAT DOES IT ALL MEAN?

What seem to be the most marked differences in this school? How does it differ most from traditional patterns of secondary schooling? In what ways are its assumptions most different? How are its aims different?

The most fundamental difference seems to lie in the assumptions that practically all young people can learn and that practically all want to learn. It follows that these same young people are seen as capable of exercising great initiative in carrying forward their own learning, with the school climate and school agencies being geared to that realization. The development of responsibility is a primary school goal.

Education Not a Contest

Education is not seen as a contest in this school. The classroom is not likened to the football field or the track, where competition is properly cultivated. Rather, in this school no two students are seen as playing precisely the same game. There is a minimum of emphasis upon the idea of trying to see who can get to any given goal first. It must be stressed, though, that individual divergence does not become a divisive force in the school. It is seen as contributing to community interests, for it means that the students have more to say to each other. They are thereby better qualified to contribute to the education of each other. This is, however, never permitted to descend to the level of, "Do you want to view my slides on Patagonia?"

The side trails taken by individuals and small groups are emphasized in Deauville High. Cooperative ventures, however, and the teaching of cooperation are emphasized more, not less, than in the traditional high school. It is not that common experiences of some kinds are emphasized less. Rather, it is that each individual student is expected to draw different values from these common experiences, values that are compatible with his own unique interests and goals. Common experiences are expected to develop great capacity for cooperation while encouraging each student to draw from them meanings that are personally relevant to him.

Other Student Responsibilities

Students at Deauville serve their total school in ways not found in traditionally organized schools, too. The cafeteria, for example, is managed by a student board of directors, two from each house.

The cafeteria board members are elected by their fellow students in their respective houses. Their faculty adviser at present is a health teacher. At times in the past the adviser has been a home economics teacher, a business education teacher, a mathematics teacher. The board selects its own faculty adviser, with the approval of the principal.

Cafeteria board members may be required to stand against new nominees at any time one-third of the students express by petition disapproval of cafeteria management. The board has practically complete control of the cafeteria, with responsibility to the principal for businesslike procedures and a balanced budget. It has menu committees, wage and employment committees, and quite a large committee on control and decorum. Students soon realize that money spent to replace broken dishes is not available to buy better food. Board and committee members are gaining maturity and insight into many aspects of social and financial management.

A safety and security council is quite similar to the cafeteria board in design and selection. It is made up of two elected students from each house. One hundred "lookouts," selected with care by the council, have no authority to act but always have the responsibility to report observations to the judicial committee of the Council. This committee investigates, weighs evidence, and when necessary recommends discipline to the house principal. Theft and related problems are rare in the school. Care has been taken to establish in all students the understanding that any community is responsible for its own welfare and that of all its individual members.

Effect Upon Teacher Attraction and Retention

A senior teacher in the school helps us to understand the impact that this kind of school has upon individual faculty members. She has been in the school for twenty-three years, has seen the changes come, and is well qualified to appraise the situation. After listening to her for a while, we are forced to a conclusion that might be simply stated as follows: Teachers of resourcefulness and imagination, those interested in studying their students as well as their subjects, like this school. Several of them have turned down better offers to stay with it. Those not so disposed tend to eliminate themselves, to seek employment in more traditionally organized schools or to leave teaching.

What Kind of Graduate?

What kind of graduate leaves Deauville High? In what respects is he most likely to be different from the high school graduate of twenty years earlier?

The 1990 graduate of Deauville High School is likely to have a more complete but realistic view of himself. He understands himself better and is more often sure of himself. He is more mature, in the best sense of that word; and he is more responsible. His social conscience is sharper. He has a keener awareness of the pressing needs of his society. He is more often determined to try to do his share in meeting these needs. He has a more fully cultivated respect for his fellow man. He respects all kinds of people, even those with the severest problems.

Finally, the Deauville graduate of 1990 has a better sense of direction. He more often knows where he wants to go and why. His individual interests and strengths have been more fully identified. He is less apologetic about going to college or not going to college. If he goes, he knows more clearly what he is seeking. If he doesn't go, he is able to justify his alternative more rationally. He has a keener appreciation of self and his potential. He is a more highly motivated and a more determined adult. His school has helped him to learn more about the world of work. His guidance and his curriculum have been merged.

Above all, this 1990 graduate is more often idea-oriented. He has seen many ideas born in his school, and he has observed their spread, their power to move others. He has had the thrill of seeing some of his own ideas harnessed and put to work to better the school, the community, to improve human relations or the human condition. He has gained self-esteem and the esteem of others. His mental health, as a consequence, is robust.

This graduate is convinced that one person can make a difference, anywhere and upon any issue. Having proved in school his usefulness to himself and to others, he looks to the life ahead, confident that it will give him abundant opportunities further to develop and enlarge his usefulness.

This high school of 1990 is by no means perfect. It has done much, however, to sweep aside many of the impediments that had persistently blocked needed school reform for almost a century.

Bibliography

Abramson, David A. "The Effectiveness of Grouping for Students of High Alibity," Ohio State University, *Educational Research Bulletin*, 38 (October 14, 1959).

Bloom, B. S., *et al. Taxonomy of Educational Objectives.* New York: Longmans, Green, 1956.

Boyer, William H., and Paul Walsh. "Are Children Born Unequal?" *Saturday Review* (October 19, 1968).

Broudy, Harry S., and John R. Palmer. *Exemplars of Teaching Method.* Chicago: Rand McNally, 1965.

Broudy, Harry S., B. Othanel Smith, and Joe R. Burnett. *Democracy and Excellence in American Secondary Education, A Study in Curriculum Theory.* Chicago: Rand McNally, 1964.

Brown, Elmer E. *The Making of Our Middle Schools.* New York: Longmans, Green, 1905.

Brown v. Board of Education of Topeka, 347 U.S. 483 (1954).

Bruner, Jerome S. *The Process of Education.* Cambridge: Harvard University Press, 1960.

_____. *Toward a Theory of Instruction.* Cambridge: Harvard University, Belknap Press, 1966.

Butman, Alexander, *et al. Paperbacks in the Schools.* New York: Bantam, 1963.

Callahan, Raymond E. *Education and the Cult of Efficiency.* Chicago: University of Chicago Press, 1962.

Clark, Ramsey. "Man v. The State." *The Center Magazine* 3:2 (March 1970).

A Climate for Individuality: Statement of the Joint Project on the Individual and the School. Washington, D.C.: American Association of School Administrators, Association for Supervision and Curriculum Development, National Association of Secondary

School Principals, and National Education Association Department of Rural Education, 1965.

Coleman, James S. *Adolescents and the Schools.* New York: Basic Books, 1965.

College Entrance Examination Board. *A Guide to the Advanced Placement Program.* Princeton: College Entrance Examination Board, 1966.

Commager, Henry Steele. "Our Schools Have Kept Us Free," *Life,* October 27, 1950.

Conant, James B. *The American High School Today.* New York: McGraw-Hill, 1959.

_____. *The Comprehensive High School: A Second Report.* New York: McGraw-Hill, 1967.

Cook, E. T., and Alex Wedderburn, eds. *The Works of John Ruskin,* XVIII. New York: Longmans, Green, 1905.

Cook, Walter W. "The Gifted and the Retarded in Historical Perspective," *Phi Delta Kappan,* 39 (March 1958).

Cousins, Norman. "Out in the Open," *Saturday Review,* April 2, 1960.

Cremin, Lawrence. *The Transformation of the School.* New York: Knopf, 1961.

Cubberley, Elwood P. *Public Education in the United States.* Boston: Houghton Mifflin, 1919.

_____. *A Brief History of Education.* Boston: Houghton Mifflin, 1922.

Dewey, John. *Democracy and Education.* New York: Macmillan, 1916.

Diederich, Paul B. *Adapting a College Type of Schedule to High Schools.* Princeton, New Jersey: Educational Testing Service (mimeographed release), December, 1966.

_____. "The Conant Report," in John A. Dahl *et al.* (eds.), *Student, School and Society, Crosscurrents in Secondary Education.* San Francisco: Chandler, 1964.

Downey, Lawrence W. *The Secondary Phase of Education.* New York: Blaisdell, 1965.

Dyer, Henry S. "The Art of Unwrapping Curriculum Packages," National Association of Secondary School Principals, Bulletin 328 (May 1968).

Eliot, Charles W. "Shortening and Enriching the Grammar School Course," in *Proceedings,* National Education Association, Department of Superintendents, Washington, D.C.: 1892.

Eliot, Charles W., *et al. Report of the Committee of Ten.* New York: American Books, 1894.

Evans, William H., and Jerry L. Walker. *New Trends in the Teaching of English in Secondary Schools.* Chicago: Rand, McNally, 1966.

Federal Supplement 269 (Judicial Digest) 401 (1967).

Finch, F. H. "Are High School Pupils of the Present Day Inferior to Those of an Earlier Period?" *The School Review,* 52:2.

Flesher, W. R., *et al. Public Education in Ohio.* Columbus: Cooperative Educational Enterprises, 1962.

Gardner, John W. "Education and the Great Society," in *Addresses and Proceedings,* National Education Association, 104 (1966).

————. "But What of the Dream?" A speech at the University of North Carolina.

Gibbon, Maurice. "Changing Secondary Education Now," National Association of Secondary School Principals, Bulletin 342 (January 1970).

Glatthorn, Allan A. "How to Sabotage 'Teacher-Proof' Curricula," National Association of Secondary School Principals, Bulletin 328 (May 1968).

Goodlad, John I., R. Van Stoephasius, and M. F. Klein. *The Changing School Curriculum: A Report from the Fund for the Advancement of Education.* New York: Ford Foundation, 1966.

Goodson, Max R. "Differentiating the Profession of Teaching," *School and Society,* 86 (May 24, 1958).

Gorman, Burton W. "The Teaching Profession Tomorrow," *School and Society,* 82 (October 29, 1955).

————. "Every Day Must Be 'Career Day,' " *The High School Journal,* 43 (May 1958).

————. *Education for Learning to Live Together.* Dubuque, Iowa: Kendall-Hunt Publishing Company, 1969.

Gorman, Burton W., and William H. Johnson. "Pupil Activity in Study Halls: An Inventory and Implications for Progress," National Association of Secondary School Principals, Bulletin 293 (September 1964).

Hall, G. Stanley. *Adolescence, Its Psychology, and Its Relation to Physiology, Anthropology, Sociology, Sex, Crime, Religion and Education.* V. 2. New York: D. Appleton & Company, 1916.

Hall, Mary Harrington, "A Conversation with Polanyi," *Psychology Today,* May 1968.

Halleck, S. L. "Hypotheses About Student Unrest," National Education Association, *Today's Education,* 57 (September 1968).

Havighurst, Robert J. "High Schools for the Future," National Association of Secondary School Principals, Bulletin 328 (May 1968).

Hemphill, John K., James M. Richards, and Richard E. Peterson. *Report of the Senior High School Principalship.* Washington, D.C.: National Association of Secondary School Principals, 1965.

Henry, Nelson B., ed. *Individualizing Instruction,* Yearbook, National

Society for the Study of Education. Chicago: University of Chicago Press, LXI, Part 1, 1962. (Chapters by Walter W. Cook, John I. Goodlad, Fred T. Wilhelms and others.)

Holt, John. *How Children Fail.* New York: Dell, 1964.

Hullfish, H. Gordon, and Philip G. Smith. *Reflective Thinking: The Method of Education.* New York: Dodd, Mead, 1961.

Hunt, Douglas, *et al.* "Preparation for Reality: Induction of Beginning Teachers," National Association of Secondary School Principals, Bulletin 319 (May 1967).

————. "Teacher Induction: A Key to Excellence," National Association of Secondary School Principals, Bulletin 52:328 (May 1968).

Hunt, Maurice P., and Lawrence E. Metcalf. *Teaching High School Social Studies: Problems in Reflective Thinking and Social Understanding.* 2nd ed. New York: Harper & Row, 1968.

Husen, Torsten, and Nils-Eric Svenson. "Pedagogic Milieu and Development of Intellectual Skills," *The School Review,* 68:1 (Spring, 1960).

Hutchins, Robert M. *Education for Freedom.* Baton Rouge: Louisiana State University Press, 1943.

————. *The Learning Society.* New York: Praeger, 1968.

Johnson, Earl. *Theory and Practice of the Social Studies.* New York: Macmillan, 1956.

Kandel, I. L. *William Chandler Bagley, Stalwart Educator.* New York: Columbia University, Teachers College Press, 1961.

Keller, Charles R. "Can the Humanities Catch Up?" National Association of Secondary School Principals, Bulletin 291 (April 1964).

Kelley, Earl C. *In Defense of Youth.* Englewood Cliffs, N.J.: Prentice-Hall, 1962.

Kennedy, John F. *Profiles in Courage.* New York: Harper and Brothers, 1955.

Koontz, David E. "Professional Attitudes of Beginning Teachers and Their School's Personnel Policies." Unpublished doctoral dissertation, Kent State University, 1967.

Krug, Edward A. *The Shaping of the American High School.* New York: Harper & Row, 1964.

Learned, William S. *Realism in Education.* Cambridge: Harvard University Press, 1932.

Learned, William S., and Ben D. Wood. *The Student and His Knowledge.* New York: The Carnegie Foundation for the Advancement of Teaching, 1938.

Lieberman, Myron. *Education as a Profession.* Englewood Cliffs, N.J.: Prentice-Hall, 1956.

_____. *The Future of Public Education.* Chicago: University of Chicago Press, 1960.

McGregor, Douglas. *The Human Side of Enterprise.* New York: McGraw-Hill, 1960.

MacLeish, Archibald. "The Great American Frustration," *Saturday Review,* July 13, 1968.

McMurrin, Sterling. "What Tasks for the Schools?" *Saturday Review,* January 14, 1967.

Marchwardt, A. H. "Dartmouth Seminar: Anglo-American Conference on the Teaching of English," National Association of Secondary School Principals, Bulletin 51 (April 1967).

Melby, Ernest O. "Needed: A New Concept of Educational Administration," *The Community School and Its Administration.* (Mott Program of Flint Board of Education) 3 (July 1965).

Merton, Robert K. "Bureaucratic Structure and Personality," in Amitai Etzioni (ed.) *Complex Organizations: A Sociological Reader.* New York: Holt, Rinehart and Winston, 1961.

Mitchell, Anne. "The Crux of the Matter," *Saturday Review,* January 15, 1966.

Monroe, Paul. *Founding of the American School System.* New York: Macmillan, 1940.

Murphy, Geraldine. *The Study of Literature in the High School.* Waltham, Mass.: Blaisdell, 1968.

North Central Association of Colleges and Secondary Schools. *Policies and Criteria for the Approval of Secondary Schools.* Chicago: 1960–1961.

Ohio State School Survey Commission. *Report of the Ohio State School Survey Commission: A Cooperative Field Study.* Columbus, Ohio: F. J. Heer Company, 1914.

Peddiwell, J. Abner (Harold R. W. Benjamin). *The Saber-Tooth Curriculum.* New York: McGraw-Hill, 1939.

Pfeiffer, Isobel L. "Teaching in Ability-Grouped English Classes: A Study of Verbal Interaction and Cognitive Goals," unpublished Ph.D. dissertation, Kent State University, 1966.

Phenix, Philip. *Education and the Common Good.* New York: Harper and Brothers, 1961.

Pierce, Truman M. Personal letter to the author. January 20, 1964.

Pino, E. C., and W. L. Armistead. "Toward a More Relevant and Human Secondary Curriculum," *The North Central Association Quarterly,* XLIII-3 (Winter, 1969).

"Price Fixing Brings Jail Terms," *Business Week,* February 11, 1961.

Pusey, Nathan M. *The Age of the Scholar.* Cambridge: Belknap Press, Harvard, 1964.

Richmond, W. Kenneth. "A Britisher's View," *Nation,* 186 (May 10, 1958).

Roberts, Paul. *English Syntax.* New York: Harcourt, Brace & Company, 1964.

Rosenthal, Robert, and Lenore Jacobson. *Pygmalion in the Classroom.* New York: Holt, Rinehart and Winston, 1968.

School Survey Service of Kent State University. *A Study of the Alliance School System.* Kent, Ohio: Kent State University Press, 1964.

Silberman, Charles E. *Crisis in the Classroom.* New York: Random House, 1970.

Spencer, Herbert. *Education: Intellectual, Moral, and Physical.* New York: D. Appleton & Company, 1860.

Tanner, J. M. "Earlier Maturation in Man," *Scientific American,* January, 1968.

Tompkins, Ellsworth, and Walter Gaumnitz. *The Carnegie Unit: Its Origin, Status, and Trends.* Office of Education Bulletin 7, 1954.

Trump, J. Lloyd, and Delmas F. Miller. *Secondary School Curriculum Improvement.* Boston: Allyn & Bacon, 1968.

Ulich, Robert. *Three Thousand Years of Educational Wisdom.* Cambridge: Harvard University Press, 1950.

U.S. Office of Education: Bulletin 35, *Cardinal Principles of Secondary Education.* 1918.

Ward, Barbara. *Spaceship Earth.* New York: Columbia University Press, 1966.

Whitehead, Alfred North. *The Aims of Education.* New York: Mentor Books, 1949.

Wines, Donald B. "A Challenge, Not a Choice," *The High School Journal,* 50 (November 1966).

Index

About the Author

Prior to holding his present position as Professor of School Administration and Supervision at Kent State, Burton W. Gorman was, from 1954 to 1969, Chairman and Professor of the Department of Secondary Education. Before that he was head of the Education Department at DePauw University. Earlier in his career he served as high school principal in schools of various sizes and as county and city superintendent of schools. He was the first holder of the Knudson Doctoral Fellowship from George Peabody College for Teachers.

Not only has Professor Gorman had wide experience with the day-to-day operation of the American high school but he also has had considerable opportunity to study secondary schools abroad. He has participated in field seminars in eight European countries, including the Soviet Union.

His published works include *Education for Learning to Live Together* (1969) and numerous contributions to such professional journals as *American School Board Journal, Educational Forum, National Association of Secondary School Principals Bulletin, School and Society, Educational Leadership, Peabody Journal of Education,* and *The High School Journal.*